A Useful Art

The Wesleyan Centennial Edition
of the Complete Critical Writings
of Louis Zukofsky

Volume I
A Test of Poetry

Volume II
Prepositions +

Volumes III and IV
Bottom: On Shakespeare

Volume V
Le Style Apollinaire

Volume VI
A Useful Art

A Useful Art

Essays and Radio Scripts
on American Design

Louis Zukofsky

Edited with an Introduction by
Kenneth Sherwood

Afterword by John Taggart

Wesleyan University Press

Middletown, Connecticut

Wesleyan University Press
Middletown, Connecticut
Published by Wesleyan University Press
Middletown, CT 06459

This edition © 2003 by Paul Zukofsky, Sole Heir to and Executor
of the Estate of Louis Zukofsky and Celia Thaew Zukofsky

Preface and Introduction © 2003 by Kenneth Sherwood
Afterword by John Taggart © 2003 by Wesleyan University Press

Library of Congress Cataloging-in-Publication Data

Zukofsky, Louis, 1904–1978.

A useful art : essays and radio scripts on American design / Louis Zukofsky ; edited with
an introduction by Kenneth Sherwood ; afterword by John Taggart.

p. cm. — (The Wesleyan centennial edition of the complete critical writings of Louis
Zukofsky ; v. 6)

Includes bibliographical references.

ISBN 0-8195-6639-x (cloth : alk. paper) — ISBN 0-8195-6640-3 (pbk. : alk. paper)

1. Decorative arts—United States—History. 2. Design—United States—History. I.
Sherwood, Kenneth, 1969– II. Title.

NK805.Z85 2003 745'.0973—dc21   2002041180

Printed in the United States of America
5 4 3 2 1   1 2 3 4

The National Gallery of Art has granted permission to reproduce the following illustrations:

1. "Baron" Stiegel Stoveplate. Elmer G. Anderson, Pa. German Stove Plate. Photograph © 2002
Board of Trustees, National Gallery of Art, Washington, D.C.

2. Henry Clay Figurehead. Mina Lowry, Figurehead: "Henry Clay". Photograph © 2002 Board of
Trustees, National Gallery of Art, Washington, D.C.

3. N.Y. Manumission Water Pitcher. Clayton Braun, Silver Water Pitcher. Photograph © 2002 Board
of Trustees, National Gallery of Art, Washington, D.C.

4. "Wide Awake" Lantern (square). Lazar Rubenstein, Square Lantern. Photograph © 2002 Board of
Trustees, National Gallery of Art, Washington, D.C.

5. "Wide Awake" Torch. Herman Bader, Swing Torch. Photograph © 2002 Board of Trustees, National Gallery of Art, Washington, D.C.

6. Dutch Kas. Isadore Goldberg, Kas. Photograph © 2002 Board of Trustees, National Gallery of Art,
Washington, D.C.

7. Caswell Carpet. Dorothy Lacey, Caswell Carpet. Photograph © 2002 Board of Trustees, National
Gallery of Art, Washington, D.C.

8. Friendship Quilt. Mary Berner, Appliqué Quilt. Photograph © 2002 Board of Trustees, National
Gallery of Art, Washington, D.C.

Contents

vi · *Contents*

Preface

What distinguishes the worker from the best of the bees
Is that the worker builds a cell in his head
  before he constructs it in wax.
The labor process ends in the creation of a thing,
Which when the process began
Already lived as the worker's image.—("*A*"-8, 61)

A Useful Art collects previously unpublished cultural criticism written between 1938 and 1940 by poet Louis Zukofsky, as a senior researchist and writer for the WPA-sponsored program, the Index of American Design. The final volume in The Wesleyan Centennial Edition of the Complete Critical Writings of Louis Zukofsky, it makes available the one, known book-length work by this significant American modernist that remained unpublished.

The Index of American Design was itself designed to assemble a comprehensive pictorial and descriptive catalogue of American craft objects. Yet its scope and ambition make it kindred to more well known projects, such as the Federal Theater Project or, beyond the cultural realm, to the public works construction of the period. Officially a work of historical documentation to record the national patrimony and permit contemporary artists to build on tradition, the Index was informed by a powerful nostalgia for a preindustrial past. How physical materials, social conditions, and industrialization shape what artists make were of compelling interest to the project. The extant contributions made by Zukofsky, herein collected, provide historical information about the development of American handicrafts, but they are also interesting for the aesthetic appreciation Zukofsky lavishes on quotidian objects. Throughout the work but particularly in the scripts, Zukofsky provides thoughtful attention to the production, formal qualities, and continuing expressivity of these objects of useful art.

Of equal interest to students of twentieth-century poetics, cultural critics, and social historians, these essays and radio scripts reward readers by:

1) fleshing out the cultural context within which Objectivist poetry of the 1930s developed, particularly with respect to the question of the relation of art and the artist to society; 2) documenting a mid-twentieth-century imagination of art and domesticity in early America; and 3) providing insight into the Index of American Design, the WPA, and more generally the workings and products of depression-era arts and culture programs. Readers of Zukofsky's poetry will also value this volume for its revelation of parallel trajectories in the poet's thinking about poems and handicraft objects as products of devoted labor; they will encounter material directly and indirectly incorporated into the masterful, long poem *"A"*.

Literary critics increasingly count Louis Zukofsky among the major American modernists. From almost the first, his poetry showed the influence and gained the approval of Ezra Pound and William Carlos Williams. In addition to poetry, Zukofsky translated, wrote critical prose (essays, books on Shakespeare and Apollinaire), and edited (both the teaching anthology *A Test of Poetry* and the first collections of Objectivist poetry). Critical attention blossomed only in the 1970s, continuing to grow since his death; but his work powerfully and steadily influenced other American poets, including peers—George Oppen, Lorine Niedecker, Basil Bunting—and later poets, notably those associated with Black Mountain College and Language writing.

In both *A Useful Art* and his poetry, Zukofsky several times indulges in a doubled trope (personification and metalepsis) he knew from the poetry of Omar Khayyám and the philosophy of Karl Marx. He imagines what historical artifacts themselves might say could they speak cogently to the present about their life, times, and makers; one hopes he would be pleased to know that the pages of this volume may now do likewise for the reader in 2003.

Kenneth Sherwood

Acknowledgments

THANKS ARE DUE TO MANY for advice, guidance, and assistance in completion of this project, but most especially to: Robert Creeley for renewing and deepening my interest in Zukofsky through his Buffalo reading group; Mark Scroggins for sharing advice and information from his own biographical research; and Dawn Smith-Sherwood for lending her eyes and ears to proofreading and for her steady encouragement. The Louis Zukofsky archive is housed at the Harry Ransom Center for the Humanities, The University of Texas at Austin, where staff facilitated work with archival materials. Charlie Ritchie and the staff at the National Gallery of Art, Washington provided generous assistance in locating relevant illustrations. A faculty research grant from the University of Texas of the Permian Basin contributed to this project in its final stages. Finally, I extend thanks to Paul Zukofsky for inviting me to edit this project and for engaging in helpful dialogue through the long process.

INTRODUCTION

Kenneth Sherwood

As the narrative of American poetry during the 1930s has it, writers of otherwise incommensurable camps came to see the relation between art and society as a central issue (Nelson 17). While for many the choice between aestheticism and realism dichotomized the possible responses, Louis Zukofsky's poetry of this decade reflects the intersection between a high modernist aesthetics and a left-wing politics with a deep concern for history (Scroggins 49, 54). In this light, his "Program 'Objectivists' 1931"—the foundational essay for what has subsequently seemed a heterogenous group of writers—defines the Objectivist poem as enmeshed in "the direction of historic and contemporary particulars" (268). Recent critics of Objectivist writing tend to agree on at least one characteristic: that it is "aware of its own historical contingency and situatedness" (DuPlessis and Quartermain 6). A little-noted sheet of paper held among Zukofsky's archives at the University of Texas conceives of the relation of art and society in a scenario perhaps only articulable at the precise moment in the course of American poetry and history:

> It's obvious a poet lives in his time and can't escape it, and he writes because he lives in his time. Today obviously he can't escape even to the so-called ivory tower, for he's likely to find it's in the Chrysler Bldg. A poet's technique keeps up with the working materials of his time, just as other craftsmen and workers keep up with theirs. . . . It is unfortunate that the poet to-day has [not] carried over into his job the business of the division of labor as other workers, because good poetry is a product [*sic*] more of dealing with specific tasks, than of poetic sentiment. . . . Yes, it would be nice if poets could forget themselves get together and one do this about a poem, and one suggest this

[1]

and the other cadence, etc. and produce a cooperative poem which would be a product of their combined labor and not of individual sentiment.[1]

The statement indicates Zukofsky was thinking about the poem in social terms circa 1937, as an object produced by and reflecting on historical and social conditions. Interesting for its content and context as a public intervention, it advances an image of the poet working alongside other laborers, rather than as a bard speaking for nation or tribe.

It is in this respect that Objectivist poetry can be situated in the loosely defined tradition of the American epic that begins with the democratic vistas of Walt Whitman, moves through the "poem including history" of Ezra Pound, and arrives at a labor theory of poetics in the first half of Zukofsky's "*A*," which works toward the constitution of a "social voice" for poetry (di Manno 297). According to Yves di Manno, the development of a "social voice" for poetry (297), or what might with equal aptness be called the social epic, reflects the Objectivist interest in "reclaiming the possibility of a collective song, a social voice, putting the emphasis on the bonding of a poet to a community" and exists "in contradistinction to a strictly individual trajectory of development" (297). Objectivist poetics is social to the extent that "the poem weaves, knots, and unravels the fibers connecting the artist to a particular place and time" (298). As it combines the characteristic Objectivist interest in a poetry of historical particulars with an artisanal dynamic of production worthy of the eighteenth- or nineteenth-century craftsman, Zukofsky's social vision might be contextualized in terms of his reading of Marx. The commonly identified source for Zukofsky's thinking about labor, production, and all things economic, Marx, along with Thorsten Veblen, invites the analogy with mechanical production that leads to the idea that poetry is ideally an impersonal art that might be practiced communally. Zukofsky adopts the Marxist labor theory of value to the extent that poesis becomes a "subcategory of production" and poetry "a commodity" in his

---

1. A reconstructed transcript of Zukofsky's response to a question about the relation between social consciousness and poetic technique, it marks his contribution to a League of American Writers panel on New York radio station WOR (with a "nationwide hookup") broadcast on June 7, 1937. From the Zukofsky collection of the Harry Ransom Humanities Research Center of the University of Texas, this unpublished document is copyright Paul Zukofsky and quoted by his permission. It may not be quoted by third parties without the express permission of the copyright holder.

poetry and correspondence of the 1930s (Marsh 105). But another source at work here in fomenting this equation between craftsmen and poets is Zukofsky's extensive, firsthand research into the tradition of American handicrafts.

One of five divisions of the Work Projects Administration (WPA) established on May 6, 1935, the Federal Arts Project (FAP) engaged Zukofsky and some six thousand other individuals in its employ. The Index of American Design, a program of the FAP, aimed to recover and diffuse information about U.S. culture, at a time when interest in handicrafts had just begun to emerge; like all Federal One programs, it aimed at once to create jobs and provide a public service. Envisioned as an eventual publication of encyclopedic scope, the Index of American Design now exists as an archive at the National Gallery of Art, including "approximately 18,000 watercolor renderings of American decorative arts objects from the colonial period through the nineteenth century" (National Gallery of Art). While visual artists worked to illustrate characteristic craft objects, "researchists" such as Zukofsky compiled information from primary sources as well as publications geared toward collectors.

Zukofsky wrote the pieces collected and published for the first time in this volume as contributions to a highly institutionalized national project. Readers will be interested in noting what light they cast upon the cultural, political, and historical context of Zukofsky's contemporaneous poetry, and perhaps also will want to assess their relationship to his other works of critical prose. The mission and scope of the project itself provide a starting point. The Index Editorial Director, Constance Rourke, wrote in 1937 that the work then being done "under the Federal Art Project by the Index of American Design, in recording sequences of examples in the useful and decorative arts, suggests both the richness of this phase of our inheritance and the slenderness of our knowledge" (n.p.). She depicts the Index as responding to a particularly American need for a cultural vocabulary that might be absorbed through the "strong and natural association with evidences of the past" more typical of European experience; the assembly and eventual publication of the Index, she argued, would allow for citizens and prospective artists to "saturate themselves with a knowledge of forms which have been essential to us in the past, getting a sense of these into their minds and eyes and at the ends of their fingers, without any immediate purpose." Zukofsky's own summation of the Index in the "Henry Clay Figurehead" radio script reprinted in this volume represents the ideals of the project in terms congruent with those of Rourke:

> The artists, research workers, and writers of the Index, a division of the New York City Art Project, are preparing for publication a monumental history of American handicrafts. The whole field of manual and decorative crafts in America will be summed up in colored and black and white plates together with written descriptions of the objects rendered. The Index of American Design promises to be a new history of our country from the earliest days down to the present revival of handicrafts. (149)

We do not know precisely how Zukofsky came to undertake the job of Index researchist, but it is consistent in some ways with his known interests. Examples include the articulation of a kind of craft aesthetic in "Program: 'Objectivists' 1931" cited at the outset, and the poem "To my wash-stand" (1932), which meditates on a quotidian household object in anticipation of the Index. So too, through the process of writing "A"-8, he began to incorporate details from his research on craft in the poem as historical information, and on a more subtle level began to investigate the models of artistic production in the labor of the craftsmen he studied. "A"-12 provides corroborating evidence (256–57) that Zukofsky planned both a story, "The Hounds," and critical study, "About Some Americans," derived from his Index research (Ahearn, "Marxism" 83).

In a 1937 letter to fellow poet Ezra Pound, Louis Zukofsky wrote, "I am now outlining the economic, political background of American Design (useful arts)—and with a chance to read and study history" (Pound 193). His appreciation of this research job—"a responsible position while it lasts"—is at first begrudging. The drain on his poetic energy must have been compounded by what he perceived as the political inequity of the fact that so many of his contemporaries had been invited to take part in the Federal Writers' Project, employed to do their own writing (Ahearn, "Marxism" 81). Zukofsky was presumably comfortable with the Index's mission to represent a national, cultural heritage, but it is also clear that he found a personal use for the job. As evidenced by specific poetic borrowing from his research, he gradually came to appreciate the fact that the work might contribute to his poetry, both as information and in giving a model of artistic laboring; it "could contribute to his concern with the labor process, and to beauty, for he was studying objects that combined elements of both" (Ahearn, "Marxism" 83).

In one of two studies indispensable to those interested in Zukofsky's Index work, "Zukofsky, Marxism, and American Handicraft," Barry Ahearn argues that Zukofsky's Index research documents a tradition in which productive labor of craftsmen was not dissociated from issues of form and aesthetics—a tradition, that is, which essentially confirms Zukofsky's own poesis (84). Zukofsky's preoccupation with complex form, rather than the transparent social messages of poetry popular in venues such as the left-wing periodical *New Masses,* troubled his own relation with American Marxism. While the popular and institutional interest in American craft tradition proceeded largely out of a desire for "totems of a pure-blooded American past" (88–89), Zukofsky finds that "these artifacts illuminate the social and economic life of the common people" (89)—and can, should be recovered so as to speak of and for the same. Thus, Ahearn observes, "the attraction Zukofsky finds in American handicrafts and design that predate industrial manufacture is the attraction of an artist who sees his own work as comparable to theirs. The same values he finds in their craft exist in his. . . . *"A"* itself . . . is an American handcraft" (90). Research into American Design bears on Zukofsky's poetics because he found the handicraft tradition applicable by analogy to poetic method, and historical information about labor, fit subject.

Rather than seeing these Index essays as an isolated example of an American poet doing cultural research, Ira Nadel argues they should be placed in the context of kindred work by William Carlos Williams, *In the American Grain,* and Ezra Pound, *Guide to Kulchur* (114). In his critical study, "'Precision of Appeal': Louis Zukofsky and the *Index of American Design,"* Nadel observes that a central lesson Zukofsky derived from the Index was the discovery, or, arguably, the confirmation "that materiality and its preoccupation with making is the very heart of a craft" (117). Nadel summarizes the importance of Zukofsky's work on the Index as follows:

> it immersed him in American history; it confirmed the method initiated by the Objectivist "movement"; it underlined the value of citation and keen observation; it united a poetics of detail with the plot of history; it clarified Zukofsky's emerging social and political thought; and finally, it reflected an aesthetic that required the proximity of lost or forgotten objects . . . (115)

As Nadel concludes, the methodology that Index writing entailed led to those methods which Zukofsky would "elaborate in sections of *"A"*: research, documentation, definition, history, and fact, vying with each other in poetic statement" (121).

Zukofsky began his work for the Index in January of 1936, although the earliest surviving text is from the middle of 1938. First composed were the essays on Ironwork, Chalkware, Tin Ware, and Kitchenware; nearer the end of his tenure, he completed eight radio scripts and researched three more dealing with exceptional objects of Index research. Given their comprehensiveness, the essays hold obvious scholarly value in their indication of the poet's reading and research preoccupations during the period. At points they grow heavy with data. The format of the radio scripts, in which Zukofsky would himself have spoken the part of the researcher, allows for freer play, a livelier tone, and limited editorialization. Zukofsky's class politics are most clearly revealed here through his own direct observations. The occasionally political tone is particularly remarkable given that the composition of the scripts coincides with the culmination of the Dies Committee hearings into "Communist" influence in Federal One programs. Perhaps the political climate influenced Zukofsky's decision to omit this passage from the radio script "A Pair of New York Water Pitchers":

> Advocating the theory that wealth consists not in labor and its products, but in the quantity of hard gold and silver in a country, mercantilism encouraged mining and importation of these metals by the state and the exportation of goods as well as people who make them. It sought to increase national rather than common individual interests, and as such especially influenced the legislative policy of Great Britain. The first extensive use of indenture, as of modern slavery, occurred in the British colonies. (165)

Without proposing a constant or unidirectional influence of the Index on the poetry, we can discern a number of familiar themes and issues, including: labor, craft, and the art object in the following pages. Most specific instances have been addressed in notes to the body of the text. A few cross-referenced examples will suffice to establish how integral Zukofsky's Index work is to the remainder of his writing.

Zukofsky addressed such related issues as labor conditions, the division of labor, and the effects of industrialization on craft tradition with seemingly heightened attention in the Index. A passage in the "Ironwork" essay and another from the radio script, "Two New York Water Pitchers" bear comparision with a selection from "*A*"-8:

> And skilled, like unskilled labor, was not always free. Extant copies of early colonial indentures are the same word for word as those of England. Colonial apprenticeship, except for differences of training compelled by different conditions, bears the stamp of a system taken over from abroad. (26)

> History has minimized the evils of this brand of slavery by giving it another name - indenture. . . . Indenture was really a means by which the growing mercantilism of the 17th and 18th centuries employed government sanction to transfer labor to undeveloped colonies. (165)

> By what name you call your people
> Whether by that of freemen or of slaves . . .
> That in some countries
> The laboring poor were called freemen,
> In others slaves . . . ("*A*"-8; 89–90)

In this next Index passage, Zukofsky gives an idealized description of the organic nascence of American craft. It dramatizes Ahearn's observation that "the items Zukofsky writes about in his notes for the *Index of American Design* and in his radio broadcast scripts are not products of alienated labor" (88). Passages from "*A*"-8 and "*A*"-9 evoke a similarly approving attitude toward the products and activities of a preindustrial laborer:

> Given an unsettled landscape, they would try to order it, work the land and build on it. Having built houses, they would fashion iron to supply their daily demands. Once these were satisfied, increasing comforts would permit them the luxuries of decoration and playthings for their children, tho it is true that sensitive craftsmen would find even these luxuries a need from the beginning. (38–39)

> How entirely different the relation between theoretical learning
> And practice was in the handicraft,
> From what it is in large-scale industry. ("*A*"-8, 74)

Hands, heart, not value made us, . . .

. . . .

Lives worked us slowly to delight the sense. (*"A"*-9, 107)

The Index essays pose an implicit critique of industrialization on the basis of its effects on craft production in the next passage. Celia Zukofsky's *American Friends,* a commonplace book of quotations drawing from Zukofsky's published writings, notes, and library, offers a passage from Alexander Hamilton, which she correlates with the subsequently quoted lines from *"A"*-9:

> For in a society with a limited labor force, one individual was often called upon to do numerous tasks. In the individually managed households of the rest of the country, however, craftsmanship was fast becoming a mere pastime. (107)

> ". . . there is scarcely anything of greater moment in the economy of a nation than the proper division of labor."
>
> Alexander Hamilton
> *Report on Manufactures*

> "The foci of production: things reflected
> As wills subjected; formed in the division
> Of labor"
>
> L. Z.
> from *"A"*-9 (23)

The inclusion of poetic artifacts, often doggerel, reveals these Index essays to be the work of a poet, not to mention the editor of the unpublished *Workers' Anthology* and the subsequently published *A Test of Poetry*. Zukofsky uses this quatrain to illustrate the particular historic quandary faced by a congregation modernizing its house of worship with the addition of a cast-iron stove or foot-warmer:

> Extinct the sacred fire of love
> Our zeal grown cold and dead
> In the house of God we fix a stove
> To warm us in their stead. (77)

In another instance, the poet and future translator offers a cleverly rhyming version of a stove-maker's signature couplet. "Baron Stiegel ist der Mann /

Der die ofen Machen Kann" becomes: "Bard Stiegel is the cove / Who can make an iron stove" (52). The acknowledged "Briticism" Zukofsky supplies to preserve the rhyme means fellow or man. This use of illustrative period verse carries out the convictions expressed in Zukofsky's *A Test of Poetry* that poetry "is one of the arts—sometimes individual, sometimes collective in origin—and reflects economic and social status of peoples ..." (99) and that "... Good poetry is definite information on the subject dealt with ..." (89).

In several instances, Zukofsky observes the simple fact that "the majority of craftsmen and their masters left no personal record." Of itself unremarkable, the observations anticipate Zukofsky's own courting of a kind of anonymity in his *Autobiography* and his use of his own initials and those of family members throughout *"A"*:

> The ironwork and the industry they established tell the story of most of them. Occasionally their names were engraved or stamped on an object, most often only their initials. (50)

> Like most of the American designers of the 17th, 18th and early 19th centuries, the majority of craftsmen who worked in tin remain anonymous. There exist only the wares they made and some few traditions connected with these. ... (77)

> As a poet I have always felt that the work says all there needs to be said of one's life. (*Autobiography* 5)

The craft object or poem should apparently speak for itself, saying all that need be said, and the artist contents himself with a simple "L. Z." This reflects not only an effacement of the artist as person but also relates to Zukofsky's well-known positions on the sincerity of good craft. In a remarkable passage from the radio script, "Remmey and Crolius Stoneware," Zukofsky suggests that the high-quality craftsmanship of the object itself confirms the good character of its maker:

> Int.: - . . . Mr. Z. do we have so much faith in the accuracy of Clarkson Crolius' statement on the origin of his pottery?
> Mr. Z.: - For one thing, no authorities have denied it. And, if for no other rea-

son, we will see when we presently look at his work, that he must have been sincerely interested in the tradition of the craftsmen he followed. (196)

In a similar fashion, after paying Duncan Phyfe the high compliment of calling him "a distinguished and sincere craftsman," Zukofsky notes that while Phyfe declined to sit for a portrait, the furniture Phyfe made substitutes:

> And the symbol of his career is almost summed up in the horizontal curves of his table tops, chairs, seats and sofas. . . . His best art, like his time, was given over to order and freedom, simultaneously as it were. Phyfe's furniture reflects the virtues of his life and age. (184)

It is but a few steps from this celebration of the immutable artifact to the poetic animation of history suggested in these lines:

> Mr. Zukofsky: - In objects which men made and used, people live again. The touch of carving to the hand revivifies the hand that made it. (149)

which cannot help but recall: "Measure, tacit is. / The dead hand shapes / An idea . . ." ("*A*"-12, 131).

Of course, the first half of "*A*"-9 has long been celebrated as a masterfully Objectivist exercise in reanimation. Its speaking objects are introduced with the lines: "So that were the things words they could say: . . ." (106), in a section Zukofsky likely completed in November 1939. This passage from the "Remmey and Crolius" script, completed in February 1940, provides an interesting context and points to a possible source for "*A*"-9's masterful conceit:

> If the stoneware shown on our Index plates could speak, like Omar Khayyám's pots, they would say: "Who *is* the Potter, pray, and who the Pot?" It doesn't matter really which Crolius or Remmey made us. The tradition is unbroken. (198)

The Persian poet, whose *Rubáiyat* was famously translated by Edward FitzGerald and included in Zukofsky's *A Test of Poetry*, also wrote of handicrafts that speak for themselves. Did the Index research lead to "*A*"-9? Did the decision to include Omar Khayyám quatrains in *A Test of Poetry* predate the Index? Perhaps it does not matter; Zukofsky participates in a tradition that is unbroken.

. . .

The pertinent biographical and bibliographical information can be summarized concisely. From January 1934 to March 1935, Zukofsky worked for a Civil Work Administration program doing research at Columbia University; he then moved to another federal job, where according to his (April 8, 1935) letter to Ezra Pound, he worked as a "feature and continuity writer and special researchist for WNYC, the Municipal Broadcasting Station of the City of New York" (Pound 166). His employment by the FAP on the Index probably began as early as January 1936; letters confirm that by December 7, 1937, Zukofsky was actively engaged in historical research. Of the surviving writings, his first essay "American Ironwork," is dated August 27, 1938; the last, April 28, 1939; the first radio script, November 16, 1939; the last radio research piece, April 4, 1940. Those readers interested in tracing correspondences between Index work and Zukofsky's other contemporaneous writings should refer to "Year by Year Bibliography of Louis Zukofsky," by Celia Zukofsky, or *A Catalogue of the Louis Zukofsky Manuscript Collection,* by Marcella Booth. Key Zukofsky works include *A Test of Poetry* (1935–40); "Modern Times," "Arise, Arise," "*A*"-8 (August 1935–July 1937), First Half of "*A*"-9 (1938–39), and "Aids and Restatement for the First Half of 'A'-9" (subsequently omitted from "*A*").

The manuscripts that this volume presents were all conserved by Louis Zukofsky and sent to the archive at the University of Texas. The initial essays required the least editorial intervention. An Index typist had produced clean copies, with minor corrections in pen, which bear Zukofsky's signature and a date signifying he had proofread them. Beginning with the third radio script, "A Pair of New York Water Pitchers," I worked from holographic manuscript in Zukofsky's hand, sometimes heavily revised. These later works, produced near the completion of Zukofsky's Index tenure, are thus not edited to the standard of the initial essays. I have made no effort to conceal this.

Errors of spelling, obvious internal inconsistencies, and other mechanical infelicities have been silently corrected. Except where confusion might arise, antiquated or obsolete usages (e.g., "adaption") have been retained in the spirit of the text and as indicative of Zukofsky's erudition. Inconsistent usage has in most cases been resolved in favor of the more contemporary usage. Informal spellings such as "thruout" have been retained if consistent; when possible the preference has been confirmed with the style in other published writings. Zukofsky's use of two elipsis points to indicate omissions within quotations has been modernized. In the cases of questionable or marginally legible passages, the original manuscripts at Texas have been consulted. In the infrequent instances when a passage was reconstructed or based partially on conjecture, I have bracketed it. I have allowed Zukofsky's preference for parentheses to mark the editorial insertion within a quotation to stand, so as to distinguish his insertions from my editorial modifications. Other changes or questionable readings are addressed in the editorial notes.

Works Cited

Ahearn, Barry. "The Adams Connection." Terrell 113–27.

———. "Zukofsky, Marxism, and American Handicraft." Scroggins 80–93.

———. 1983. *Zukofsky's "A": An Introduction.* Berkeley: University of California Press.

Booth, Marcella. 1975. *A Catalogue of the Louis Zukofsky Manuscript Collection.* Austin: Humanities Research Center, University of Texas.

di Manno, Yves. "Land's End." DuPlessis and Quartermain 294–300.

DuPlessis, Rachel, and Peter Quartermain, eds. 1999. *The Objectivist Nexus: Essays in Cultural Poetics.* Tuscaloosa: University of Alabama Press.

———. "Introduction." DuPlessis 1–22.

Leggott, Michelle. 1989. *Reading Zukofsky's 80 Flowers.* Baltimore: Johns Hopkins University Press.

Marsh, Alec. "Poetry and the Age: Pound, Zukofsky, and the Labor Theory of Value." Scroggins 95–111.

Nadel, Ira. "'A Precision of Appeal': Louis Zukofsky and the *Index of American Design.*" Scroggins 112–26.

National Gallery of Art. 1 August 2000. <http://www.nga.gov>.

Nelson, Cary. 1989. *Repression and Recovery: Modern American Poetry and the Politics of Cultural Memory, 1910–1945.* Madison: University of Wisconsin Press.

Pound, Ezra, and Louis Zukofsky. 1987. *Pound/Zukofsky: Selected Letters of Ezra Pound and Louis Zukofsky.* Ed. Barry Ahearn. New York: New Directions.

Quartermain, Peter. 1992. *Disjunctive Poetics: From Gertrude Stein and Louis Zukofsky to Susan Howe.* Cambridge: Cambridge University Press.

Rourke, Constance. "American Traditions for Young People." *Bulletin of the American Library Association* 31, 12 (1937): 934. *New Deal Network.* Ed. Thomas Thurston. 1996. Institute for Learning Technologies, Columbia University. 11 August 2000. <http://newdeal.feri.org/index.htm>.

Scroggins, Mark. "The Revolutionary Word: Zukofsky, *New Masses,* and Political Radicalism in the 1930s." 45–64.

——, ed. 1997. *Upper Limit Music: The Writing of Louis Zukofsky.* Tuscaloosa: University of Alabama Press.

Terrell, Carroll F., ed. 1979. *Louis Zukofsky: Man and Poet.* Orono: National Poetry Foundation, University of Maine.

Zukofsky, Celia. 1979. *American Friends.* New York: C. Z. Publications.

——. "Year by Year Bibliography of Louis Zukofsky." Terrell 385–92.

Zukofsky, Louis. [1978] 1993. *"A."* Baltimore: Johns Hopkins University Press.

——. 1946. *Anew.* Prairie City, Ill.: Press of James A. Decker. Collected in *Complete Short Stories.*

——. [1948] 2000. *A Test of Poetry.* Hanover, N.H.: Wesleyan University Press.

——. 1970. Autobiography. New York: Crossman.

——. [1963] 1987. *Bottom: On Shakespeare.* Berkeley: University of California Press.

——. 1990. *Collected Fiction.* Elmwood Park, Ill.: Dalkey Archive Press.

——. 1991. *Complete Short Poetry.* Baltimore: Johns Hopkins University Press.

——. 1981. *Prepositions: The Collected Critical Essays of Louis Zukofsky.* Expanded Edition. Berkeley: University of California Press.

——. "Program 'Objectivists' 1931." *Poetry: A Magazine of Verse* 37, 5 (February 1931): 268–72.

PART ONE

Essays

I. American Ironwork, 1585–1856

1

Old World Traditions

The entanglements of influence affecting production and design in the spread of iron from the ancient East into the beginnings of modern Europe form a complicated history. The difficulties increase in an attempt to disentangle it with respect to the ironworkers in the Colonies. To realize that their immediate needs demanded quick adaption of what they knew to what ores they found in the new land is a convenience. The Indians who had yet to learn the use of iron from the white immigrants could not help them. For the rest, considering it is often difficult to tell if very early "American" ironwork was made in the Colonies or brought over by the different nationals, one can only look back to Europe of the tenth to the fifteenth centuries as a beginning.

The work of French Renaissance blacksmiths is evident in the hinges and latches of Maine, New Hampshire, Vermont and New York (Crown Point and Ticonderoga, originally Forts Carillon and Vaudreuil, built 1755–56). New York also shows the influence of the Dutch; Pennsylvania, New Jersey and Delaware, of the Germans and Swedes. The names of craftsmen in Charleston, S.C.—Thibaut, Justi, Werner, Ortman Sr., Johnson—indicate that they were Latin, German and English. The traditions of sixteenth and seventeenth-century French and Spanish iron flourished in the Vieux Carré of New Orleans. The houses in the old quarter of this city had door-knockers of French and Venetian designs that the ironworkers could carry out, though the knockers may have been imported. Nearer to hand, in the Metropolitan Museum of Art, is a Connecticut specimen of Suffolk latch of Turkish motif.

The church continued as a force in the new land. For example, an ecclesiastical wafer-iron used at St. Mary's Catholic Church at Doylestown, Pennsylvania (1850) is stamped, or probably engraved, with two crosses upon a grassy hill, between two thorn bushes, and surrounded with a double rimmed border enclosing twelve little stars, and two small, singly rimmed circles containing small crosses composed of dots. The use of the wafer-iron was known not only to Luther and twelfth-century France, but in Carthage of the sixth or seventh century.

To work the metal, the craftsmen of seventeenth-century Pennsylvania built forges or bloomeries like the Catalan forge first used in Spain in the tenth [century] and subsequently thruout western Europe. Without even the crude wind furnaces, let alone the foot-bellows, of their forbears, the English who discovered iron ore on Roanoke Island, North Carolina (1585) faced the most primitive conditions.

Looking back, it seems poetic justice that the first book published in Virginia (1623) was Mr. George Sandys' translation of Ovid's *Metamorphoses*[1] with its legendary description of the Iron Age. The colonists had to start from scratch: make tools of iron to break the ground, and nails and cooking utensils for their houses. The dense forests of the colonies were an advantage in the process of smelting. There were no legal restrictions as to their use, as in England, when during Elizabeth's reign statutes prohibited not only the cutting down of trees, but the erection of ironworks in specified districts. Lord Dudley's[2] attempt to substitute pit-coal for wood in the mother country, in 1620, was abandoned on expiration of his patent (1634) and not* revived till a century later. The leaders of expeditions at the time were evidently not concerned with Dudley's method, though they were aware of the fact that working the iron in the Colonies would demand money, labor and protection on the part of the authorities at home.

1. (Bibliographic information for the footnotes on the following pages can be found in Works Cited following the Introduction.)

George Sandys, 1578–1644 (1664 according to Library of Congress; Britannica), poet, translator, director of Virginia industry and agriculture, also traveled to the Middle East. The Library of Congress holds the 1626 London edition of his Ovid translation. Zukofsky's interest may be explained by the suggestion of *"A"*-12 that he once intended to write an opera: "Ovid's *Metamorphoses* / That would sing Golding" (254). Again, in *A Test of Poetry*, Zukofsky includes a passage from Arthur Golding's 1565 translation of Ovid (53–54).

2. Presumably Thomas Dudley 1576–1653, four-time governor of the Massachusetts Bay Colony.

2
Iron Districts (1585–1790)

North Carolina and Virginia

The early English colonists on the Atlantic coast were at once interested in the iron they discovered. The unsuccessful Raleigh expedition of 1585 sent home a small quantity of the ore for expert examination. There is no sequel to this event, and North Carolina does not figure in the production of iron till 1728 when pig iron was exported and several furnaces were in existence.

The Virginia settlers found bog ore near Jamestown in 1608, and two years later Sir Thomas Gates testified before the Council in London that some of the ore which "had been sent home had been found to yield as good iron as any in the world." The Virginia Company of London was then formed to exploit it. An early record of 1620 mentions among tradesmen sent out to the colony "men for ironworks," about forty of whom came from Sussex. In the same year, the treasurer of the company, Sir Edwin Sandys, in a speech on affairs of the colony, relates the attempts made to turn the settlers from the cultivation of tobacco to other more useful commodities, and notes that 150 persons had been sent to set up three ironworks. Beverly's *History of Virginia* gives the details of the venture: "an *iron-work* at Falling Creek (seven miles below Richmond) in Jamestown River, where they made proof of good iron ore, and brought the whole workes so near a perfection that they writ word to the Company in London that they did not doubt to finish the work, and have plentiful provision of iron for them by next Easter." The next year, 1621, three of the master-workmen having died, the Company sent over Mr. John Berkeley and his son Maurice, both commended as skillful ironworkers, with twenty other experienced craftsmen. "The iron proved reasonably good," says Beverly, but on May 22, 1622, before the workers "got into the body of the mine," the ironworks were demolished and the people executed by the Indians. The production of iron in Virginia was not resumed till about 1715, though E. W. Gent suggests a much earlier date: "Neither does Virginia yield to an other province whatsoever in excellency and plenty of this oare: and I cannot promise to myself any other than extraordinary successe and gaine if this noble and useful staple be but vigirously followed." In 1650, when this statement appeared in London, the scene of the pioneer industry had already shifted to New England.

Massachusetts and Rhode Island

Thomas Dexter of the Massachusetts Bay Colony discovered bog-ore at Hammersmith, now Saugus, near Lynn. The small quantity of ore which he persuaded Captain Robert Bridges to take with him to England proved fine enough when reduced to effect† the organization in the mother country of "The Company of Undertakers for the Iron Works," in 1642. Eleven or more stockholders, contributing a capital of £1000, sent Richard Leader as their agent to Boston with a group of workers trained in mining, smelting and fabrication of iron, to work under the machinist and inventor, Joseph Jenks. John Winthrop Jr., son of the governor, was immediately interested in the enterprise and applied to the Massachusetts General Court for a charter. This was granted in 1644, and included special privileges respecting the use of wood, ore and other materials needed for the working of iron. Winthrop himself travelled down the New England coast from Maine to Connecticut to find a suitable location for the project. He decided in favor of Braintree, Massachusetts, but construction of blast furnaces and bloomery forges seems to have been begun at the same time in both Braintree and Hammersmith. It took about three years to complete these works. Local stock subscriptions were authorized by the General Court in 1644, and about £1200 to £1500 were spent on construction. In 1647, the records of the Court have it that £1500 more were required. In any case, the enterprise was successful, for one of the operators wrote to Winthrop in Connecticut, in 1647: "We have cast this winter some tons of pots, likewise mortors, stoves and skillets." A year later, the governor wrote to his son, as follows: "The iron works goeth on with more hope, and now yields about seven tons per week", and "The furnace runs eight tons per week, and their bar iron is as good as Spanish." The Hammersmith furnace continued to operate till 1688, and the Braintree furnace till 1653.

By 1720, Massachusetts was said to be the main iron district in the Colonies. The Plymouth Colony followed the example of the Massachusetts Bay in the construction of furnaces, and it is recorded that Plymouth and Norfolk counties alone had twenty ironworks using both pond- and bog-ore. The industry branched out to Rhode Island where the first furnace was built as early as 1675.‡

Connecticut

When John Winthrop Jr. received the royal commission as Governor of Connecticut in 1657, his sponsorship of the iron industry did not stop with the Braintree and Saugus projects in Massachusetts. He became the first ironmaster of the colony of Connecticut. A deposit of bog-ore in North Haven, like that of Hammersmith,§ and sufficient water-power from two streams emptying into Long Island Sound at nearby East Haven, offered an obvious opportunity for the development of iron production. The governor and Captain Thomas Clarke therefore built a blast furnace at the site, and some hundred feet away, a refinery forge (1658), which produced pig iron and pots from 1663 till perhaps 1680. The deposits of ore seem to have been too shallow for mining to have continued after that time—as seems also to have been the case, during the next fifty years, with a number of small ironworks using bog- and pond-ore in central Connecticut and magnetic sand found along the shore of Long Island Sound at the eastern end of the state.

The second landmark in the history of Connecticut iron-mining was effected** by Daniel Bissell and Thomas Lamb who opened Ore Hill mine (1732) and built the bloomery forge at Lime Rock, (Litchfield Cy., N.W. Conn.), even before the town was settled, thus beginning the extensive mining of the famous Salisbury District. Salisbury ore, limonite or brown hematite, was found in stratified mica slate remarkably free of other materials and mined at first for the most part in open pits or sometimes in horizontal drifts not more than about thirty-five feet below the surface. The workmen who received concessions from the owners paid them a royalty for the privilege.

The deposits first discovered at Ore Hill, later Salisbury, at Lakeville, were of large extent, and were soon being worked in an area reaching from southern Vermont through western Massachusetts and Connecticut, New York east of the Hudson and down into New Jersey. At the peak of its productive history, the Salisbury District in Connecticut had twenty-seven blast furnaces, besides forges, puddling furnaces and foundries making small castings, within thirty miles of Lakeville and Lime Rock alone; and the out-of-state mines in Massachusetts and New York exceeded those of Connecticut. Most of the yield of the local mines was usually consumed by local furnaces. It is reasonable to assume that in isolated, inland settlements of the seventeenth century, the local iron was intended for consumption by local purchasers. Local legislation often enforced this intention as will be seen later.

New Hampshire, Vermont, New York

No furnaces were worked in Vermont before 1775; and in New Hampshire and Maine, before about 1795. In New York, the Ancram Furnace, owned by Philip Livingston, was operated at Ancram Creek, Columbia County, fourteen miles east of the Hudson River, near Connecticut "Ore Hill," as early as 1750. It was thus part of the Salisbury mining district, as were the furnaces operated in Orange, Duchess, Rockland and Westchester Counties between 1750 and the Revolution.

New Jersey and Pennsylvania

The year 1682 marks the beginning of the third change in the center of iron production in the thirteen colonies; New Jersey and Pennsylvania were to exceed, in the first seventy-five years of the eighteenth century, the prestige of New England in the seventeenth and the promise of Virginia before the Jamestown massacre. Shrewsbury Furnace at Pinton Falls, South Monmouth County, New Jersey, is recorded as in operation under the management of Colonel Lewis Morris, in 1682. The same year, William Penn, who owned iron furnaces at Hawkurst, in England, arrived in Pennsylvania, with high hopes of encouraging the manufacture of iron in his new world province. His writing noted the existence of "mineral of iron and copper in various places," the following year, 1683. There is a tradition that ca. 1707 the colony had iron mines run by the king of the Shawnee Indians, a Swiss and Governor Evans. But this was later denied by James Logan, Secretary of the Province [under]†† Penn. Possibly the copper mines on Mine Ridge, several miles south of Lancaster, where in 1843 a very old shaft was still to be seen, were meant instead of iron mines. However, the smelting of iron in the province at a very early date, 1692, is supported by Richard Frame's rhymed "Description of Pennsylvania" published that year by Bradford:

> A certain place here is where some begun
> To try some mettle and have made it run,
> Wherein was iron absolutely found
> At once was known some forty pound.

The first successful attempt to establish ironworks in Pennsylvania was made by Thomas Rutter, an English Quaker, at Pool Forge, Philadelphia County, later Berks County, in 1716. Jonathan Dickinson described this project, in 1717: "This last summer one Thomas Rutter, a smith, who lives not far from Germantown, hath removed further up in the country and of his own strength hath set about making iron. Such it proves to be as is highly set by, by all the smiths here, who say the best of Swedes' iron doth not exceed it, and we have heard of others that are going on with iron works. It is supposed there is stone (i.e. ore) sufficient for ages to come—and in all likelihood . . . iron may be improved and transported home . . . if not discouraged."

Rutter founded the Colebrookdale Furnace at Ironstone Creek, eight miles west of Pottstown, Colebrookdale Township, Berks County, Pennsylvania in 1720. His share owners were James Lewis and Anthony Morris. Later, the furnace owned by Morris, Alexander Wood, Samuel Preston, William Atwood, John Leacock, Nathaniel French, George Mifflin, Thomas Potts, George Boone (the pioneer's ancestor) and descendants of Rutter and Potts, supplied not only Pool Forge as the original Thomas Rutter had done, but at least four other forges in the vicinity, until about 1765. Other furnaces were founded soon after 1720, notably Christine-Redding Furnace, in Chester County, Pennsylvania, by William Branson and Samuel Nutt (1728); Keith's Furnace, Newcastle County, Delaware, then Pennsylvania, by Sir William Keith, Governor of the Province (1725-8); Kurtz's Furnace, Lancaster County, by Kurtz, said to be an Amish Mennonite, who for religious reasons refused a grant of 1000 acres from the Proprietaries; Abington Furnace, South bank of Christiana Creek, Delaware, originally Pennsylvania, by Samuel Nutt, John Rutter, Caspar Wistar and others (1727); Durham Furnace, Bucks County, by Anthony Morris, James Logan (Penn's secretary) and others (1727); Mount Pleasant Furnace, Berks County, by Thomas Potts, Jr., (1738); Warwick Furnace, Chester County, by Anna Nutt & Co., (1738); Cornwall Furnace, Lebanon County, by Peter Grubb, (1742); Popadicken or Potts Grove Furnace, Berks County, (before 1745); Elizabeth Furnace, Lancaster County, by Hans Jacob Huber (1750, sold to H. W. Stiegel and partners in 1757).

During the eighteenth century, Philadelphia was the commercial center of the chief region of iron production in the Colonies. The names of the English founders and owners of furnaces in Pennsylvania already mentioned show that their interests in iron production were not confined to one district of the province. Their property rights spread out and were taken over by their descendants. The same facts hold true of other nationals and in other colonies. Thus, Peter Hasenclever and John Jacob Faesch owned a number of furnaces in several counties of New Jersey about 1768. Tho there was as yet no question of [the] restriction of individual enterprise by domestic or regional monopoly, obviously the interests which could establish furnaces and forges had money to invest and very often valuable European experience in the industry which they furthered and centralized.[3] But other factors contributed to the concentration of iron districts in Eastern Pennsylvania and New Jersey: changes in the smelting process, which will be discussed later; the physical features of the region which the owners selected for their iron works—streams and rivers for their use as power and transportation; and the migratory temper of the iron masters and ironworkers.

The Swedish traveler Acrelius, writing in 1758, regarded Durham Furnace as the best ironworks in the country, and one of its chief claims to distinction was its success in commercializing the Delaware, on which the ore was transported in Durham boats. Andover Furnace (1760) in Sussex County, New Jersey made use of the river in the same fashion, as did the other furnaces of the region transporting ore to the established commercial center, Philadelphia, which in turn shipped the iron to England.

However, the pioneer element among the colonial ironworkers was seeing further than the achievements of the ironmasters and the consequent difficulties which involved them with the mother country, and seeking to better their‡‡ own situation in the West. About 1760, furnaces were established in central and western Pennsylvania, in the Allegheny coal region. Wyoming Valley, for example, was settled by colonials from Connecticut, among them two brothers called Gore, blacksmiths who were the first to use anthracite coal in their forge fires, between 1768 and 1769. But even before that date the Pennsylvania Germans who earned a good part of their reputation by

---

3. Passages such as this perhaps indicate the concern for economic issues Zukofsky brought to this project. In a letter to Ezra Pound (Dec. 7, 1937) Zukofsky writes about his "responsible position" with the WPA, and notes, "I am now outlining the economic, political background of American Design (useful arts)—and with a chance to read and study history" (*Pound/Zukofsky: Selected Letters* 192). Alec Marsh ("Poetry and the Age," *Upper Limit Music*) gives detailed treatment to Zukofsky's economic thinking, which is especially evident in "*A*"-8, "*A*"-9, and the letters.

casting stove plates from ca. 1740 to ca. 1760 had been migrating, the simple German ironworkers often carrying their molds from furnace to furnace.

Other States

The impetus given to iron manufacture by the undertakings of New Jersey and Pennsylvania spurred its development in the south and west, especially towards 1760. One of the most important American Colonial furnaces, the Principio, was established as early as 1724 in Cecil County, Maryland by an English Company which also owned the Accokuck Furnace in Stafford County, Virginia in 1726, thus reviving the Virginia industry. There were furnaces in North and South Carolina about 1728, exporting pig iron, but their names are not extant. There were no furnaces in Georgia till 1832, and none in Tennessee and Kentucky till 1790–91 respectively, about the time that the introduction of steam and the use of coal in blast furnaces was beginning to confine the iron industry to regions yielding mineral coal. In the first quarter of the nineteenth century, these were to be western Pennsylvania, and West Virginia, eastern Tennessee, north Alabama, and northern Ohio in the Cleveland region where rich ores from the Lake Superior district would meet the coal, shipped by water, from the Alleghenies. However, confining interest to the original colonies, the description of establishment of furnaces before the Revolution may end by calling attention to the ironworks near Baltimore, owned by Mr. Carter of Nomini-Hall estate, Westmoreland County, Virginia. He was a leading social light of his time, and his position suggests a discussion of the economic and social life which developed around the iron centers already mentioned.

Iron Plantations

The typical community where working iron was a flourishing industry fostered by gentlemen of means like Mr. Carter thrived extensively in eastern Pennsylvania during the eighteenth century. Practically self-sufficing, the iron plantation embraced several thousand acres of land, resembling in general aspect the small, feudal, manorial holding of medieval Europe. From the mansion house of the ironmaster as a center, secluded in environs that gave the leisure and distinction necessary for his circle of intimates and interest, spread the outlying homes of the workers; removed somewhat from these, the furnaces and forges where they labored, the iron mines, and, in the dense woods, the charcoal house storing the fuel for their operations. Also part of the community of the workers were their orchards and grain fields to sustain them, barns, a common grist mill, perhaps a common bake oven, a store, the ironmaster's or his representative's office, and a blacksmith's shop. Emanuel Swedenborg who visited the Christini-Redding and Keith's furnaces (ca. 1725) saw the kind of community described here and wrote about it in his "Regnum Subteranneum sine Minerale de Ferro."[4] George Whitefield also visited the district and preached Methodism at Warwick and neighboring townships. Very likely his audience consisted of farmers who did their own ironwork, freeholders but not men of wealth, as well as of ironworkers hired for their immediate skill, who did some farming on the rich ironmasters' estates, if they had contracted for it.

Labor

Skilled labor for ironworks was not usually in demand except in towns and on plantations devoted to specialized manufacture. And skilled, like unskilled labor, was not always free. Extant copies of early colonial indentures are the same word for word as those of England. Colonial apprenticeship, except for differences of training compelled by different conditions, bears the stamp of a system taken over from abroad.[5]

An advertisement in Bradford's New York *Gazette* for June 10, 1728 gives these facts: "The ship *Happy Return* is lately arrived at the City of New York, from Dublin, with Men and Women Servants: many of the Men are Tradesmen as Blacksmiths, Carpenters, Weavers, Tailors, Cordwainers, and other trades, which servants are to be seen on board said Vessel, lying over Mr. Reads Wharff, and to be disposed of by John S. and Joseph Read on reasonable terms."

---

4. Emmanuel Swedenborg, 1688–1772, well-known Swedish philosopher and religious writer. His *Regnum subterraneum sive minerale* appeared as one volume of the book entitled *Opera Philiosophica et mineralia* (Leipzig, 1734), a work of natural philosophy that theorized particles in motion. Swedenborg is referenced—". . . Emanuel's 4 Angels with Hats / on their Heads . . ."—in *"A"*-13 (394).

5. See *"A"*-8: "By what name you call your people / Whether by that of freemen or of slaves . . . / That in some countries / The *laboring* poor were called freemen, / In others slaves . . ." (89–90). The general concern with labor here has relevance for Zukofsky's poetry and politics. The letters, *"A,"* the original publication of the first half of *"A"*-9, "27 / Song - 3/4 time" (*Complete Short Poetry* 58–61) and the concluding notes to *Anew* (*CSP* 102–4) make the Marxist elements of his thinking clear. Drafts of subsequent Index work give evidence that explicitly editorializing statements about economics were cut.

Sent on to the iron plantations from New York, or direct from nearer ports, and supervised by the ironmaster himself or his manager, these servants lost their liberty for a specified time. For the negroes among them the loss of liberty was perpetual, tho in the seventeenth century they were considered servants rather than slaves and were not called so till the eighteenth century when slavery became widespread in colonial society. In the North, many of the negroes were skilled blacksmiths.

Blacksmiths

The services of the blacksmith, whether rendered to an iron plantation or to the community of a township, conferred upon him what amounted to a special social distinction. On the plantation, as a worker and often decorator in iron, he attained to the position of a recognized artisan, whose skill was specialized and rewarded accordingly; in the town, where he often combined craftsmanship with shopkeeping, he was in a class with the tradesman, as the advertisement quoted from Bradford's New York *Gazette* of 1728 has shown. The *American Weekly Mercury* published at Philadelphia, Sept. 5, 1734, further supports the fact of the blacksmith's commercial achievements: "Lately set up at Trenton in New Jersey, a Planing and Plate Mill by Isaac Harrow, an English smith, who makes the under named goods"—e.g. dripping pans, frying pans, chafing dishes, broad axes, falling axes, knives, spades, shovels, ladels, pans, shears, saws, coffee roasters, etc.,—"likewise also too, iron plates fitted for Bell Making and any other Use."

The blacksmith's appearance in colonial history occurs early: in 1643, at Hartford, Connecticut, Thomas Hurlbut and Peter Bassaker; in 1657, in New York, on lists of burgers and freemen in old civic records, names like Claes Pieterzen. In Delaware, a state historian records the early smiths as well paid—"one who with his negroes, by working up old iron at sixpence per pound, earned 50 shillings a day." Sometimes the practice of the craft descends through a family, as John Pratt's of Essex, Connecticut, the line beginning in 1678 and running to 1870.

Before and during the Revolution, the blacksmith's ability to cast cannon was honored, as an old epitaph on a tombstone in St. Paul's Churchyard in New York attests: "James Davis Late Smith to Royal Artillery, / d. Dec. 17, 1769."

So that by the end of the Revolution, the blacksmith is a citizen enjoying the social life of the new country: "Notice All White and Black-Smiths in the

City of New York are requested to meet at the City Tavern Tomorrow Evening at 6 o'clock" (*American Magazine,* July 9, 1788. White smith—worker in white metal—tin or silver—or galvanizer of iron). Or he is to be found with his "forges, anvils and sledges at work" in a procession in Portsmouth, New Hampshire, celebrating the adoption of the Constitution of the United States.

The blacksmith is also of especial interest in relation to a study of legislative provisions that furthered his social position and the growth of the iron industry in general. Thus the records of Middletown, Connecticut, refer to a special grant of land to workers in iron, April 16, 1663: "George Durant allso doth engage himself to be hear resident the next micelmus, insueing the deat hearof and also to inhabit upon it and to do the towns worek of smithing during the term of four years befor he shall mac sale of it to any other."

Legislation's Effect on the Iron Industry §§

Very early (1642), special legislation released the officers and employees of the Company of Undertakers for the Iron Works at Saugus, Massachusetts, from church attendance without depriving them of their voting rights. Contentions with other residents of Saugus, resulting from this dispensation, caused a local commentator to remark (1677): "instead of drawing out bars of iron for the country's use there was hammered out nothing but contentions and lawsuits." The success of the ironworks at Saugus makes the truth of this remark questionable, and undoubtedly the officers and employees of the ironworks were allowed not to go to church so that they could give more time to their work. The community needed their products, as is shown by the fact that as late as 1685, three years before the project was finally abandoned, the operating company was granted rights to manufacture cast-iron pots and other wares "on condition that the inhabitants of this jurisdiction shall be furnished with all sorts of barr iron for their use—not exceeding 20£ per ton."

But the iron districts were not always fortunate enough to benefit by local laws. The mother country interfered, as in 1718 when Parliament introduced a bill prohibiting the erection of forges and iron mills, declaring that the establishment of such works in the Colonies tended "to lessen their dependence upon Great Britain." The British manufacturers were producing smaller and finer nails than the colonials, but admitting the excellence of American spikes, bolts and large nails which, by 1740, were competing for the British market. In 1747, Col. Joseph Pitkin obtained from the authorities of East Hartford, Connecticut, the right to set up an iron slitting-mill, only to have the British Parliament revoke it by prohibiting Colonial ironworks in the Iron Act of 1750. However, cities like Birmingham demanded American iron, and claimed that England produced only half enough for home consumption. The Iron Act was thus partly a concession to home demands and the colonies, for it removed British duties from colonial pig and bar iron in order to encourage colonial exporters to replace Swedish iron supplying England's industrial centers. But it insisted that the colonial iron be worked up in Britain instead of at home, and specifically forbade not only mills that slit bar iron into nail rods, but plating forges using trip-hammers, and all steel-tool furnaces,—altho existing works were allowed to continue in operation.

The law had little effect. Iron exports to England, between 1750 and 1771, rose only from 3,000 to 7,520 tons. In 1757, the Sheffield decree prohibited the importation of American iron. From the time the Iron Act was passed, Pennsylvania, New Jersey and Massachusetts flagrantly disregarded it and opposed its mercantile principles by granting bounties for the building of new ironworks.

By 1775, the colonies had more furnaces producing pig iron, and more forges smelting pig iron into bar and wrought iron, than England and Wales combined. After the Declaration of Independence, the young country continued to fight the English prohibitions on American iron manufacture with concerted revolutionary action. The quotation which follows is from the proceedings of the Connecticut General Assembly for December 1776: "Whereas it is of greatest importance for the safety and defense of this, the United State of America, that the foundery of cannon should be continued at Salisbury, and in order thereto that some proper persons should be appointed to procure wood and coal and other material for that purpose— . . . Resolved by this assembly that Mr. Benjamin Henshaw be and is hereby appointed and directed to repair forthwith to Salisbury and apply to Col. Joshua Porter, manager of said foundery, and afford him all the assistance in power." Fifty men worked at the Salisbury foundry for about five years and produced mortars, cannon, swivel guns, hand-grenades and camp-kettles which were distributed to the American armies.

In 1789, the efforts American iron manufacturers would exert to influence protectionist legislation, in order to develop their industry in the next half century, are already apparent. Mr. Hartley, from the iron district near York, Pennsylvania, thus advocated the levying of a national tariff: "We had then (1783) but few manufactures among us, and the vast quantities of goods that flowed in upon us from Europe at the conclusion of the war rendered those few useless."

The "vast quantities of goods" from abroad were still flowing in 1791, as a notice of Mr. Anthony Ackley, "At the Sign of the Gold Mill Saw, No. 7 Broad Street," in the *N.Y. Journal and Patriotic Record* for November 12, 1791, attests: "JUST IMPORTED Hardware, Ironmongery and Cutler Consisting of the Following Articles, viz . . . 4 d. nails, spades and shovels, sheet lead and sheet iron, Smoothing Irons, long and short handle frying pans . . . iron wire, shovels and tongs . . . bellows . . . iron candlesticks . . . locks, brads and clout nails, crosscut and tenant sawfiles . . . thumb latches, locks of all sorts . . . iron window pulleys, etc. etc. etc."

Nevertheless, in the very first session of Congress, the protectionists had begun a struggle which was to form the main historical interest of American iron production till the invention of the Bessemer process—aside, that is, from the more lasting interest to be found in the objects made by the iron workers and their own lives.

3

Ironworking and Ironwork: (1645-1856)

Furnaces and Foundries

Mercer (*The Bible in Iron* 144) notes the differences between furnace and foundry which are often confused in descriptions of ironworking in the colonies:

"It was the important process of smelting iron direct from the ore, as pigiron or raw material, rather than remelting the metal thus previously produced, that distinguished the blast furnaces properly so called not only from the secondary blast furnaces called foundries or 'cupolas,' which did not smelt but remelted iron for manufacturing purposes, but also from the forge, where iron was hammered into the raw material for wrought ironwork, known as bar iron. Because the forge was also built in the forest equipped with a massive smoke stack and blast bellows on a waterwheel, it has sometimes been confused . . . with the furnace; but the forge as a blacksmith shop on a large scale, which only softened the metal without smelting it, equipped with a huge hammer attached to another waterwheel, which hammered the metal into shape either directly from the ore (a bloomery), or by reheating the previously smelted pig iron, had nothing to do with the casting of iron, or with the manufacture of any such thing as a stove plate made of cast iron." It is true "that forge and furnace were sometimes owned, managed and accounted for together." And "though it appears that the 'air furnace' of Colonel Spotswood, at Massaponax, in Virginia, working in 1732 . . . may properly be called a foundry, and though the name foundry was loosely, if not incorrectly applied to blast furnaces in the United States until the middle of the 19th century, . . . before 1820 there were no true foundries in Pennsylvania, so that during the period of their artistic decoration (ca. 1670–1770) . . . the making of stoves was confined to the furnaces; that is to say, . . . the stove plates . . . were cast, not at stove works and foundries in small remelting furnaces called 'cupolas,' but direct from the ore at its first melting, in the original furnace, and close to the site of its excavation from the earth; so that the chemical analysis of these plates, when agreeing with certain deposits of ore, might sometimes show, without further evidence, which furnace made them."

The plant at Saugus, Massachusetts (1642), already discussed here under iron districts, may serve as a typical example of iron manufactories operating in the colonies until about 1750:

"To provide power for the blast a dam ten feet high was built across the Saugus River about 2000 feet up-stream from the furnace; this raised the water level six or eight feet, and flooded a thousand acres. From this dam a canal fifteen or twenty feet wide and six to eight feet deep conducted the water to a small pond near the furnace and only a little lower than the main reservoir, though fifty feet above the level of the river opposite. This gave about thirty feet of head to the thirty foot water-wheel. The floor from which the charge was fed into the top of the furnace was nearly level with the water of this pond. The raw material was bog-ore, the fuel charcoal, and the flux oyster shells. The molten iron was drawn direct from the blast furnace into V-shaped trenches in the sand of the casting floor, producing long triangular bars which were designated as 'sowes'; at that time (1645) no branches were made to produce 'pigs.' Small castings were made from remelted sowes; wrought iron was made in the adjacent bloomery forge; when required the machine shop carried the work to further perfection" (H. C. Keith, *The Early Iron Industry in Connecticut* 5).

The principle involved in the metallurgy of blast furnace and forge is that iron ores "are either oxides, or, by comparatively simple treatment, can be converted to oxides," which "suitably heated with carbon readily give up their oxygen to it, leaving spongy metallic iron. In the forge this is practically the extent of the reactions; the resulting gases at once escape into the air, while the mineral matter associated with the ore, and known as the 'gangue,' melts, part remaining in the forge as cinder, and part filling the pores in the spongy iron, from which some is later removed by hammering or squeezing." This process involving the direct extraction of wrought iron from the ore goes back to prehistoric times.

"The reduction of the ore, however, is but the first step in a series of reactions, in the case of the blast furnace. The function of the latter is not only to deoxidize the iron, as is done in the forge, but also to carburize and melt it; and to convert the gangue into a fusible slag which, as far as practicable, will carry off all the undesirable matter, the process depending upon a general, though not invariable principle underlying most metallurgical operations: that if both reduced and oxidized substances are melted together, the reduced substances will unite in one group, and those oxidized in another, but the two groups will remain entirely separate."

"The blast furnace is essentially a tall container, filled to the top with fuel, ore, and flux, with the lower part of the contents maintained at an intense heat by a blast of air, which furnishes the oxygen to burn the fuel, and then, by the products of that combustion, aided by the heat produced, first effects the reactions which must precede the melting of the iron and the slag, and then becomes 'tunnel-head gas,' burned in the early days to get rid of it, but later utilized to heat the blast and to generate steam."

"The solid contents of the stack, eaten away at the bottom by the burning of the fuel and the melting of other constituents, move slowly downward, the top of the column, by the more or less continuous addition of fresh material, being kept close to a fixed level, the 'stock line.' As the ore descends, it is first reduced to spongy iron, as in the forge; then, continuing down into regions of increasing heat, but still solid, it slowly absorbs carbon, thus lowering its point of fusion from the 2786 degrees Fahrenheit required for pure iron, until at about 2200 degrees it melts, taking up, as the temperature continues to increase, more carbon, until it has absorbed a total of nearly 5%, together with such silicon, manganese and phosphorus as have also been reduced, and such sulphur—as iron sulphide—as has not been converted to calcium sulphide, the compound collecting in the bottom of the hearth as a molten mass of that material of rather widely varying composition known under the general name of 'pig-iron.'"

"In the meantime, the limestone, the amount of which, in the early days was determined by the combined results of experience, experiment, and then an 'informed guess,' has burned to lime, part combining with the iron sulphide present, to form calcium sulphide and free the iron, the rest uniting with the silicious matter of the gangue, and the ash, to make a fusible silicate of lime with more or less magnesia and alumina, which, on melting, collects all the oxidized material and the calcium sulphide, and settles on top of the much heavier molten iron, to flow out over the 'cinder notch,' as soon as it reaches that level."

"The various reactions are controlled by mixing different ores, by varying the proportion of flux used, and by changing the temperature of the hearth, to all of which the resulting metal is very sensitive. That the early iron-masters—and not so early ones at that, for it is only within comparatively recent times that the assistance of the chemist has been accepted—working almost entirely by rule-of-thumb methods, were able to turn out the quality of iron that they did, is little short of miraculous" (C. R. Harte, "Connecticut Blast Furnaces" in Keith and Harte, *Early Iron Industry of Connecticut*).

"The stack of Cornwall Furnace (Lebanon Cy., Pa.), built in 1742, was 32 feet high, 21 1/2 feet square at the base, and 11 feet square at top; . . . a Lakeville, Connecticut, furnace, built in 1763, . . . its greatest diameter inside the egg or 'bosh,' 9 feet, and a height of 21 feet. It was lined with slate smeared with yellow clay, against which the outer wall was constructed of white lime-stone. The bottom of the interior was built of a special refractory stone."

"Swedenborg describes the old furnace stacks in general as 25 feet high, with oblong openings near the top about 4 feet long for charging the ore, charcoal and flux. He says the largest bellows were 5 feet wide, that the ore was roasted at the rate of 18 pecks to 24 bushels of charcoal, that oyster shells, when convenient, were used for flux, and that the furnace was tapped every 8 hours."

"Some of the lower hearths for about three feet up were lined with sand-stone, higher with brick, and every six days was a 'found day.'"

"Federal Furnace, Massachusetts, built in 1794, had a stone stack 20 feet high, 24 feet square at base, 7 feet thick, and an inside diameter of 10 feet. It was lined with a soft slate called firestone and had a brick funnel at the top.

It was arched on the oven front above the tap-hole and also on the side for the two tuyers of the two leather bellows."

"The blowing apparatus of the old blast furnaces was of these kinds, 1, the leather bellows, first used; 2, the blowing tub, or wooden box bellows, and 3, the tromp, or water blast . . . Two bellows, rather than one, were used, driven by water power communicated by means of a cam arrangement on the shaft of the great water wheel."

"In general . . . the leather bellows were 22 feet long and made of oak plank two inches thick, at the Scotch furnaces in 1809."

"The blowing-tub . . . invented by Hans Lobsinger, of Nurenburg, about 1550, (and) used in England in the 18th century, (was) introduced in Pennsylvania shortly before the Revolution and continued in the United States in many furnaces as late as about 1870. . . . This apparatus . . . held to be cheaper and more durable than the leather bellows . . . consisted of two large close-fitting wooden boxes, one of which raised and lowered upon the other, and being kept air tight along the cracks by what might be called very flexible wood and leather weather strips set on steel springs, forced out the air which had entered through valves in the bottom box through the tuyer or blast pipe. . . . These tubs or boxes of short stroke, three feet, . . . generally had one tuyer and rarely two."

"The tromp or water blast . . . was a very ancient invention by which air was forced or pumped in through a wooden pipe about 8 inches square, by the down-rush of water from a tank above and forced into a box 5 feet long by 2 1/2 high by 1 1/2 deep, where incoming water compressing it, forced it out through the tuyer in a continuous steady blast. The apparatus had been long used in Southern Europe . . . with the . . . Catalan forge . . . Professor Lesley in 1856 describes it as surviving in the Southern States" (ibid. Mercer, 149–150).

Bog ore

"Men in boats with an apparatus resembling oyster tongs used to pull the lumps of bog ore out of Assawamsett, Carver and Middleboro ponds in Massachusetts, the latter of which yielded from three to six hundred tons a year at six dollars a ton . . . bog ore occurred along the margin of ponds where there were springs and . . . grew or formed in from seven to fifteen years, if the digger covered the hole with leaves and rubbish, but . . . would not form if the water were drained off. Some other ore called 'pond ore' was dredged out of ponds at depths of from two to twenty-five feet with tongs, and 'grew' again in twenty-five years. A man could raise half a ton a day, consisting of three kinds, the so-called 'short,' reddish brown and of the size of large bullets; the 'pancake,' resembling Turkey figs, and the 'black,' in cakes from the mud bottom. Dr. Forbes asserted in 1793 that 'the time will come when it will be as easy to raise a bed of bog ore as a bed of carrots'" (ibid., Mercer 150).

Iron, wrought, steel and cast

Until the invention of the Bessemer open-hearth process, American iron, like other iron, included three important classes: wrought, steel and cast. This classification was based on the carbon-content or on the properties it effected. *Wrought iron* was slag-bearing, malleable and contained 0.30% or less carbon. It did not harden much when cooled suddenly. The carbon content of *steel* was moderate, between .30 and 2.2%, enough to render the metal hard and brittle when cooled suddenly, yet not excessive, so that it was malleable when cooled slowly. *Cast iron* contained at least 2.2% of carbon and was not usefully malleable at any temperature. One might distinguish further between cast iron in the form of *castings* or remelted cast iron suitable for such castings, and *pig iron,* i.e., the molten cast iron as it issued from the furnace, or the 'pigs' into which it was cast. *Malleable cast iron* was cast iron made malleable by subsequent treatment without fusion.

Wrought iron and certain types of steel contained a great deal of slag or cinder, since they were made by welding together pasty particles of metal in a bath of slag, without fusing them afterwards. But the best steel, crucible steel, was freed from slag by fusion in crucibles, and therefore called *cast steel.*

The Bessemer process introduced a new class of iron known now as "mild" or "low-carbon steel," without the characteristic hardening property of steel, but differing from wrought iron in freedom from slag, and from cast iron in being extremely malleable. Bessemer "steel" was thus really more in the class of wrought iron than steel as of before 1856. But wrought iron was considered a cheaply priced material at the time, and the manufacturers, instead of inventing a new name for their new product, contented themselves with appropriating the name "steel" which connoted "superior quality" to the public mind. The new product, however, did resemble *cast steel,* as of before 1856, in its freedom from slag.

Technological improvements

The working of these three important classes of iron was advanced largely by English inventions between 1611 and 1856, which the American manufacturers took over, in certain cases almost immediately and generally within a decade of their use in Europe. The leading dates follow:

1611 - Simon Sturtevant patented the use of mineral coal for iron-smelting.

1619 - Lord Dudley used coal to make both cast and wrought iron. He was opposed by the ironmakers who employed charcoal, as has already been noted*** in the first part of this essay.

1625 - A similar attempt to Lord Dudley's was made be Straddain Hainaut in France.

1728 - Payn and Hanbury established rolling mills for sheet iron. Previously all sheet iron, tinned or not, was hammered with heavy hammers run by water-wheels; it could be rolled in small narrow strips, or smoothed by rolling after hammering, but could not be squeezed out into broad, flat sheets, hot or cold, between rollers.

1735 - Abraham Darby made cast iron with coke in a high furnace, really a blast furnace.

1760 - John Smeaton used cylindrical cast-iron bellows in place of wooden and leather ones.

1762 - John Roebuck converted cast iron into malleable, by reviving the use of a hollow-pit coal fire urged by a powerful artificial blast.

1783 - Cast grooved rolls were used for rolling bars and rods.

1784 - Henry Cort simplified the conversion of cast into wrought iron by employing a reverberatory puddling furnace. The iron was kept in a chamber apart from the fireplace and thus protected from the carburizing action of the fuel.

1811 - Aubertot, in France, used furnace gasses rich in carbonic oxide for heating steel.

1828 - J. B. Neilson of Glasgow invented the process of heating the blast, thus saving fuel and increasing production of iron.

1834 - William Henry continued Neilson's experiments at Oxford, New Jersey.

1856 - The Bessemer open-hearth process proved cheaper and yielded more useful products than Benjamin Huntsman's "crucible process" of melting steel in small crucibles and freeing it from slag, introduced as early as 1740.

Steam and the Railroad

But the inventions which most stimulated the growth of iron manufacture were the steam engine (1760–70) and the railroad (1825). They created a demand for iron products, both for themselves and the iron industries. The steam engine aided the iron master by giving him convenient motor power and caused a revolution in iron mining. The railroad helped him to assemble his raw materials and to distribute his products. Thus, before the railroad, the use of coal for iron manufacture tended to be confined soley to smiths' forges.

It is true that the best wrought iron work today is still done almost entirely by hand, and that prior to the introduction of the machine era in the nineteenth century the crude charcoal methods of fashioning wrought iron since the middle ages were still in use. But obviously the machine meant a great difference to the production of the ironwork itself, and the kinds of objects manufactured always kept pace with inventions and current needs as new uses were found for old resources. For example, pokers were seldom made for colonial fireplaces before the use of coal became common, towards 1750.

4

The Ironwork

The first casting in the colonies is said to have been a small iron kettle, made at Saugus probably about 1645, for "The Company of Undertakers for the Iron Works." The kettle was given to the original owner of the land on which the stockholders had built their plant. His descendant later presented the kettle to the city of Lynn.

The same company also cast the dies for the famous "Pine Tree Shillings," one side of which bore the legend "Massachusetts" encircling a tree. Mrs. Jenks, the wife of the Master Mechanic Joseph Jenks, had made the drawings. Mr. Jenks himself received a patent for an improved scythe, much better than the English scythe of his time. The machine shop that manufactured these objects also produced the first fire engine in America, for the "Towne of Boston."

Given a sufficient supply of iron, the objects that the colonists made are already determined by their needs by the middle of the seventeenth century: household articles, dies for coinage, agricultural implements, a machine like the fire engine which would protect what they were building. They would need iron for the vehicles in which they traveled, for the hoops and spiders of wheels, and for their sleighs on winter journeys. They would overcome the isolation of New England snows by making sleighs standing "upon two pieces of wood that lyes flat on the ground like a North of England sled, the forepart turning up with a bent to slyde over stones on any little rising and shod with smooth plates of iron to prevent their wearing away too fast," as an††† early chronicler records.‡‡‡

They would need arms for hunting and fighting, keep up with the latest foreign inventions and yet preserve mediaeval arms for a long time to come. A military halberd, now in Bucks County Historical Society Museum, Pennsylvania, was still used during the Revolution. Its head, ferrule and collar are made of wrought iron, the work of a blacksmith rather than an armorer, and it is evidently more a badge of rank than an offensive arm. But Baron Von Steuben's "Tasties" (Phila. 1776) continually mentions the halberd as the sergeant's arm and gives a complete manual for its use. There is no question that the English, Germans, French and Americans who fought in the War of Independence used it. The Pennsylvania "Springfield Pioneers" used pikes as late as August 16, 1856.

During the Revolution, the ore for a chain that spanned the Hudson to prevent Lord Howe's fleet from passing West Point was mined in Orange County, New York. It was forged there at the Stirling Iron Works, and carried in sections to West Point, and its 180 tons put in place May, 1778.

Washington and staff are said to have negotiated for army equipment with John Jacob Faesch, one of New Jersey's principal ironmasters. The general's father had been a manufacturer of pig iron at Accokuck Furnace, Virginia. A Massachusetts ancestor of Lincoln was also in the iron industry near Hingham.

The objects of ironwork would multiply with the needs of the people and their increasing knowledge of working the metal. Given an unsettled landscape, they would try to order it, work the land and build on it. Having built houses, they would fashion iron to supply their daily demands. Once these were satisfied, increasing comforts would permit them the luxuries of decoration and playthings for their children, tho it is true that sensitive crafts-men would find even these luxuries a need from the beginning.[6]

The expert might study the development of design in ironwork, from the functional aspect of the objects in their relation to period design in architec-ture—exteriors of buildings and landscaping—and architectural interiors. A general survey can only list the different things made, where they were made, and describe in detail some of the more unusual objects. They fall perhaps into five convenient classes: Architectural ironwork (nails, door hardware, ties, etc);[7] Weathervanes; Fire and kitchen implements; Lighting devices; Decorative and miscellaneous.

I. Architectural Ironwork

A. Nails - As has already been noted, colonial spikes, bolts and large nails, because of their excellence, were competing for the British market by 1740. Knight's *American Mechanical Dictionary*[8] lists that "Jeremiah Wilkinson of Cumberland, Rhode Island, about 1775, cut tacks from sheet metal and af-terward (n.d. given) made nails also." Two handwrought iron nails from roofing boards of the old Derby Academy, Hingham, Massachusetts, built in 1784, were still good in 1930 after 145 years of use, and attest to the care spent by the early Americans on their houses.

In 1790, Pennsylvania, New Jersey and Delaware were making 600 tons of nails and nail rods annually, and exporting these articles. A Notice in the *New York Journal and Patriotic Record* for April 2, 1791, gives these details of a nail factory of the time:

---

6. One finds these echoing lines in *"A"*-8: "How entirely different the relation between the-oretical learning / And practice was in the handicraft, / From what it is in large-scale indus-try" (74). The faint editorializing behind this passage lends itself well to an argument that Zukofsky the poet writes this research and that Zukofsky the researcher adopts the notion of craft to his poetry writing. Zukofsky is clearly the sensitive craftsman who sees a need for the luxury of art despite the demands working "to supply their daily demands." See Barry Ahearn's "Zukofsky, Marxism and American Handicraft," in *Upper Limit Music* (especially pp. 90–91).

7. [Zukofsky's note:] The limited scope of this essay does not permit a study of the larger ar-chitectural ironwork such as gates, railings, bannister posts, stairways, balconies, etc., for which New Orleans, Charleston, S.C., Philadelphia and other American cities are famous.

8. Edward Henry Knight. Published in New York: Hurd and Houghton, 1877.

To Be Sold

Or Exchanged for Property in the Country, on Advantageous Terms.

THAT well known Manufactory and Smith Works, No. 22 Cherry Street, now in compleat repair with Tools and implements sufficient to employ 28 workmen—These works are so well known and established, that the proprietor may, with propriety assert that his nails have a more universal circulation than any others manufactured in America. Any person wishing to purchase the above works, and employ the hands now at work, will be enabled to keep up the credit of this manufactory as is now established. And the subscriber assures the public that the business bears a more flattering prospect than it ever has since its commencement.

As he wishes to enter in a line of business more retired is his only motive for disposing of the same. For particulars, apply to the subscriber on the premises.

Jacob Foster

N.B. If the above works are not sold by the 1st of April next, they will then be Let on moderate terms, together with the house in front.

The Tariff enacted July 1789 laid an import duty on nails, of 1¢ per pound. The price of iron itself had increased from $64 per ton before the Revolution to $80 per ton in 1791. Hamilton's *Report on Manufactures,* published that year, attributed the rise in price to increased production and recommended further encouragement of American establishments by favoring still higher duties on foreign iron.[9] By 1794, the tariff on rolled iron and steel imports in American vessels was 15%; on hardware 10%; on all other iron products 15%, with an addition of 10% when imported in foreign bot-

9. Alexander Hamilton (1757–1804) presented the *Report on Manufactures* to the House of Representatives, December 5, 1791, which subsequently ordered it published by Childs and Swaine, 1791. Officially titled: *Report of the Secretary of the Treasury of the United States, on the subject of manufactures.* Celia Zukofsky's *American Friends,* a commonplace book drawing from Zukofsky's notes and library, correlates a passage from Hamilton—". . . there is scarcely anything of greater moment in the economy of a nation than the proper division of labor." (23)—with these lines from *"A"*-9: "The foci of production: things reflected / As wills subjected; formed in the division / Of labor" (*"A"* 106).

toms. These rates continued until 1816, despite the fact that the neglect of superior slitting and rolling mills in Vermont, Pennsylvania, Maryland and Virginia caused their owners to request a reduction of the prohibitive duties in 1810, so that they might import Russian iron, a cheaper product. Heavy importations from Russia followed, but American iron manufactures received a new impulse during the War of 1812. In 1816, the tariff on hammered iron made in Russia and Sweden was $9 per ton; on rolled iron made in England, $30 per ton. Between 1816 and 1842, cyclical depressions in the iron industry, due to increased importations, were repeatedly counteracted by higher tariffs. The building of the Erie Canal, in 1825, also spurred American production by effecting the establishment of engine works and iron furnaces in Buffalo.

B. Door Hardware - Under this head are included hinges, hasps, latches, bolts, knobs, keys, key-plates, locks, knockers and combined handles and knockers.

1. Hinges - The most common type in the colonies was the plain strap which had some bevelling but little other ornamentation. The washers were usually of leather in brilliant colors. The finials were mostly round or oval. The Dutch smiths of New York, New Jersey and Long Island hammered out the hinge, near the eye end, into a circle. Rarer shapes included spear or cusp single and triple, heart, fish tail, tulip, fleur-de-lis, ox shoe, butterfly, eagle, and strap with side member. Examples of the plain strap hinge were made in the New England and Middle colonies as early as 1650 (Dutch strap, Green Cy., N.Y.) and thruout the eighteenth century.

Another type of hinge, the Cross Garnet, was decorated for strength rather than beauty. The *Cockshead Hinge,* of which there were few in the colonies, was a simplification of an English type dating back to Roman days. Its head resembled a crowing cock. It was sometimes called a *pin joint hinge* and coated with pewter to prevent rusting. Examples have been found in Ipswich, Mass. and Berlin, Connecticut dating from 1665 and 1670 respectively.

The *Butterfly* or *Dovetail Hinge* came in various sizes and was used as frequently on small pin boxes, desks and cabinets as on great doorways, thruout New England, Pennsylvania and the South.

The H and L hinge, which was often painted, was the cheapest to make, and distributed thruout the colonies. The tradition is that H L stood for the

Holy Land, and that this hinge used on a door would protect the house from evil.

The *Side Hinge* was particularly popular in Pennsylvania, about 1790. Heavy and more ornamented than the others, it was used for all purposes.

All the hinges were wrought and none of them decorated to any great extent except for their main contours. There more unusual hinges did not differ from general types in basic construction. Thus a strap hinge from Phillipse Manor, New York, 1745, has the novelty of an attached decorated plate; a cupboard hinge from Doylestown, Pennsylvania, is hammered out in the shape of a rat rail. The strap hinge was used also on shutters in Charleston, South Carolina in the eighteenth century.

2. Hasps - These were probably not met with on colonial doors till ca. 1780. In any case, a new feature of a serpentine shaped hinge made in Harrisburg, Pennsylvania about that time—and used mainly for wagon chests and boxes—is the hasp, opening in the hinge for the ring, which was attached to the box to enable the fixing of the padlock.

3. Latches - Colonial wrought iron latches for outer doors were large and their ornamentation varied. There were three types, designed after English originals: Escutcheon-Lift, Suffolk and Norfolk latches. The Escutcheon-Lift, to be found occasionally in Pennsylvania, ca. 1700, became less rare towards 1776. The Suffolk latch, generally of the cusp type (but some with tulip or pear-shaped design), measured in some cases eighteen inches from cusp to cusp. It was used for the most part in central New England and eastern New York, but also occasionally in Pennsylvania and Virginia. There was a special type of Suffolk Latch near East Haddam, in the Connecticut Valley, ca. 1794. The Norfolk latch, used in Pennsylvania for both inside and outside doors, was imported from England in the early seventeenth century.

The latches for inner doors were not ornamented and [were] made with plain or triangular cusps. The lifts were all straight before about 1800. The first latch with a curved lift, found by Mercer, dates from 1803.

Some of the Suffolk latches were made with swivel lifts and thumb presses, large and dished, bearing the initials of the maker—as "C. L." on a latch made in Kingston, New York, ca. 1703.

A unique Pennsylvania-German, Suffolk latch has an upper cusp resembling the cockshead pattern and a thumb-press tooled in a shell design. It probably dates from the late eighteenth century or early nineteenth century, when the ornamentation of Suffolk latches became more complicated and embraced such variations of the cusp type as the ball and spear pattern of a latch from Martinsburg, New York.

4. Knobs and door-pulls - A latch lock of a knob type, originally from Newington, Connecticut, and now in the Metropolitan Museum of Art, marks perhaps the transition from latch to knob (ca. 1750?). Door-pulls, of which there exists an early Pennsylvania specimen in wrought iron, were common enough in Europe, but rare in the colonies.

5. Locks - A pair of lock escutcheon plates representing Hessian soldiers, cast by some Pennsylvania-German craftsmen ca. 1776, are a fine example of the craft of locksmithing in the colonies. Other Pennsylvania types such as the cockshead escutcheon, recently unearthed in the ruins of old Ft. Ticonderoga, N.Y., were probably the work of soldiers in the Hessian contingent of British forces stationed at the fort in 1777. Undoubtedly, the keys fitting these plates were decorated to match.

6. Knockers and knocker-latches - The wrought iron door-knocker was never so popular in the colonies as in Europe. The New England type of knocker-latch was used in the other colonies, but the Dutch type of New York and New Jersey was never used in New England. Knocker-latches date from 1698 in New England, and from 1658 in New York. The latch and knocker combination consisted of a grasp pin-hinged below the upper cusp of the latch, so that the pendant grasp and lower cusp could be used for rapping against the door.

A beautiful example of Philadelphia ironwork of the eighteenth century is a door knocker made up of the finely modelled head of a lady on a fluted base and the grasp pendent [hanging] from her ears.

C. Footscrapers - Philadelphia is also noted for its footscrapers of wrought iron, used in the doorways of its houses in the eighteenth century. The designs were various: scrolls, winged lions and cats, wings and lyres.

D. Fire Insurance Badges - Also marked the facades of insured buildings in the same city at that time. The badges were cast iron plates, the insignia of representative insurance companies, like the United Fireman, Green Tree Insurance Co., Guardian Insurance Co., etc., [in the forms of]: an engine, a tree, a female figure, a monogram framed in four logs, etc.

E. Tie Irons - Were used by the Dutch early in the seventeenth century, to reinforce the ends of beams and to pull the masonry of walls towards them. They were made in the form of figures giving the date of buildings or the owners' initials. Occasionally abstract devices were also employed

F. Hitching Posts - The hitching post was a necessary convenience in colonial times, and wrought iron posts in the shape of horses heads, etc., continued to be characteristic accessories of urban and country houses, in all states well through the first half of the nineteenth century.

II. Weathervanes

Partly practical—since it showed the direction of the wind—, partly architectural decoration, the weathervane was finally the result of the craftsman's desire to make art, like the wood sculpture of the ship's figurehead. The carver who made figureheads and store signs very often cast weathervanes, and during the nineteenth century the latter also found [their]§§§ forms in the popular art of Currier and Ives. The painted "Horse and Sulky" weathervane of hammered sheet copper, horse's head of cast lead and wheels and reins of iron wire, made in New York, modelled its horse after a print of a well-known race horse of the time.[10] The anonymous folk painters, in their turn, painted horses that resembled cast-iron weathervanes in their metallic contours against brilliantly colored landscapes.

The weathervanes of ca. 1700 had their stocks ornamented with scrolls and tendrils. The vanes themselves carried devices, like the mitre on the vane of Christ Church, Philadelphia, and the heraldic birds on the turrets of Mulberry Castle, South Carolina. A wrought iron vane from a mill built by William Penn and others at Chester, Pennsylvania, 1699, was pierced with the initials of the owner and the date. Representations of fish, birds and domestic animals followed the abstract designs of early weathervanes, in the eighteenth century, towards the end of which the gilding and painting of

10. Given the well-known Zukofskian conceit that he resembled a horse, the frequent Index references to various equine pieces are vaguely humorous. See for example the *"A"*-8 description of a cheese ". . . bearing the imprint of a horse's head, / The trademark of the original manufacturer" (65); all of *"A"*-7; *"A"*-12: "The horse sees he is repeating / All known cultures. . . . The shape of his ground seems to have been / A constant for all dead horses / His neigh cultural constant / Also his sniff— . . ." (174; also 179–80); and *"A"*-22: "old in / a greenhouse the stabled horse / sings sometimes . . ." (535).

stocks and vanes became popular. The following list gives an idea of the variety of subject matter and materials:

- Vane from Residence of Sir William Keith, Graeme Park (near Phila.), Pa.; wrought iron, L. 38", pierced with 'W. K. 1722.'

- Little Heiskell, colonial ranger aiming his gun, on Courthouse in Hagerstown, Md.; hand forged wrought iron (bolted together by hand and hammered), ca. 1800.

- Horse, Pennsylvania; sheet iron, cut in silhouette and painted. H. 21 1/4" - L. 23 1/2". Late 18th c.

- Cock with base, Pennsylvania; sheet iron, cut in silhouette. H. 20 1/2" - L. 18". Late 18th c.

- Angel Gabriel, Riverhead, L.I.; Iron [3]**** inch plate) cut in silhouette. L. 41". Early 19th c.

- Prairie Horse, Pennsylvania; sheet iron, hammered; mane and part of tail in silhouette. L. 40 1/2". Early 19th c.

- Formal Rooster, New England; hollow cast iron body; applied sheet-iron tail, cut in silhouette; traces of original polychrome. H 32 1/2" - L. 36". 19th c.

- Steer, Massachusetts; sheet iron, cut in silhouette; painted red. H. 26" L. 41". Early 19th c.

- Galloping Horse, New Jersey; wooden body with applied cast iron legs; horsehair tail. L. 19 1/4". Early 19th c.

III. Fire and Kitchen Implements

The earliest of these implements were determined by the need for strict domestic economy, such as was exercised in self-sufficient New England households of the seventeenth century, and scarcely concerned with decoration for itself. The first interiors of colonial houses, like the exteriors, were obviously for use, and it was not till the middle of the eighteenth century that a variety of gratuitous motifs developed.

A. Firebacks - The first colonial fireplaces, practically identical with those of England, may very well have used imported firebacks as patterns for their own castings. The firebacks were placed at the back or sides of open fireplaces to protect the bricks or mortar. The designs were the simplest. The fireback in the entrance hall at Harriton, Bryn Mawr, bears the date

MDCCXXVI (1726) and a true lover's knot at the side; another fireback, found in West Chester, Pennsylvania, dated 1734 and possibly cast at Durham Furnace, [bears] a foliage and fruit design. Others had armorial designs.

B. Firedogs or Andirons - Like the firebacks, seventeenth-century and early-eighteenth-century andirons were of cast iron, and more or less abstract in outline,—the alternative name of firedog suggesting the tendency to represent animals such as deer and dogs. The late eighteenth-century andirons were frankly realistic and portrayed not only animals, but marching Hessians, grotesque blackamoors and heads and busts of women. While many of these andirons were of cast iron, some combined cast iron bodies with feet and tops of brass, copper, steel and even silver.

C. Implements - for fireplace and kitchen use included spit-dogs, chimney cranes, trammels, trivets with pierced foliation, baking irons, skewer holds, toasters, waffle, wafer and gridirons, [gridle]†††† plates, goffering irons, cauldrons, skillets, tongs and shovels, most of these designed on English lines, tho other European styles had their influence. One unusual trivet of the eighteenth century had the handle turned upwards and supports at the top for long spoon handles, fashioned after the implements of Carpathian nomads.

The spit-dogs at Mt. Vernon (ca. 1750) were massive and angular, with four hooks on the face of the upright. The American spit-dogs were commonly distinguished from foreign types by the flattening out of the stem at the base of the goose neck.

The wafer irons were made up of two iron baking-plates set on long handles hinged near the plates, so that they could be pressed together when baking the wafer—a thin, dry cake about the thickness of blotting paper. The wafer irons were rimless, unlike the waffle irons, and the faces of the plates stamped or engraved with tulips, stars, zig-zags, fleurs-de-lis, hearts, symbols, ecclesiastical formulae, monograms, dates and inscriptions, reproduced the designs of the iron onto the wafer. These irons varied in length from 26 to 35 inches. The tapered handles, 20 1/2 to 29 1/2 inches long, were always of wrought iron. The plates—circular or oval, 4 1/2 to 7 inches in diameter, 3/16 to 9/16 inches thick—were sometimes forged or hammered out of the same piece of iron as the handles, and sometimes cast, in which case they were fastened to the wrought-iron handles by screws or rivets. Wafer irons were not generally used in the post-colonial period, and then usually to make ecclesiastical wafers.

Most of the implements mentioned in this section survived until the middle of the nineteenth century, but in Pennsylvania and New Jersey where the German stove had replaced the fireplace, they became obsolete about seventy-five years earlier.

D. German stoves and stoveplates - Benjamin Franklin, who invented and improved the type of fireplace named after him, described the stove of the Pennsylvania Germans in his "Account of the New Invented Pennsylvania Fireplace," published in 1744: "The German stove is like a Box, one side wanting. 'Tis composed of five iron plates scru'd together and fixed so that you may put Fuel into it from another room, or from Outside of the House. 'Tis a kind of oven reversed, its Mouth being without, and Body within the Room to be warmed by it."

The German workmen who settled in Pennsylvania and New Jersey no doubt caused the English ironmasters in the region to manufacture these jamb stoves. The ironmasters knew nothing about them, but the German immigrants knew how to make them and preferred them to the English fireplaces. Mercer believes that some of the German colonists arrived in America with broken stove plates and that the first attempts to make recasts from the wooden moulds which they carried with them, ca. 1728, resulted in the assembling of single plates into stoves ten years later, when a complete stove was first sold.

The stove plates were cast in low relief by stamping the moulds directly upon open sand, without the use of flasks. The finest designs were produced between 1740 and 1760. The six-plate stove, introduced towards the end of this period, differed from the five-plate in standing out into the room and having a stovepipe, fuel door and draught opening at one end. But it was still used only for heating and not for cooking. The latter function was assumed to some extent by the ten-plate stove which appeared in Pennsylvania about 1765 and displaced the old five-plate stove, thus ending some of the best artistic casting in the colonies.

The individual plates were approximately two feet square. The top and bottom plates were plain. The designs of the embellished plates were for the most part the stories of the Bible retold in iron. But legendary, symbolic, and contemporary Pennsylvania German scenes were also used. The traditions displayed were those of the peasant craftsmen of the Rhine country, medieval and country-like, with a sense of humor that could emphasize the gravity of a wedding scene naively carved with the inscription—"Let him who will only laugh at this, make it better; many can find fault, but the real fun is to do better." The religious plates—such as the Adam and Eve (1741), The Dance of Death (1745), and the Peaceable Kingdom (ca. 1750)—were perforce more serious. The recurring tulips and hearts framed in architectural forms like the arch and column made for a formalism which was at once strict and graceful.[11] Warwick and Durham furnaces produced the best of these plates.

In the last quarter of the eighteenth century, when flower, leaf and tendril motifs were being used indiscriminately, without the poetic qualities of religious and legendary subjects to offset them, as at Baron Stiegel's Elizabeth furnace, an‡‡‡‡ up-to-date subject matter for the stove plates was sought out. Stiegel had already manufactured "The Hero," probably a self-portrait, in 1769. By the end of the century, stove plates carried portraits of Washington, surrounded by the thirrteen stars and the inscription "First in Peace." About 1812, stove plates cast at Cumberland Furnace, New Jersey, which were sent to Troy, New York to be mounted, merely bore the name of the furnace across the top and two plain oval medallions underneath.

IV. Lighting Devices

Wrought iron grissets for rushlights used in the colonies in the seventeenth century were made after English forms. In the eighteenth century, pierced, conical lamps were made out of sheet iron. Other lighting objects of the time included the steel betty lamp, a candle pendant of wrought iron, and a sheet-iron lantern decorated with gilt and bronze.

V. Decorative and Miscellaneous Iron

Most of the objects under this head date from about the first quarter of the nineteenth century. They form a miscellaneous group illustrating the abun-

---

11. A passage like this implies a general aesthetics; compare Zukofsky's note in *A Test of Poetry:* "Folk art occurs with inevitable order as part of the growing history of a people.... The *essential* technique of folk art ... —its simplicity, its wholeness of emotional presentation—*can* serve as a guide to any detail of technique growing out of the living processes of any age" (70).

FIGURE 1. "Baron" Stiegel Stoveplate

dance of American ironwork, so that a wrought iron tobacco pipe tongs of the early eighteenth century may be thrown in for good measure:

- Ca. 1828, an iron fire fighting apparatus, called The Hydraulion: a narrow box, 6 1/2 feet long, containing a force pump operated by levers mounted on a structure in the middle of the box, the whole was mounted on four wheels.

- Said to have been put up, Feb. 22, 1826, made by Samuel Cooper and painted by Samuel Moor, at Logan House, New Hope, Pennsylvania: an Indian figure of heavy sheet iron on a pole ten feet high, strengthened by bars of the same metal. The Indian holds his bow fully drawn, and the general pose and proportions have sculptural character.

- Ca. 1830 (?), a copy of Leonardo da Vinci's *Last Supper,* cast directly from pure ore, in common sand and oiled, at Windsor Furnace, Berks County, Pennsylvania, then under the management of Jones, Keim and Co.

- A nineteenth-century bootjack from Maryland: the cast iron figure of a female circus performer done in half-round, length 10 inches.

The year 1834 witnessed increased skill in casting, particularly at Albany. Bishop notes that the holloware of Bartlett, Bent and Co. was preferred to the best of Scotch ironwork, and mentions the stoves of Dr. Nott and the machine castings of Maury and Ward "equal to those of any country." Five factories at Albany, melting annually 2,500 tons of iron and employing 4,000 workmen, produced fruit dishes decorated "with open flowerwork, cast and then made malleable so as not to break. Breast pins of Napoleon and other iron ornaments rendered fashionable in Europe by the Queen of Prussia were made at Seth Boyden foundry, Newark, N.J." Francis Alger of Boston made small statuary. Philadelphia foundries manufactured wrought iron tubes for gas fittings, steam and water works.

James Beebe and Co's Illustrated Catalog, ca. 1858, contained plates of eagles, fountains, urns, lions, deer, pigs, wholves [sic], sheep, dogs, human figures such as knights and ladies and a George Washington—all lawn statuary. The popular demand for these objects had been increasing for some time.

Tables in Bishop, showing the tariffs on ironwork for the years 1842, 1846, 1857, and 1862, list the following objects, which one may infer were also made in the States: anchors, anvils, axles; malleable iron in castings; band, hoop and slit rods; bars; bed screws and wrought hinges; blacksmith hammers and sledges; boiler plates; cables; chains; cast-iron vessels; sads; tailors and hatters; stoves and stove plates; cast-iron pipe, steam, gas and water; cast-iron butts and hinges; chains, trace, halter and fence; cut tacks, brads, sprigs; galvanized or zinc coated; hollow ware glazed or tinned; iron liquor; nails, spikes, rivets, bolts, wrought; horshoes; pig, railroad, sheet, slabs, blooms, loop, taggers iron; iron wood screws; wrought iron for mill, mill-cranks, ships, locomotives, steam-engines; wrought railroad chairs, nuts, punched washers; wrought tubes, steam, gas and water, etc.

5

Ironworkers and Ironmasters

The majority of craftsmen and their masters left no personal record. The ironwork and the industry they established tell the story of most of them. Occasionally their names were engraved or stamped on an object, most often only their initials.[12]

12. The motif of nameless craftsmen recurs in the Index essays. It bears directly on the poetry of Zukofsky: in his insistence that the poems (craft objects) speak for themselves, in place of

The workers and masters came to the colonies from England, France, Germany, Holland and other European countries. Despite the system of indenture, some of the workers undoubtedly had the opportunity to become masters, when they migrated from the coastal colonies to the frontier. This essay has already called attention to the special status of the blacksmith. A letter from Col. William Johnson to Governor Clinton, dated August 10, 1748, mentions a smith instructing the Senecas. As for the ironmasters, it is very likely that most of them at sometime in their lives had been apprentices in their trade and that many of them continued to work and supervise their foundries in person. A few ironmasters attracted the interest of travellers in the colonies, so that some biographical detail remains. Swedenborg recorded that Sir William Keith produced large quantities of iron at his smelting works on Christiana Creek, Pennsylvania, during the first two years of their existence, but that he abandoned these works because of the difficulty of smelting the ore (1725–1728).

"Baron" (Henry William) Stiegel, famous for his glassware as well as his ironwork, has had at least one full length biography written about him.[13] He purchased an interest in Jacob Huber's ironworks at Brickersville, Lancaster County, Pennsylvania, in 1757. He tore down the old building and established himself with his partners, John Barr, and Alexander and Charles Steadman, in a larger and more efficient plant which he called Elizabeth Furnace in honor of his wife, Huber's daughter. From about 1765 to 1778 he made stoves with great success, introduced the "Baron Stiegel" 10-plate wood stove and another stove which was an improvement over Benjamin Franklin's open hearth. He manufactured various other castings and supplied sugar planters and refiners with castings for the West India trade. He died in 1783, impoverished at the end of the Revolution.

---

autobiography or critical exegesis, and in his alliance with craftsmen working at a labor of love. In *Autobiography,* one reads, "As a poet I have always felt that the work says all there needs to be said of one's life." (5). Further, the initials of L. Z. and other family members recur liberally as markers in *"A,"* as if the poem were also a craft object.

13. Born Heinrich Wilhelm Stiegel (1729–85), the Baron emigrated from Germany in 1750. A prosperous ironmaster, he operated Elizabeth Furnace and Charming Forge in Pennsylvania and is thought to have lived extravagantly. Glassware produced at his American Flint Glassworks in Manheim, Pennsylvania—a town he designed and founded in 1762—remains collectible; a restored glassworks exists there now.

His stove plate "The Hero," said to be a self-portrait, bears in the corners the masonic emblems—square, plumb rule, and compasses—testifying to his connection with freemasonry at the time it was made in 1769. One of two copies left of this stove plate spells his name "STIGGHEL"; the other uses only his given names "Heinrich Wilhelm." The plates are also stamped with the tulip and heart motifs of the Pennsylvania Germans. He seems to have been especially proud of his career as manufacturer of stoves, for some of his plates still show the legend:

> "Baron Stiegel ist der Mann
> Der die Ofen Machen Kann."

Considering the vicissitudes of his fortunes, the "Baron" who adopted this title for himself as a young man, might, at the end of his career, not have found this free translation ungenerous:

> "Baron Stiegel is the cove[14]
> Who can make an iron stove."

In 1795, one Whetstone used anthracite for iron near Pottsville. In 1827, one Elihu Burritt, blacksmith, scholar and linguist, was working in New Britain, Connecticut.

The names are isolated, as isolated as the lives of the early ironmasters seem to have been, according to "The Legend of the Hounds," a verse narrative by George Boker of the eighteenth century: the owner of Colebrook Furnace, Pennsylvania, returns from a fox hunt, enraged by the falseness of his hounds, and with whip in hand, drives the whole pack of them into the blazing tunnelhead. Evidently a lifetime devoted to building up an industry against odds could produce extreme personalities. The consistent craftsmanship of American ironwork itself, however, betrays nothing of the restlessness of such lives.[15]

Louis Zukofsky
8/27/38

14. Sixteenth-century Briticism for a man or fellow.

15. Consider the manner in which this conclusion separates the eccentricity of the personal from the sincerity of craft. The analogue of poetry seems clear, although it contradicts somewhat the sense (as noted above) that poetry may serve as autobiography—unless by autobiography we mean a kind of selective self-presentation. A further note, "*A*"-12 (256) suggests Zukofsky once intended to write a story entitled "The Hounds" that would presumably have adapted this history.

Bibliography

Ironwork

Albree, Chester B - The Use, Design and Manufacture of Iron in Ornament (Proceedings of Engineers' Society of Western Pennsylvania, vol. XV, pp. 150–173), Pittsburgh, Pa., 1899.

Allison, Archibald - The Outline of Steel and Iron, London: N. F. and G. Witherby Ltd., 1936. (191 pp.)

Alteneck, Hefner - Artistic Wrought Iron Works from the Middle Ages and Renaissance Period, II. series, Helburn and Hogen, New York and Chicago, n.d. (84 plates)

Anderson, John A. - Interesting New Hope Relics (Bucks County Historical Society, Coll. of Papers, vol. IV, pp. 75–84) Easton, Pa. 1917.

Bining, Arthur Cecil - The Iron Plantations of Early Pennsylvania (Reprinted from the Pennsylvania Magazine of History and Biography, April, 1933) Published by the Historical Society of Pennsylvania.

Bining, Arthur Cecil - The Rise of Iron Manufacture in Western Pennsylvania (Reprinted from the Western Pennsylvania Historical Magazine, Nov. 1933)

Boyer, Charles S. - Early Forges and Furnaces in New Jersey, Philadelphia and London, 1931 (287 pp.).

Braddock, Rogers K - Fragments of Early Industries in South Jersey - The Bog Ore Industry in South Jersey Prior to 1845 (The General Magazine and Historical Chronicle, vol. XXXXV, no. 111. pp. 337–362) April, 1932.

Bucks County Historical Society, A Collection of Papers Read Before. Published for the Society by B. F. Fackenthal, Jr., 6 vols, Riegelsville and Easton, Pa., 1908–1932.

Davis, W. W. H. - Links in the Chain of Local History (Bucks Cy. Hist. Soc. Coll. v. 3. p. 398–404) Easton, Pa. 1908

Davis, W. W. H. - William Penn's Home Life at the Manor House (Bucks Cy. Hist. Soc. Coll. v. 1., p. 28–38) 1908.

Dyer, Walter A. - American Iron, Brass and Copper, The New York Sun, Sat., Mar. 29, 1930.

Eberlein, Harold Donaldson and McClure, Abbot - The Practical Book of American Antiques, Garden City, N.Y., 1927 (390 pp.)

Fackenthal, B. F. Jr. - Classification and Analyses of Stove plates (Bucks Cy., Hist. Soc. Coll. v. IV, pp. 55–61) 1917.

Forges and Furnaces in the Province of Pennsylvania, Publications of the Pa. Society of the Colonial Dames of America III, Prepared by the Committee on Historical Research. Philadelphia, Printed for the Society, 1914. (204 pp.)

Gardner, J. Starkie - Ironwork. 3 vols. London, 1896–1922 (v. 1, 138 pp.; v. 2, 202 pp; v. 3, 198 pp.).

Gillingham, Harrold E. - The Fascinating Fire-Mark (Antiques, vol. IV, no. 6, pp. 277–280) Boston, Dec. 1923.

James, Beebe and Co. 356 Broadway, New York, Illustrated Catalog of Ornamental Ironwork (1858).

Keith, Herbert C. and Harte, Charles Rufus - The Early Iron Industry of Connecticut, Reprinted from the Fifty-first Annual Report of the Connecticut Society of Civil Engineers, Inc. (New Haven, 1935) 70 pp.

Lathrop, W. L. - Stove Plate from Batsto Furnace, New Jersey (Bucks Cy., Hist. Soc., Coll. v. IV. pp. 382–4). 1917.

Laubach, Charles - The Durham (Pa.) Iron Works (Bucks Cy., Hist. Soc. Coll. v. I, pp. 232–9) 1908.

Lindsay, J. Seymour - Iron and Brass Implements of the English House, Illustrated by the Author, with an introduction by Ralph Edwards. The Medici Society, London and Boston, 1927 (pp. 194–207, Some remarks on American Colonial Implements.).

Mercer, Henry C. - The Bible in Iron on the Pictured Stoves and Stove Plates of the Pennsylvania Germans. Published for the Bucks County Historical Society, Doylestown, Pa. 1914 (174 pp.)

Mercer, Henry C. - The Dating of Old Houses (Bucks Cy. Hist. Soc. Coll. vol. V, pp. 536–549) Meadville, Pa., 1926.

Mercer, Henry C. - Light and Fire Making (contributions to American History by the Bucks County Historical Society, no. 4.) Philadelphia, 1898.

Mercer, Henry C. - A Lost Stoveplate Inscription (Bucks Cy., Hist. Soc. Coll. Papers, v. V, p. 388–400) 1926.

Mercer, Henry C. - Notes on Wrought-Iron Door Latches (Old-time New England Jan. 1923, p. 139)

Mercer, Henry C. - The Tools of the Nation Maker (Bucks Cy. Hist. Soc., Coll. v. II, p. 480) 1909

Mercer, Henry C. - The Tools of the Nation Maker, a Descriptive Catalogue of Objects in the Museum of the Historical Society of Bucks County, Penna. 1897. Printed for the Society at the office of the Bucks County Intelligence, Doylestown, Pa. (87 pp.)

Mercer, Henry C. - The Tools of the Nation Maker (address del. Doylestown, Pa. May 28, 1907) (Bucks Cy. Hist. Soc. Coll. v. III, pp. 478–481) 1909.

Mercer, Henry C. - Wafer Irons (Bucks Cy. Hist. Soc. Coll. v. V, pp. 245–250) 1926.

Mott, J. L., Iron Works Catalog. New York 1893.

Nelson, William - Beginnings of the Iron Industry in Trenton, N.J. 1723–1750. Historical Society of Pennsylvania, Phila. 1911.

Nutting, Wallace - Early American House Hardware I (Antiques, v. IV, no. 2, p. 78–81) Aug. 1923.

Owen, B. F. - Pennsylvania German Stoveplates in Berks County (Bucks Cy. Hist. Soc. Coll. v. IV, p. 50–54) 1917.

Pearse, John B. - A Concise History of Iron Manufacture of the American Colonies up to the Revolution and of Pennsylvania Until the Present Time. Phila. 1876 (282 pp.)

Rice, H. H. - Stoveplate Hunting (Bucks Cy. Hist. Soc. Coll. v. IV, p. 606–611) 1917.

Shellenberger, Fred J. - The Military Halberd of the Eighteenth Century (Bucks Cy. Hist. Soc. Coll. v. III, p. 521–5) 1909.

Sonn, Albert H. - Early American Wrought Iron with 320 plates from drawings by the Author, 3 vols, Charles Scribner's Sons, New York, 1928. (v. 1, 262 pp; v. 2, 204 pp; v. 3, 263 pp.)

Stewart Iron Works, Architectural and Structural Ironwork Catalogue, No. 36. Cincinnati, O. (1902) 74 pp.

Stow, Charles Messer - A Portrait in Irons: Stiegel (The Antiquarian, vol. XIV, no. 6, pp. 29–31) New York, June 1930.

Swank, James M. - Cambria County Pioneers, Philadelphia, 1910. (138 pp.)

Swank, James M. - History of the Manufacture of Iron in All Ages and particularly in the United States from Colonial Times to 1891. Philadelphia: The American Iron and Steel Association, 1892 (540 pp.)

Swank, James M. - Progressive Pennysylvania, Phila. 1906.

Wallace, Philip B. - Colonial Ironwork in Old Philadelphia, Measured Drawings by Wm. Allen Dunn, Introduction by Fiske Kimball. Architectural Book Publishing Co., Inc. New York, n.d. (147 pp.)

Wrot [*sic*] Iron Designers - Art in Iron, 12 vols. of Plates, Published by the Wrot Iron Designers, 541 W. 35 St., New York, 1932–4.

Wrought Iron Record (The) - Published by the Wrought Iron Research Association, Union Bank Building, Pittsburgh, Pa., v. I, nos. 1–4. 1928–1930.

General History

Andrews, Charles M. - Colonial Folkways, New Haven: Yale University Press, 1919. (255 pp.).

Andrews, Charles M. - The Colonial Period of American History, New Haven: Yale University Press, 1934 (vol. I The Settlements, 581 pp.).

Bassett, John Spencer - A Short History of the United States 1492–1929, New York: The Macmillan Co., 1935 (976 pp.).

Bishop, J. Leander - A History of American Manufactures from 1608 to 1860, 3 vols, 3rd ed. revised. Philadelphia and London 1868 (v. 1 - 702 pp; v. 2 - 654 pp; v. 3 - 574 pp.).

(Cahill, Holger) - American Folk Art, The Art of the Common Man in America 1750–1900. The Museum of Modern Art, New York, 1932.

Dow, George Francis - Domestic Life in New England in the 17th Century, Topsfield, Mass. 1925 (48 pp.).

Hart, Albert Bushnell (editor) American History Told by Contemporaries, The Macmillan Co., New York, 5 vols.

Hart, Albert Bushnell - Social and Economic Forces in American History. From the American Nation: a History n.d. (523 pp.).

Mercer, Henry C. - Folk Lore, Notes Taken at Random (1896), (Bucks Cy. Hist. Soc. Coll. v. II, p. 406–16) 1909.

Morison, Samuel Eliot and Commager, Henry Steele - The Growth of the American Republic, 3. vols. New York, 1937. (v. 1, 702 pp.).

Tryon, Rolla Milton - Household Manufactures in the United States, 1640–1860. University of Chicago Press, 1917 (413 pp.).

Editorial Notes

* not revived] not to be revived

† effect] affect

‡ "Ironwork at Scituate, July 19, 1796; Newark, January 8, 1788." The preceding line was penned by Zukofsky into a final copy of the typescript, with a note indicating it should be incorporated into this page.

§ in North Haven, like that of Hammersmith,] like that of Hammersmith, in North Haven,

** effected] affected

†† under] to

‡‡ their] its

§§ Effect] Affect

*** noted] noticed

††† an] any

‡‡‡ Typescript pagination and subhead numbering indicate that the section that follows is a subsequent addition to the piece. There is no reason not to assume the insertion was Zukofsky's.

§§§ their] its

**** Manuscript is uncertain, overtyped.

†††† gridle] girdle

‡‡‡‡ an] and

II. Chalkware

Chalkware

American cottage ornaments of cast chalk were made by the Pennsylvania Germans between 1850 and 1870. The process of casting this chalk and decorating it later in polychrome with water or oil paints appears to have originated with the Pennsylvania Germans. There is no proof that chalkware objects found in Brewster, Massachusetts, Albany, New York, Waldoboro, Maine, and Vermont were made there, and it has been assumed that they were brought to these places by travelling peddlers or worked on by migrating Pennsylvania German craftsmen. The district near Waldoboro, Maine, was settled by Germans. The subject matter of a few chalkware pieces dates them as of before 1850.

These hollow cottage ornaments made of chalk cast in a mold are to be distinguished from contemporary products resembling them in construction and design, also made by the Pennsylvania Germans or under their influence, and loosely called "chalkware," tho their composition is thin plaster. The exact process of casting chalkware proper is still unknown. On examination, however, the chalkware ornaments seems to have been cast in molds of separate sections, which were covered on the inside with a thin mixture of the chalk. The mold, very likely of wood or plaster of Paris, was then removed from the outside. The objects were left pure white or painted in brilliant colors with water or oil paints. A striking difference between the chalkware objects and the thin plaster "chalkware" is the extreme light weight of the former.

The chalkware are genre objects and their designs are easily traceable to the genre ornaments and miscellaneous "image toys" popular in peasant and working class households in England, France and Germany, beginning about 1700 and lasting thru Victorian times. The English Staffordshire ware (1700–1850) embracing various porcelain—stoneware or salt-glaze, brown and white earthenware figures—cast in a mold and fired, found a ready market in America. From 1800 to 1870, Bennington, Vt. and other cities pursued a thriving industry, imitating Staffordshire ware for well-to-do urban consumers. The handmade chalkware of the Pennsylvania Germans, combining seventeenth-century "Dutch" tulip and fruit motifs of their peasant traditions and the more worldly elegances of Staffordshire manufacture, were an attempt to produce for the rural communities, for as little as fifteen to fifty cents per object in some cases, household ornaments as attractive as the more expensive factory wares of Bennington.

The subjects of Staffordshire ware included animals, birds, rustic, allegorical and historical figures,—specifically: two cranes with candlestick or flower-holder; a pair of hawks; jugs in forms of owls; stags; a grotesque ox; horses; sheep; elephants; a postillion on horse-back; a woman in form of a bell; musicians; a Dutch boy and girl; actors; sailors; shepherds and shepherdesses; Diana; Charity; Voltaire; Washington; King George III; etc. The beginnings of Staffordshire influence on the subject matter of American chalkware may perhaps be traced in the following advertisement which appeared in the *Boston News-Letter* for January 25, 1768: "Henry Christian Geyer, Stone Cutter near Liberty Tree, South End, Boston, Hereby informs his customers, and the Gentlemen and Ladies, that besides carrying on the Stone Cutting Business as usual, he carries on the Art and Manufacture of a Fuser Simulacorum, or the making of all sorts of Images, viz., 1st. Kings and Queens; 2nd. King George and Queen Charlotte; 3rd. King & Queen of Prussia; 4th. King and Queen of Denmark; 5th. King and Queen of Sweden, Likewise a Number of Busts, among which are Matthew Prior, Homer, Milton &c.—also a number of animals such as Parrots, Dogs, Lions, Sheep, with a number of others too many to enumerate: Said Geyer also cleans old deficient Animals, and makes them look as well as new, at a reasonable Rate. All the above mentioned Images, Animals, &c are made of Plaister [*sic*] of Paris of this Country Produce, and Manufactured at a reasonable Rate . . . any Merchants, Masters of Vessels, Country Traders, Shop keepers, &c., may be supplied with what quantity they may have occasion for by giving timely notice to said Geyer."

It is to be stressed at Geyer's "Images" in the Staffordshire tradition were made of plaster of Paris. Roughly one hundred years later, plaster of Paris genre figures and groups were still being made alongside of the newer chalkware and thin plaster groups. It is recorded that peddlers carrying trays on their heads, loaded with all of these wares, as well as with plaster casts from

Lucca, Italy, travelled about selling them from house to house in the eastern states. Very often they brought molds and cast figures and painted them while their country patrons waited. By 1870, however, the introduction of machine made articles and the revival of prosperity following Reconstruction days diminished the demand for the cheaply priced, handmade ornaments. The American sculptor, John Rogers, who began his professional career in 1860, invented his "gelatine mould" and bronze "master caster" for the accurate yet inexpensive reproduction of his fairly large red plaster groups. By the end of his life (1893) the sculptor was successful enough to have sold 100,000 copies of his works at prices ranging from $5 to $50 the piece. Contemporaries of Rogers, like Caspar Hennecke, who established a stoneware pottery business at Milwaukee at the close of the Civil War, were just as successful. Tho this genre work recalled the Staffordshire tradition of the chalkware, the more recent historic portraits, the subjects from the American contemporary theater, and the Victorian flavor of the domestic scenes which they depicted, soon displaced the older motifs of the chalkware with the popular taste. By the end of the nineteenth century this fine art of the Pennsylvania Germans was practically forgotten.[1]

The revived interest [. . .] in chalkware articles [reflects collectors' admiration of] the soft,* velvety quality of their surfaces and their brilliant, primitive colors which contrast readily with the somber glazes of Staffordshire ware. The Pennsylvania sculptured cats and dogs are "set flat" (composed in plane) as the Staffordshire, and the American country figures wear bowler hats like the English shepherds. But the art of working in chalk, which is very brittle, compels differences: as when the legs and horns of chalkware deer are made less slender than their Staffordshire models. The Staffordshire influences, however, are immediately apparent in the chalkware spotted dogs, in the colorings of the chalkware roosters, and in the color and stylization of the decorative ornament employed on most of the chalkware figures. Thus a bust of Mrs. Jackson has its base decorated with a Staffordshire design of mock-orange and leaves.

1. Note that here Zukofsky implies a sentiment of regret that popular taste does not foster the maintenance of a worthy craft. Ahearn observes that it was "the passing of American handicrafts that gave them new value toward the end of the nineteenth century," and addresses the complicated relation of popular taste and aesthetics in Zukofsky's work, arguing that Zukofsky did see himself in part as working in a craft tradition ("Zukofsky, Marxism, and American Handicraft," *Upper Limit Music* 89–90).

The chalkware objects included: cats, dogs, deer, squirrels, canaries, turtle doves, roosters; composite, flat bouquets of mock-orange and leaves; fruit and leaves; rustic figurines in pairs; various other statuettes; watch pockets in which watches could be hung; clock cases; shrines and models of churches; busts and bas-reliefs. The last two classes of objects were the rarest and usually pseudo-chalkware, that is, hollow, thin plaster. The favorite colors of the chalkware objects were blue, brownish black, tomato red and ochre. The costumes of the statuettes were usually as colorful as the composite fruit and floral groups.

Most of these objects were made ca. 1850, tho one small white duck on a green base in the Nadleman Collection bears the late date 1883. The duck and a small bird in the same collection still carry their price tags—15¢. The original price of the cats was about 50¢. The prices of the more imposing busts and statuettes, tho unrecorded, were naturally in proportion to their importance and demand.

The Index of American Design has made and filed drawings and data of the following chalkware objects:

A. Collection of the American Folk Art Gallery, 113 West 13 St., New York

- Figurine of a dog, made in Pa. Found in Brewster, Mass., White with painted head and base. H. 5 1/2".

- Mantel ornament of pomegranate and leaves in stylized form on a base decorated with a floral design in relief. Made in Pa. by Pennsylvania Germans. Found in Brewster, Mass. H. 1 3/4".

- "Prince Charles Spaniel," made in Pa. Found in Pottsville, Pa. Stylized figure of a spaniel standing on an oblong base. White chalk painted polychrome. H. 7 1/2" W. 5 1/8", D. 3".

- Figure of a seated shepherd boy. Found in Doylestown, Pa. White chalk painted polychrome. H. 11 7/8". W. 4 5/8". D. 5 1/8".

- Figurine of a Bloomer Girl. Pennsylvania German. Polychrome finish. H. 10".

- Figurine of a Cock. Pennsylvania German. Polychrome finish. H. 8".

- Figurine of a Spotted cat. Pennsylvania German. H. 10 1/8".

- Figurine of a Deer. Found in Bucks Cy., Pa. White with painted head and base. H. 10 1/2", W. 10".

- Group (Sheep and Lamb). Made in Pa. Polychrome Finish. H. 6", W. 9 1/4", D. 4".

- Shrine with opening at the top for a watch. Made in Pa. White and Polychrome finish. H. 11 3/4", W. 7 1/2", D. 3 3/4".

- Figurine of Queen Victoria, Empress of India. Made in Pa. Polychrome finish. H. 7 3/8".

- "King Charles Spaniel." Made in Pa. Polychrome finish. H. 8 5/8".

- Group of two roosters in symmetrical attitudes. White and polychrome finish. Found near Albany, N.Y. H. 6 1/2", W. 8 5/8", D. 3 1/2".

- Group (Love Birds). Made in Pa. Found in York, Pa. White and polychrome finish. H. 5 3/4".

- Figurine of a Parrot. Made in Pa. Polychrome finish. H. 6".

- Figurine of a Pigeon. Made in Pa. Polychrome finish. H. 5 1/4".

- Urn with fruit and birds. Urn base with circular decorations in relief and left white. Fruit and birds, polychrome painted. Made in Pa. Found in Brewster, Mass. H. 11 3/4", W. 6".

- Pair of Mantel Stops. Formalized arrangement of fruit and leaves upon a pedestal base, painted polychrome and white. Pennsylvania German craftsmanship. Found in Brewster, Mass. H. 14", W. 10".

- Group (Fireman and Woman) Polychrome finish, mounted on a wood base (restoration). Pennsylvania German craftsmanship. Found in Brewster, Mass. H. 10 1/4".

- Cat, seated on an oblong base with incised decoration. Painted polychrome. Pennsylvania German craftsmanship. Found in Brewster, Mass. H. 7 3/8".

- Group (Mother and Child). Made in Pennsylvania. Polychrome finish. H. 8 1/4".

- Figure of a deer. "Chalkware" (plaster cast in a mold). White with painted head and belly. Figurine touched up with carving after casting. Found in Bucks Cy., Pa. H. 13 7/8", W. 15 3/4".

- Church. *Plaster* cast in a mold. White with colored paper transparencies in windows and door. Found in Holicong, Bucks Cy., Pa. H. 20 1/2", W. 10", D. 4 3/4".

B. Collection of Miss Elena Wade Jack

- Mantel ornament. Base richly decorated with rococo ornament in relief. On top, Romeo and Juliet in the round, reclining against the circular frame of a central round opening which showed the face of a watch placed behind it.

Latter half of 19th c. Found in Vt. H. 12 3/8", W. 11 3/4", D. 3 7/8".

- Madonna and Child. Draped full figure of Madonna holding infant in her left arm. Stands on a molded oblong base, with chamfered corners. The seat "A.M." (Ave Maria) appears on the front face of base in relief. Figure partly painted polychrome. Middle 19 c. Found in Vt. H. 17 1/2".

- Winged figure kneeling in attitude of prayer upon a square pedestal. White chalk originally coated with shellac. Found in Vt. H. 7 1/2".

- Figurine of an angel, winged female figure kneeling in attitude of prayer upon a high square pedestal. Found in Vt. H. 8 1/2".

- Chalice with flowers. A chalice shape with incised designs around the bowl and gadrooning around the bottom of the bowl. A round knopped stem on a square base with chamfered corners. Painted pale pink. The stems of paper flowers embedded in top of chalice. Found in Vt. H. (not incl. flowers) 5 7/8".

- "Prince Charles Spaniel" seated on an oblong base with chamfered corners. Painted polychrome. Found in Vt. H. 8 1/2".

C. Collection of Mrs. John D. Rockefeller, Jr.

- Woman on Horse. Polychrome. Found in Brewster, Mass. H. 7".

- Portrait Bust of Young man in military regalia. Made in Pa. (probably before 1850). Found in Lancaster Cy., Pa. H. 14 1/2".

- Angel Figure. Found in Bucks Cy., Pa. H. 11 1/4".

D. Collection of Helena Penrose and J. H. Edgette

- Figure of a man wearing a three-cornered hat, and seated cross-legged upon an oblong base, reading a book. Polychrome. Paint chipped. Head broken off and repaired. Found in Pa. H. 7 1/4", W. (base) 3 1/4", D. 3 5/8".

Bibliography

American Folk Sculpture, The Work of Eighteenth and Nineteenth Century Craftsmen Exhibited October 20, 1931 to January 31, 1932. The Newark Museum, Newark, N.J. 1931 (pp. 93–96, chalkware, cottage ornaments).

Barck, Dorothy C. - Rogers Groups in the Museum of the New York Historical Society, in The New York Historical Society Quarterly Bulletin, vol. XVI, no. 3 (pp. 67–68, John Rogers' groups).

(Cahill, Holger) - American Folk Art, The Art of the Common Man in America 1750–1900. The Museum of Modern Art, New York, W. W. Norton & Company, Inc., 1932. (Preface, chalkware).

Forbes, Harriet M. - Early Portrait Sculpture in New England, In Old-Time New England, vol. XIX, no. 4, Serial No. 56, April, 1929. (p. 159, Henry Christian Geyer and plaster of Paris ornaments).

Gould, Mr. and Mrs. G. Glen - 18th Century Cottage Ornaments, in House and Garden, vol. LVII, no. 5. N.Y. May, 1930. (pp. 124–148, chalkware).

Gould, Mr. and Mrs. G. Glen - Plaster Ornaments for Collectors, in House and Garden, vol. 56, August, 1929, N.Y. (p. 84, plaster and chalkware ornaments)

Larsen, Peter - Chalkware, Index of American Design, Data Sheets. New York, 1938.

Read, Herbert - Staffordshire Pottery Figures. Duckworth, 3 Henrietta Street, London, 1929. (24 pp., 70 plates, Staffordshire ware).

R., W. S. (Rusk, William Sener) - John Rogers, in Dictionary of American Biography. Edited by Dumas Malone, vol. XVI, New York, Charles Scribner's Sons, 1935. (p. 102–3, John Rogers' plaster groups).

Wright, Richardson. Hawkers and Walkers in Early America. Strolling Peddlers, Preachers, Lawyers, Doctors, Players and Others. From the Beginning to the Civil War. Philadelphia, J. B. Lippincott Co., 1927. (317 pp., chalkware and plaster ornaments).

Prepared for the Index of American Design
by Louis Zukofsky
completed Sept 26/38

Editorial Note

* The revived ... admiration of the soft] The revived interest of collectors in chalkware articles admires the soft ...

III. American Tinware

1

Manufacture

The early American tinsmith—or whitesmith, as he was often called in the eighteenth and nineteenth centuries,[1] to distinguish him from the blacksmith who worked in iron—imported from England sheets of pure iron which he later tinned for his wares. Even today, the United States must obtain most of the tin used for commercial purposes from other countries.

A few bare facts give the history of the mining of tin in this country. The early New England historian, Nathaniel Morton, listed tin among the minerals found in these states in 1632. According to Bishop, tin mines were known to exist about that time in New England. William Hubbard noted, for the year 1680, that "Staten Island produces tin and store of Iron ore." These three facts are all that come out of the seventeenth century, relating to the extraction of tin.

In 1700, the Huguenot Andrew Faneuil, whose co-religionists had worked tin and steel extensively in France at the turn of the century, arrived at Boston to sell imported lanthorns, dishes, pans and kettles of tin at a very high price. Governor Winthrop possessed a few of these articles, as did also some southern planters. But the rarity of this tinware may be judged from the fact that a common utensil like the tin pail was still unknown at the time.

Edmund Billington, whitesmith, worked in Philadelphia in 1718. Between him and the first important manufacturers of tinware in the United States—the Patterson brothers of Berlin, Connecticut, (ca. 1740)—there is a gap in the record. The contribution of the Pattersons' is more than a date and will be discussed in its proper place, as part of the story of craftsmen whose lives are known.

1. [Zukofsky's note:] (In England, the word *Whitesmith* is still current.)

The next date is of special interest in connection with one that follows it almost twenty years later. The Provincial Congress of Massachusetts, realizing that the importation of tin plate would be stopped by the Revolution, recommended the domestic manufacture of tin plate in 1774. Importations had to be resumed immediately after the Revolution, and three tin plate workers were listed in Winchester, Virginia, by 1792.

The first verifiable discovery of tin in the United States was made by Professor Edward Hitchcock of Amherst, Massachusetts, at Goshen, Connecticut, ca. 1830 (?). He found it in a piece of granite—a single crystal of oxide of tin (cassiterite, or tin stone) weighing fifty grains. Other small quantities of the metal were found by Professor Charles Upham Shepard and Henry Darwin Rogers, about 1842. The sole deposit of tin ore (cassiterite) of any economic value, discovered about the same time, was found by Dr. Charles Thomas Jackson, state geologist at Jackson, New Hampshire. The cassiterite occurred in small crystals in mica slate and quartz.

But tin plates continued to be imported. The plates were easily workable and comparatively free from rust. A manufactory, principally for coachmakers and saddlers, employed seventy-three workmen plating tin plates at Philadelphia in 1810, doing an annual business of $100,000. Other establishments existed in New York, Baltimore, Boston and Charleston. Thomas Ewbank of New York City manufactured tinned sheet lead, and tin-plated lead pipes for stills in 1823. Tin plates, 10 inches wide by 14 inches long, were used for roofing thruout the West in dry mountainous districts, prior to the Civil War. Imported British tin plates were also run thru a bath of molten lead, as by N. and G. Taylor Co. of Philadelphia, in 1830, and used for roofing purposes. These were called terne plates.

Tho Calvin Whiting and Eli Parsons had invented a machine for working tin plate in Dedham, Massachusetts, in 1806, the decorative quality of the work of these early craftsmen hardly places it in the class of machine manufacture. Inquiries ordered by Congress, March 30, 1822 and January 27, 1824, do not contain references to the manufacture of tinware in Connecticut, but historians now consider it probable that the value of tinware made there and exported during those years exceeded that of any other product. Wide public consumption of tinware was no doubt advanced by Peck's improved machines for tin and other wares, invented in 1839, and advertised for sale in the *Norfolk Democrat* for Feb. 11, 1848 by Roswell Gleason, maker of tinware at Dorchester, Massachusetts. These machines included a full set of folding, grooving, turning and burring machines, as well as extra rollers, at a cost of $105. The rollers were adjusted for pressing half-inch and three-quarter inch beads for coffee pots.

Long before 1850, the use of water power had spurred tin manufacture in New England, so that Berlin, Connecticut, became the center of an industry consuming annually 10,000 boxes of sheet tin for culinary utensils. The machines used both tin plates and iron black plates, and stamped household articles from a single blank. The first articles made were shallow, such as pie plates and covers for pots. But ca. 1860, a machine was devised for the manufacture of deeper wares, including milk pans, washbowls, cake pans and dishpans. Tin plates were used for all of these deeper wares. Black plates were often stamped into ladles and skimmers and subsequently tinned. In the process of manufacture the original tin plates lost their lustre and the stamped articles had to be redipped in liquid tin.

The first attempt in the United States to produce tin or terne plates for the general market was made by four Welshmen who built a dipping plant in Pittsburgh, Pennsylvania. Evan H. Davies followed them at Wellsville, Ohio, and William Oak Davies at Demmler, Pennsylvania in 1873, when Rogers and Burchfield established a plant for the manufacture of black, tin and terne plates at Lechburg, Pa. The American Tin Plate Company began a similar business in 1874, but discontinued it the same year. The U.S. Iron and Tin Plate Company at Demmler, Pa. also established in 1874, suspended plating of iron and steel sheets with tin and alloy of tin and lead in 1877, continuing to manufacture black plates for show cards, tea trays and stamped ware till 1879, when the manufacture of tin and terne plates was resumed. It was again discontinued in 1880 and revived ten years later. The entrance into business of the Iron Clad Can Co. at Brooklyn, manufacturing "railroad" milk cans between 1874 and 1875; of the Monitor Tin Plate Co., at Horatio and Water Streets, New York, in 1876; of tin plating concerns at St. Louis and Detroit in 1889; and of the Anderson Tin Plate Company of Indiana in 1891—marked the end of the dominance of New England as a center of the tin industry and its shift to the Middle Atlantic and Mid-Western States in the last half of the nineteenth century. The period covered by 1740 to 1850, however, remains the dominant concern of those interested in the making of tinware as a handicraft which enriched American practical design.

2

Unpainted Tin and Its Workers (ca. 1740–1850)

The objects made by American tinsmiths, between 1740 and 1850, were both painted and unpainted, and included several main classes: table and household accessories; lighting and heating devices; weathervanes and other exterior architectural ornaments; and various interior ornaments and toys. Painted tinware, or toleware, will be treated separately in the third part of this essay.

A few facts regarding the history of European unpainted tin serve to establish the dating of the earliest American objects, and to distinguish these from the wares the colonists may have brought with them. Andrew Yarranton's *England's Improvement by Sea and Land,* 1698, relates how he learned the process of tin plating in Saxony and how he induced several German platers to come to England. He established a small plant at Pontypool in Monmouthshire, but his project was unsuccessful. In 1720, Major John Hanbury resumed the manufacture of tin plates at Pontypool. In 1728, he produced tinned sheets that were not hammered, as on the continent, with heavy hammers run by waterwheels, but rolled flat, hot or cold, between rollers. The hammered sheets made before 1728 naturally varied in thickness; the tin plates made by Hanbury were uniform. The tinsmiths of New England imported English tin plates, as has already been noted, and probably did not import them before 1740. Tinware found in America before 1740 no doubt showed the uneven thickness resulting from the hammering process, and must have been brought here from Germany or made here from imported German plates. It is possible that the Pennsylvania Germans brought a few of these objects or some hammered plate with them from their homeland.

In 1738, William and Edward Patterson (known also as William and Edgar Pattison—see Wright), natives of County Tyrone in Ireland settled at Berlin, Connecticut, to practice the trade of whitesmiths. They began importing sheets of the "best charcoal tin" packed in oak boxes, from England, about 1740. These were sheets of pure iron, two feet square and of the thickness of a sheet of paper, which the Pattersons first cleaned of their black oxide by immersing them in sulphuric [*sic*] acid. Afterwards, to plate the sheets, they dipped them in cisterns of melted tin. They worked at home. The first objects they made were cooking utensils—vessels beaten out with wooden mallets, or anvils. They sold their wares from house to house in Berlin and to the settlers of nearby communities.

The poetess Emma Hart Willard has celebrated the Pattersons in her work:

> "Oh, what's that lordly dish so rare,
> That glitters forth in splendour's glare?
> Tell us, Miss Norton, is it silver?
> Is it from China or Brazil or . . . ?"
> Then all together on they ran.
> Quote the good dame, "'Tis a tin pan,
> "The first made in the colony
> "The maker, Pattison's jest by
> "From Ireland in the last ship o'er.
> "You all can buy. He'll soon make more!"[2]

The Patterson brothers manufactured more tin plate than the local purchasers could buy. Yet they kept the secrets of their trade to themselves till 1760, when they first began training several apprentices. The Revolution, however, cut short their supply of sheet tin, and it was not till after the close of hostilities that the business of William and Edgar Patterson expanded with the help of the tin peddler.

What the tin peddler sold and who he was is ingeniously described in Hugh Peter's old Connecticut poem, "A Yankee Lyric":

> There is, in famous Yankee-land
> A class of men ycleped [*sic*] tin-peddlers
> A shrewd, sarcastic band
> Of busy meddlers:
> They scour the country through and through,
> Vending their wares, tin pots, tin pans,

---

2. This use of poetry mirrors the spirit of Zukofsky's *A Test of Poetry,* which includes folk ballads and other anonymous songs; here poems provide information and local color on the history of tin smiths and tin peddlars. This 'unconventional' manner of illustration tips a hand as to the author's affinities. Compare with two statements from *A Test of Poetry.* "Poetry does not arise and exist in a vacuum. It is one of the arts—sometimes individual, sometimes collective in origin—and reflects economic and social status of peoples . . ." (99). Characterized at its best by "sincere convictions . . . [and] the art of simplicity," folk poetry "is not the property of the few 'arty,' but of everybody" (103).

Tin ovens, dippers, wash-bowls, cans,
Tin whistles, kettles, or to boil or stew
Tin dullenders, tin nutmeg graters,
Tin warming-platters for your fish and 'taters!

In short
If you will look within
His cart,
And gaze upon the tin
Which glitters there,
So bright and fair,
There is no danger of defying
You to go off without buying.
One of these cunning, keen-eyed gentry
Stopped at a tavern in the country
Just before night,
And called for bitters for himself, of course,
And fodder for his horse:
This done, our worthy wight
Informed the landlord that his purse was low,
Quite empty, I assure, sir, and so
I wish you'd take your pay
In something in my way.

Now Boniface supposed himself a wag -
And when he saw that he was sucked,
Was not dispirited, but plucked
Up courage and his trousers too!
Quoth he t'himself, I am not apt to brag,
'Tis true
But I can stick a feather in my cap
By making fun of this same Yankee chap.
"Well, my good friend,
That we may end
This troublesome affair,
I'll take my pay in ware,
Provided that you've got what suits

My inclination."
"No doubt of that," the peddler cried,
Sans hesitation:
"Well, bring us in a pair of good tin boots!"
"Tin boots," our Jonathan espied
His landlord's spindle shanks,
And giving his good Genius thanks
For the suggestion,
Ran out, returned, and then - "By goles!
Yes, here's a pair of candle-moulds!
They'll fit you without question!"

The original Yankee peddlers travelled on foot or on horseback, with their dishes and other wares packed in two tin trunks weighing about fifty pounds each slung over their backs or over the backs of their horses. About 1790, carts with boxed tops were substituted, giving the peddlers more room for their products and making their journeys less burdensome. Their sales territory, no longer limited to Berlin, Farmington, and other nearby towns in Connecticut, became nation wide. Timothy Dwight records meeting them on Cape Cod and Lake Erie, and in Detroit, Canada and Kentucky. The peddlers are known to have made their way to St. Louis and New Orleans. Their scheduled trips covered two main routes, the northern and southern. Since five tinsmiths working at Berlin, Connecticut, could supply enough wares for twenty-five peddlers on the road, about that many would leave in the late summer or fall for the South, stopping at the important manufacturing centers—Richmond, Charleston and Savannah—through the winter. The peddlers carried their tinker's tools with them, as well as their wares, so that they could repair their patrons' old utensils, and, if necessary, embellish their current stock to suit local taste. Sometime during their winter sojourns they would turn over their profits to an agent of the tin manufacturers, who would give them new supplies for their spring and summer routes taking them back to the north. The peddlers now travelled by water, if possible. They met in New York at the beginning of the summer, sold their teams and wagons there, and returned on foot or horseback to Connecticut. On the northern route, peddlers started out early in the spring, made their way to Albany, then to Massachusetts and the important Bay State ports, and up to Montreal. Most of these centers had temporary tin factories established during the summer. A good deal of the Yankee peddlers' trade was barter—especially when he first began to sell tin. He had exchanged linen for potasheries, for iron pots, etc., long before that time.

By the turn of the eighteenth century, temporary and permanent tin establishments were manufacturing the following articles: candle boxes, candlesticks, candle moulds, lanthorns, sconces, sand shakers, foot-warmers, teacaddies, bread trays and small tin boxes for various purposes, most of them still unpainted. The decoration—aside from scalloping and embossed or repoussé work, respectively effected by pressing and hammering—was accomplished by etching designs on the surface of the tin or by pricking them into the surface. The last two processes were completely distinct and may have arisen in different places. In any case, different workmen would be likely to confine themselves to either one method or the other. E. A. Barber believes the etched designs "to have been outlined by metal wheels with serrated edges, the figures afterwards being filled in my hand with short strokes of the graver. These serrations and lines were cut thru the thin film of tin which covered the sheet iron beneath. By this treatment the ornamentation appeared darker in tint than the bright tin of the surrounding ground, producing a pleasing effect without the use of applied coloring. A coffee pot (probably early nineteenth century) in the (Pennsylvania) Museum Collection is embellished in this manner with tulips, birds and waving bands of etched work." The other method of pricking the designs into the surface of the tin was carried out with a sharp metal point, and prepared stencils were employed to guide the work.

In the case of punched or pricked lanthorns and foot-warmers, the decorations served the practical purposes of radiating light and heat. The foot-warmer consisted of a tin-box body contained in a wooden framework with turned spindles at the corners and often a wire handle. It held coal or heated bricks or stones and was used on winter rides and during church services.

Among the early makers of tin coffee pots and tin lanthorns was Eli Parsons, originally from Connecticut and later of Dedham, Massachusetts. The *Columbian Minerva,* a Dedham newspaper, for August 1, 1799, printed the following advertisement:

ELI PARSONS
Takes this method to inform his friends and the public that he has newly set up the / Tinning Business / in the town of Dedham, about three quarters of a

mile west of the Court house near Messrs. Whiting and Newell's store; where he determines to carry on the Manufacturing of Tin Ware in all its various and particular branches—likewise particular pains taken to do justice to all those who will oblige him with their custom. All kinds of Tin Ware warranted good and on the good terms as can be had in this state. Eli Parsons.

The following year another advertisement appeared in the *Columbian Minerva:*

Eli Parsons
Respectfully informs his friends and the public that he continues to carry on the Tin Ware Making near the usual place in Dedham; also that he makes all kinds of Sheet Iron Stoves and Funnels, and Lead Pipes for conductors to Houses. Any Gentlemen who wishes to furnish himself with any of the above will be faithfully served on the shorteth (sic) notice by applying as above.

He likewise wants immediately a LAD about 15 years oa [*sic*] age who can be well recommended as an Apprentice.

December 25, 1800.

About 1803, Parsons, investing his tools, tin carts and other effects, enlarged his tin business by entering into partnership with Calvin Whiting, no doubt the Whiting mentioned as of "Messrs. Whiting and Newell's store" in Parsons' advertisement of 1799. The original member of the firm brought with him his skilled workers and peddlers from Connecticut, and it is possible that the following note, found among the papers of Calvin Whiting, marks the beginning of the Parsons and Whiting partnership:

Boston, June 6, 1803
Major Whiting Sir, I have a distant relative a very clever fellow but as I have no tin here any more than I want myself if you have any tin unsold if you will let him have a load out of your shop I will be answerable for the same in so Doing you will oblige him & me & not disoblige yourself. I am Yours &c. Divan B. Yate tin Pedlar.[*sic*]

The partnership prospered and very shortly the Upper Village section of Dedham became known by the name of Connecticut Corner, calling attention to the state, and center of the tin industry, from where Parsons had come.

Another slip of paper also in Yate's handwriting and again dated "Boston, June 6, 1803" might indicate the kind of wares Parsons and Whiting sold:

'Japann'd Ware/ 36 Sugar Boxes of Difrent [*sic*] sizes/ 60 Bread Baskets/ 6 Large Coffee Pots/ 6 2nd size Do/ 6 L graters/ 6 Flour boxes/ 60 Harts and rounds/ 12 Graters/ 12 Gill cups." The name "Caleb Downing" is written on back of this note, and he may have been the bearer, calling on the Dedham tinsmiths for wears for the Boston peddler, Divan B. Yate.

Whiting, who had been a successful merchant of West India goods, seems also to have had inventive ability. The *Norfolk Repository,* a weekly newspaper of Dedham, advertised for May 9, 1806:

> Patent Machine for Working Tin Plate. The public are respectfully informed that a machine has lately been invented by Calvin Whiting and Eli Parsons of Dedham (in the county of Norfolk and commonwealth of Massachusetts) for working Tin Plate into the various kinds of ware necessary for use, for which a patent is obtained according to law. The Machine is considered by those who have had an opportunity to examine it to be one of the most useful and important inventions that ever originated in our country and worthy the attention of every Tin Plate worker who considers his time of any value. Although it is simple in its operations above described it will make from ninety to one hundred and twenty revolutions in a minute. Those who incline to purchase patent rights to the above machinery may have opportunity by applying at the Patent Tin Manufactory a little west of the Court House Dedham where shopkeepers and others may be supplied with any quantity of Japanned and Gilt Tin Ware at the most reduced prices of any in the United States.
>
> Dedham, May 9, 1806.

An idea of these prices may be obtain[ed] from the following bill of a few years earlier:

> Wm. Herman Mann / to C. Whiting, Dr.
> 1802 - Dec. 11 to mending stove funnel $0.17
> 1803 - April 26 To tin kitchen   3.25
> July 17 to a skimmer   17

And the following record on three scraps of paper, dated Dedham, Feb. 17, 1803, suggests a sequence of business as conducted at the time:

> Madam please to deliver to Calvin Whiting or order the tin ware which I left locked in your stable.
> Mrs. Clark. Yours Alpheus Cleveland.

Madam please to deliver to Calvin Whiting or order the tinware which I left in your care.

Mrs. Sally Curtis Yours Alpheus Cleveland.

R'cd of Calvin Whiting Forty Dollars being in full of all demand.
Alpheus Cleveland.

In the same year that Eli Parsons first advertised his business at Dedham, 1799, a maker of tinware of another generation was born at Putney, Vermont—Roswell Gleason. Leaving his birthplace in the autumn of 1818, Gleason journeyed to Dorchester, Massachusetts, where he became an apprentice to a Mr. Wilcox, a manufacturer of block tinware, then another name for pewter. Gleason began his own business at the age of 23, working at first in pewter, then tin in 1825, and britannia ware in 1837. His career may be traced in manuscript letters discovered in the Gleason homestead. A letter dated 1825 negotiates for a quantity of tin, considerable for the time. Invoices addressed to him from Connecticut were sometimes still figured in pounds, shillings and pence, representing, however, not English, but New England, currency of the time—£1 = $3 1/3 and 6 sh = $1.

In 1837, the Massachusetts charitable Mechanics Association Awarded Gleason a medal and diploma for his block tinware. In 1840, he received a request from Haverhill, New Hampshire asking him to permit his correspondent to sell "tin tippers" for the pay of $26 a month. He took his sons into partnership when they reached their majority, and one of them after a business tour returned with a number of new ideas and a few skilled workers to assist his father in the opening of the first silver-plating establishment in the United States. Critics have called Gleason's silver decadent, but have praised his pewter, which often bears one of Gleason's marks: a coat of arms of Massachusetts, sometimes stamped on the bottom of a piece, and sometimes on a separate disk soldered to the metal sides.

As a maker of tinware, Gleason successfully adapted his products to the current public demand for machine manufacture. As has already been noted (66), he used and sold Peck's machines for making tin in 1839. He advertised his trade in the *Norfolk Democrat,* Feb. 11, 1848: "Britannia Ware, Lamps etc. . . . Tin Plate, sheet Iron and Japaned Ware of every description made to order and warranted."

By 1837, a typical large-scale manufacturer of the time, Gleason had built a mansion and stables on Washington Street, in Dorchester. He joined his town's Rifle Company and became its captain. He gave money to the Gibson School, and free milk from his cows to the children of his employees. He was eulogized in a book entitled *Rich Men of Massachusetts*. The end of his life was sad. The Civil War destroyed his southern market, and saw the death of his two sons. When a boiler explosion damaged his plant in 1871, he was seventy-two, he never re-opened it. He died sixteen years later.

Other tin manufacturers, contemporaries of Gleason, included Thomas Smith (born in England, 1791, d. 1876) and David B. More (1807–1882), who founded the firm of Smith and Morey in Boston, at 4 Market Street, which ceased operating in 1886; and Timothy Bailey and James Harvey Putnam, whose business thrived from about 1825 to 1850.

Bailey was born in Westmoreland, New Hampshire, September 20, 1785. He first worked as a farmer and teacher, and subsequently accepted an offer of Burrage Yale, a tinsmith of South Reading (now Wakefield, Massachusetts) to enter his employ as a peddler. He described his experiences later: "I went from town to town and from state to state peddling wares until I sold my load; then I went home for another load. I had to drive a two-wheel horse cart with a box made fast on the shafts and axle-tree to hold the wares. The harness for the horse to draw it with was a saddle, leather breastplate and rope tugs and a wooden whiffle-tree, and a bridle without reins. I had to walk beside the horse all day, hot or cold and put up at night with private families as I could find them. I drove the same cart and harness for Mr. Yale for eight years in succession with the exception of the cold season of the winter. I walked beside my horse to average about two thousand miles a year for eight years."

Bailey left his employer in 1815, and established his own business in Roxbury. After marrying in 1817, he settled at Malden where he bought a house on Main Street, which was later moved to number 20 Madison. He set up his shop in the rear of his house, and tradition has it that his back yard was always filled with piles of shining scrap tin. He employed eight workmen in his shop and sixteen peddlers on the road. He died November 19, 1852,— his partnership with James Harvey Putnam lasting from about 1830–1835.

Putnam, who was born in Charleston, N.H., 1803, was the son of Bailey's sister. He came to Malden, Massachusetts, probably soon after his uncle had established his business there, and served him as an apprentice before he joined him in partnership, mainly to make pewter. Their firm endured only about five years. The state census of Massachusetts, after 1836, lists two tinware shops in Malden, employing twenty workmen and manufacturing goods valued at $31,000. Since the census records no other tin establishments of the kind in Malden at that time, and since Bailey was known to have employed eight workmen, it is probable that the other twelve were in the employ of Putnam. After the dissolution of the partnership which very likely was conducted at Bailey's house, Putnam opened a shop on Haskins Street (now Main and Eastern Avenue). He devoted most of his time to the manufacture of tinware, but also made pewter and britannia later in his career. He died May, 1855.

Like most of the American designers of the seventeenth, eighteenth and early nineteenth centuries, the majority of craftsmen who worked in tin remain anonymous. There exist only the wares they made and some few traditions connected with these, such as a quatrain from the *Boston Evening Post,* 1783, recording a religious objection to the use of footwarmers in churches:

> Extinct the sacred fire of love
> Our zeal grown cold and dead
> In the house of God we fix a stove
> To warm us in their stead.[3]

Collectors have preserved, and written about, the following objects of table and kitchenware interesting for their use and design:

- A coffee pot, natural color, punched design, ea. nineteenth century of Pennsylvania Dutch make, now at the Metropolitan Museum.
- Another of the same period, also with punched design, and the lower part of its spout fluted.
- A nursing can or bottle, shaped like a coffee pot with handle, horizontal spout, flat lid, made of wrought tin, in Pennsylvania in the nineteenth century. This nursing device worked on the principle of an inner tube connecting with the outer nipple and reaching to the bottom of the vessel.

---

3. Once again, anonymity is presented as a usual condition with the suggestion that the persistence of the craft object (stove, foot-warmer, or poem) obviates any sense of loss. Not necessarily presented as examples of good poetry, the quatrain above and others included in *A Useful Art* substantiate some key beliefs of Zukofsky: e.g., "A gift of description . . . may be far from great poetry, but it will do to present an image or a situation. . . . Good poetry is definite information on the subject dealt with . . ." (*A Test of Poetry* 89).

- An egg cooker, attributed to Thomas Clark, silversmith of Hingham. (Now owned by W. W. Lunt)
- A reflector baking oven with spit, nineteenth century.
- A Springele mold of sheet tin, oblong, partly filled with baked clay in which were six intaglio designs (monkey, dog, goat, cow, kicking horse, bison) within squares made by double-line divisions—L. 4 3/8", W. 6 1/8". The Pennsylvania Germans used this cake mold for their St. Nichola [*sic*] Day, ca. 1850.
- Another, with giraffe, elephant, camel, running deer, mule, cat, engraved within squares made by double line divisions.
- Another, fifteen designs in circular leaf borders—designs and borders in relief.
- Other small patterns of ladies, babies, bunnies, flowers, horses, dogs and birds, cut out of tin—suggest that they were backs of cookie molds made in Pennsylvania. (Holger Cahill collection)

Extant lighting devices made out of tin, from the seventeenth thru the nineteenth century, are numerous. The earliest objects are tin candle sticks and tin candle boxes for an extra supply of candles, which were hung on the wall ca. 1680. The "Ipswich Betty" lamp and similar lamps made by a tinsmith in Newburyport date from about the same time. Hanging lard and fluid lamps were introduced about 1700 and continued to be used till about 1830. The New York Historical Society possesses candle holders of sheet tin of the saucer type and a candlestick with a high cylindrical shape, dating from the late seventeenth and early eighteenth century.

Mercer gives a complete description of a Pennsylvania tinder box, 4" in diameter and 2" high, typical of a whole class used in colonial homes ca. 1740. It had a circular tin handle for the forefinger, an inner loose lid for smothering the smoldering tinders, and was so devised as to permit the burning and smothering of a fresh rag—placed under the lid—from an already existing fire. The flint, steel and spunks were placed over the lid, enclosed in the box. The lid had a candle-socket, unlike the earlier tinder boxes which had no candlestick attachments.

The majority of candle molds surviving from the eighteenth century are made out of tin. They were of great variety of design. Prior to 1770, the itinerant candleman made his rounds of colonial households, carrying with him molds for candles of all sizes and constructed for the making of six to sixteen candles at a time.

The early colonial lamps were not painted, their decorations consisting mostly of pierced designs. The earliest tin ones resembled the iron sconces and lanterns which they replaced. Later lamps followed Spanish and English designs of the seventeenth century, in the use of tin combined with leadwork, and of tin reflectors set with pressed glass in geometrical patterns and furnished with candle holders. One tin chandelier of the late eighteenth or ea. nineteenth century was mounted on a wooden core and braced with wooden arms.

The Index of Design has made drawings of the following lighting devices:

- A sconce of natural tin, tooled parallel lines on reflector, the top shell-shaped with tool fluting, ea. eighteenth century. (Owned by the Metropolitan Museum)

- A sconce with a faceted mirror, seventeenth or eighteenth century.

- A wall sconce, with punched design and tooled decoration, ea. eighteenth century. (Owned by the Metropolitan Museum)

- A lantern of the "Paul Revere Type," i.e. with domed top, dormer draughts, pierced design, eighteenth century. (Owned by the N.Y. Historical Society)

- A hand lantern of sheet tin, semi-circular in shape, late eighteenth or ea. nineteenth c.

- Another of hexagonal shape.

- A watchman's lantern, glass encased, with wire frame. (Owned by the N.Y. Historical Society)

- A chandelier of sheet tin painted black, with four square cups, candle sockets and reflector above, of Pennsylvania German make, ca. 1800. (Owned by the Metropolitan Museum)

- A lantern of cylindrical shape, straight sides in flat saucer, with peaked top and long handle for hanging, nineteenth c. (Owned by the New York Historical Society)

- A Betty lamp and stand, ca. 1800.

- A Watchman's lantern, punched design, with glass door, ca. 1825. (Owned by the Metropolitan Museum)

- A lantern in the shape of an eagle used on a pole ca. 1820–30. Repoussé decoration; the entire body forms a receptacle for kerosene; wick holders unscrew for filling, on top of each wing. H. 12 1/2", W. 9". (Nadleman Collection)

- A whale oil lamp, with saucer and columnar shaft, ca. 1845–60. (Owned by the New York Historical Society)
- A lard lamp with oil repository of tin in cast iron ball, dated 1851. (Nadleman Collection)
- Another, with pierced design.

Other extant lighting devices include: tin cans and lamps for burning fluid, of ca. 1850, found in Ohio; a candle sconce of sheet tin with circular plate reflector with impressed design, the bottom holding a flat U bracket supporting a circular bobecke, nineteenth century; tin peg lamps, japanned, made ca. 1812, now in the Massachusetts State House Boston; patented tin wall lamps, manufactured by W. Carlton of Boston in the nineteenth century; The Tin Tomlinson lard lamp, patented 1843; tin canting lamps, which could be maintained at a desired angle by a coil spring, ca. 1840–1862; and a tin canting lamp, invented by Dexter Chamberlain in 1854, which tipped automatically as the fluid in the reservoir was consumed, thus reverting to the device of the Porter lamp of 1804.

Weathervanes made from sheet metal hammered by tinsmiths remain an outstanding achievement of nineteenth century American architectural ornament. One of these vanes, shown at the exhibit of American Folk Sculpture at the Newark Museum, some years ago, was a gull entirely out of hammered tin, composed of separate small pieces of the metal soldered together. The realistic presentation catches the bird just descended on a small ball, with wings half spread and tail down in an effort to balance itself. Other tin weathervanes were produced in quantity, the main body of the vanes stamped out by dies made from a wood pattern, and the parts soldered. Finishing touches were accomplished by hand.

Among architectural curiosities, one collector has found an eaves spout of tin plate, in the form of a grinning cetacean, made probably by a Pennsylvania German in the first quarter of the nineteenth century. The fish's use at the end of a rain gutter under the eaves of an old dwelling in Lancaster County seems to have been purely decorative. In fact, a downspout was arranged to carry off any water before it reached its throat, which was further protected against floods by the insertion of a metal plate.

Miscellaneous interior ornaments of tin include: clock-cases, "[W]ole trees"* of a silvery appearance (as much as can be made out from the photograph) in painted tin bowls; two tin silhouette birds; and a variety of children's toys now owned by the Essex Institute and a collector of Salem, Massachusetts. The earliest of these toys, dating back perhaps to ca. 1750, are miniature reproductions of unpainted lighting devices of the time: a candlestick less than one inch high; a tiny lamp with whale-oil burner fitted as in real models; candle lanterns with rounded backs, conical tops and square projecting windows; and candle moulds for two candles, five inches high, with square bottoms and circular tops. The more recent toys of the nineteenth century also include unpainted wares, such as tiny spoons and other dinner plate, but are more notable for their imitation of the painted toleware of their time, which will be considered subsequently. In anticipation, the various toys, painted and unpainted, may be listed here, and a description of the decorative processes employed in the manufacture of the tole left to a discussion of the larger pieces. In any case, toys that were produced in large quantities would generally not follow these processes to the most refined details.

The toys of the Salem collector include, besides the lighting devices already mentioned: a tea set of ten pieces of which the lacquered tray is less than two inches in length; soup dishes; ladles; cups, spoons (ca. 1870); trays in plain colors and colored stenciling; four miniature coffee pots, two of which—one painted red, the other blue—have the spigot on the left side, so that the coffee will pour at a turn of the wrist to the left; a mixing bowl; a wash boiler of a very early type; a combination baby's rattle and whistle; dust pans with gold traces; little boxes resembling trunks, brightly colored in the manner of their larger prototypes, ca. 1825 to 1840; and three banks, one with "Savings Bank" painted over the door. Also: ten alphabet plates, fifty to one hundred years old, two and a half inches in diameter, illustrating: lasses around a mulberry bush; Aston Hall in Birmingham, England, 1680; a cavalry man and soldier; a coffee grinder operated by two men,—protruding from the opening at the top, the head and legs of a human figure, while a smaller figure is being ejected from the opening below—the legend on this plate is "grinding old into young." Another plate is decorated with a bust of Washington and thirteen stars.

The toy collection of the Essex Institute, in addition to several duplicates of the above, includes: a richly decorated tray with cut out, lacework design; tea caddies in bright colors, of 1830 to 1860; a spice box with three compartments; doll houses; chairs; tables; bath tubs; a bird cage; a water pump which actually worked; a Dutch oven; a Franklin stove with finely wrought fender and coal scuttle; a warming pan; an oil can for whale oil; lamps; etc.

Also: a tin monkey which can run up a string; an eagle; several horse drawn vehicles; a sleigh with a clownish figure, drawn by a white horse; a farm wagon drawn by a pair of white horses; a female on a buggy, driving a brown pacer; and railroad trains consisting of locomotive and coaches named New York and Boston (ca. 1850).

Helena Penrose and J. H. Edgette own miniature houses of painted sheet tin made over one hundred years ago.

As late as the mid-nineteenth century, certain American manufacturers employed hand-cut soapstone molds for casting tin soldiers, horsemen, and other tiny figures. Other manufacturers, however, making toy railway trains, boats and case furniture, cut them out from sheet metal.

Francis, Field and Francis conducted the first tin toy manufactory at 80 North Second and 19 Broad Street, Philadelphia, between 1852 and 1855, advertising themselves in a local business directory as "prepared to furnish every description of handsome Japanned Ware and Tin Toys in Great Variety, Wholesale, suitable for the City and Country Trade, which they will sell on the most liberal terms." "Orders," the end of the advertisement read, "executed with promptness and dispatch."

3

Toleware

The word *toleware* implies tableware. The very early French form, *taule,* used on the banks of the Garonne in southwestern France, meant table. The derivative, tôle, was also applied to sheet iron. Hence, tôle peinte, painted tole or painted table-ware made from sheet iron.[4]

If the iron is not used as an alloy with zinc, lead or tin, tôle rusts or corrodes. It was therefore painted. To make handling easier for the painter or enameler, several thin sheets of tole were first pressed into one under rollers and pierced with holes. The tôle was then japanned—i.e. given a desired foundation color and fired, to effect a surface that was not porous. Paint was applied over this japanned surface.

---

4. Compare this foregrounding of etymology with a passage such as this from "*A*"-12: "His legs in a *gigue* / Old French, *to dance (giguer)* or *hop* / From *gigue* (Teuton *geige*—a fiddle)" (176) or the prose piece "Thanks to the Dictionary" (*Collected Fiction*). Zukofsky's extraordinarily precise attention to word forms and meanings is manifested through the entirety of "*A*" and later poems (see Michelle Leggott, *Reading Zukofsky's 80 Flowers*).

Whatever economic reasons an English law of 1622 had in forbidding the painting and gilding of pewter, unless the objects so decorated were merely intended for presents and not the commercial market, the sense of good craftsmanship was unintentionally asserted. The surface of pewter does not need the extra embellishment of painting. Nevertheless, the earliest English tôle was painted pewter, and the inspiration for the designs came from Oriental lacquered objects and furniture first brought into England by Charles II (1630–1685).

In 1660, Thomas Allgood, a native of Northampton migrated to Pontypool in Monmouthshire, then part of Wales, and became one of the managers in the manufactory of John Hanbury (inventor of rolled tin sheets, 1728, see above, p. 36). Allgood is said to have been the first (Bradney, *History of Monmouthshire,* vol. 1, part II) to have discovered the method of japanning or lacquering iron plates, and by his own testimony recorded "a substance capable of application, under heat, to metal, which made a hard lacquer." The exact date of his discovery is unknown, but in 1688, John Stalker and George Parker published *A Treatise of Japaning and Varnishing,* at Oxford. The book, divided into two parts, took up both *Japaning* and *Lackering,* and as a recent critic has explained, the term *japaning* stood for what today is *lacquer,* and the term *lacker* for what ironmongers now call a clear golden or colourless varnish.

It remains for the specialist to decide whether Allgood's method resembled the methods of *japaning* and *lackering* found in the *Treatise*—a difficult decision to make, for when Allgood died in 1710, he passed on the secret of japanning to his sons. They carried on the industry till 1822, while collateral relations had started a similar industry at Usk in Wales. Meanwhile, the literature on japanning grew. In June, 1732, The Gentlemen's Magazine advertised: "The method of learning to draw in perspective made easy and fully explained. Also the Art of Painting upon glass, wood and metal, so as to imitate *China;* and to make black or gilt Japan ware as beautiful and light as any brought from the East Indies; with proper directions for making the hardest and most transparent varnishes; and particularly the way to cast Amber in any shape. Chiefly from the Mss. of the great Mr. Boyle. Printed for J. Peele. Price 1 s." In 1764, appeared (R. Dossie's) *The Handmaid to the Arts,* in two volumes, printed for J. Nourse in London, containing these directions: "Japan work ought properly to be painted with colours in varnish . . . But . . . for . . . greater dispatch, and in some very nice works in small, for the freer use of the pencil, the colours are now most frequently tempered in oil, which should previously have a fourth part of its weight of gum animi dissolved in it. (Etc.) In some instances water colours . . . are laid on grounds of gold. Sometimes so managed to have the effect of embossed work." (v. 1, pp. 190, 495–6). Dossie also defined *japanning* as referring to grounds of opaque colors; and *lacquer,* to transparent grounds used over brass and *tin,* so as to give the effect of color, mentioning its use for snuff boxes, coaches, screens, etc., in which "there is rivalship betwixt ourselves and the French" (p. 479).

The American makers of toleware did not follow Dossie's description of its manufacture in every detail. But Portsmouth, New Hampshire, and Newburyport, Boston and Salem, Massachusetts, imported tôle from abroad, some years before the appearance of his "handmaid," and there is no question that European pieces must have inspired the painting of tin lanterns, sold in the first "housekeepers" markets on the banks of the Delaware in 1752.

Gilded and painted lanterns were used in Colonial hallways during the first half of the eighteenth century. Ca. 1750–1775, a double chandelier with circles of tin, fluted crown and scallop-shaped† canopy, all painted yellow, could be found in a church in Hebron, Connecticut. (Collection of Mrs. J. Insley Blair)

The imported tôle Empire vases, cache-pôts, tea caddies, bread trays, egg warmers, etc., which make up American toleware collections of the present day, were formerly the property of wealthy American colonists. The mixed English, Dutch, French and German component affecting the design and manufacture of this toleware is still difficult to unravel.[5] It is uncertain whether the manufacture of tôle was started in Holland ca. 1700, or whether Allgood or Pontypool was responsible for shipments of tôle into Holland before that date. It is known that the Dutch later sent some of their pewter to Wales to be decorated, and some of the Dutch pieces very likely must have found their way thru Belgium and France, into England. At the end of the

---

5. The implication that new craft may be forged through the conjunction of various ethnic traditions finds manifestation throughout Zukofsky's poetry. "Poem Beginning 'The'" recalls the presence of Yiddish theater and literature at the turn of the century; *"A"*-6 incorporates a sampling of ethnic, vernacular voices of New York. See also the Introduction to Peter Quartermain's *Disjunctive Poetics* for an elaboration of cultural demographics as related to American modernism (9–15).

eighteenth century, Dutch shapes decorated in French styles were prevalent in both Belgium and France.

The Pontypool tôle was distinguished by a tortoise shell finish, red designs resembling seaweed forms, and butterflies. Simon Etienne Martin was the first to start the industry in Paris, having imported his lacquer from Holland, probably via Wales. In 1744, he discovered his own varnish-vernis Martin—and was granted a monopoly. His characteristic black grounds decorated with gold imitated the Chinese and Japanese lacquer. The end of the eighteenth century in France witnessed other craftsmen and a variety of grounds in tôle: mauve-pink, Rose du Barry, royal blues, creams, green and mustard yellow, sealing-wax red, and the rarer bluish-green lacquer.

The painting of these grounds, in the best pieces, with portraits, landscapes, historical and mythical subjects, demanded the art of fine painters of miniatures thruout the Continent—for the art of toleware spread to Italy, Germany and Russia about 1800. The connoisseur, like Madame Récamier (1777–1840), collected the early pieces. But the public demand for a less costly reproduction of decorated pewter led not only to the entire abandonment of the use of pewter for tole, but of the care originally given by the special artist to its decoration. The continent forgot the formula for old painted pewter sometime in the first half of the nineteenth century. A diary of 1864, found only recently, described a process requiring seven ingredients. More recent authorities list seventeen.

The American makers of toleware in the early nineteenth century, attracted chiefly by contemporary English, Dutch and German pieces, decorated the tin plate they imported from England and imitated the *lacklier-tess-zinn gefäss* (lacquered tinware) of North Germany. Pewter was not used at all. Perhaps the fact that pewter was called *tin* in Holland was in itself partly responsible for the nineteenth century manufacturer's failure to remember that originally there had been two kinds of toleware, first, painted pewter, and then, painted tin. In any case, the manufacture of toleware in the early republic became part of the craft of the tinsmith. The New England craftsman may have borrowed the subject matter for his decoration from English vignettes; the Pennsylvania German craftsman may have followed Dutch originals in the lines of his tableware—tho the lines were usually straighter and more elongated; but both used tinned iron and painted their oil colors over American-made japanned surfaces, usually black or golden brown.

The japanning was often thin, and the decoration, which would have seemed garish to the European connoisseur, was usually a matter of bold designs done in bright colors. But this toleware was exceedingly popular with the country people and the Yankee peddler fostered its distribution thruout the Union to such an extent that tinware replaced the American decorated pottery which had been in vogue for over a century. The tinned teapots and coffeepots were fairly resistant to heat, and the lightness of the tin mugs, tea canisters, fruit dishes and waiters must have had an added appeal. The earliest of this toleware dates from the first quarter of the nineteenth century; the latest, ca. 1875. And the earliest pieces of American toleware come closest to the serious artistry of the European tôle, in their care for consistency and delicacy of the grounds, and the sureness of their painting, which no ordinary apprentice could execute. Artists like Thomas Cole (1801–48) of the Hudson River school decorated japanned ware during its best period in America. When the freehand painting of the accomplished artist gave way to cruder and more obvious color treatments, this garish decoration was in time replaced by stenciling, a painstaking process in itself. One collector remembers a description of the work by an old craftsman who used stencil patterns and mixed "Japan" colors. He found his job "awful fidgety and puttering;" the first surface had to be "real tacky," before the decoration was applied; the powdered "goldy" lacquer effect was obtained by touching the design lightly with a chamois skin before it was quite dry.

The Index of American Design has made drawings of some of the best toleware pieces, all dating from the early nineteenth century. They include:

- An oblong, octagonal shaped tray, with dark japanned edge and center panel, and whitish border painted with tulip, leaf and fruit designs in red, orange, brown, green and black. L. 12 1/4", W. 8 1/2", D. 7/8". (Collection of the American Wing, Metropolitan Museum of Art)

- A coffee pot, found in Lancaster Cy., Pa., of japanned sheet tin, with brightly painted leaf bands around the lid and top of the pot, and at the base another band of fruit and leaves. H. 10 1/4", Diameter at base 6 1/2" and at top 3 7/8". (Present owner, F. M. Kline, The Early American Shop, 46 Greenwich Ave., N.Y.C.)

- A coffee pot with painted tulip design in bright colors. H. 10 1/2". (Collection of the American Wing, Metropolitan Museum of Art)

- Another, with tulip design around the base and top border, brilliantly painted over a dark background. H. 10 1/4". (Present owner, McKearin's Antiques, Inc. 136 E. 55th St., N.Y.C.)

- Another coffee pot, with conventionalized tulips and petals in red and yellow. H. 27 cm., 24 cm. from end of handle to spout. (Present owners: Mr. and Mrs. John Dashiell and Mr. Arthur W. Clement; shown at the American Gallery of The Brooklyn Museum)

- A tea canister of elliptical shape, with yellow and red floral design over dark background. H. 5 1/4", W. 3 3/8", D. 2 5/8". (Present owner, McKearin's Antiques, Inc., 136 E. 55th St., N.Y.C.)

- A Chocolate pot, top and body painted with bright floral designs over dark background. H. 7 7/8". (Present owner, McKearin's Antiques, Inc.)

All of these pieces, with the exceptions of the tea canister and chocolate pot, have been verified as of Pennsylvania German handicraft.

The Index of American Design has also made drawings of two early lighting objects:

- A Pennsylvania German oil lamp, ca. 1750–1800, of tin painted with earth colors. H. 12 1/2". "The cone cover is an oil repository fitting into the inverted cone below, leading the oil into three arms containing wicks at their ends." Bits of solder at the top edge of the inverted cone would seem to indicate that hooks or rings have been broken off and that the lamp was meant to be hung up, as its three arms testify.

- An early nineteenth century, sheet-tin lantern of cylindrical shape with cone top, entirely painted black with asphaltum, and also decorated with nail and pierced designs. Two bull's eye glasses are set in the circular windows.

As against these early painted lighting devices, there are the following all dating after 1850:

- A hanging lantern of glass and tole, with domed perforated top, painted red and blue. (Rushlight Exhibition Catalogue)

- A shelf lantern with two reflectors, used in halls and stores, 1865 patent. Tin painted red. (U.S. National Museum)

- A single-wick type of lamp, erroneously called a political torch, i.e. a flare torch with long tubular handle. Painted red. Air was blown thru the flame by means of a tube, the mouth of which projects from the handle, 24.4" long. (U.S. National Museum)

Other tin torches with brass wick tubes, 8.6" high and 6.3" in diameter, fitted on a staff, were used on mackerel fishing boats off Gloucester, Massachusetts, in 1882.

Much of this toleware was painted by women. They are said to have exceeded the number of men working in the industry, and it is certain that Pennsylvania and New England housewives made toleware painting their avocation, just as they did the painting of velvet and other amateur decoration.

The center of toleware manufacture in New England was Stevens Plains, (then Westbrook) Maine, and the career of Zachariah Stevens (1778–1856) who perpetuated its name is almost a summary of the history of American toleware in the first half of the nineteenth century. The first of four generations to abandon the paternal craft of blacksmithing, he founded an industry whose products were sold by the Yankee peddler along the seacoast from Boston to Portland, and thruout Maine and New Hampshire to the Canadian border. It is not known where Stevens spent his apprenticeship as tinsmith, but before him there was no one from Stevens Plains expert enough to teach him his craft. Family legend is that he resided for some time in Cambridge. In any case, the urban style of the tinware suggests the possibility that he may have passed his apprenticeship in a shop which furnished Japanned tea trays and other tinware sold by Paul Revere at his place in the North End of Boston. Philip Rose, Revere's nephew, is known to have stayed at Stevens Plains in 1791 or shortly after, and the Stevens family still owns two of his ornamental drawings which he made for them. One of these commemorated the marriage of Issac S. Stevens and Sarah Brackett; the other was a genealogical list of their nine children. The decorative device which Rose used for the borders of his pictures—a wriggled line made with the flat of the brush—is characteristic of the borders of painted trays. It is possible that Rose had once been employed in a shop which decorated trays, and was now (1791) young Zachariah's teacher. Another influence may have been Thomas Brisco, the first whitesmith 'from foreign parts,' who came to Stevens Plains in 1803, and bought land for his house and tin establishment from Issac Sawyer Stevens, Zachariah's father. Brisco drove his own horse and cart in which he peddled his goods, consisting of tinware japanned and ornamented by his wife, "aided later by five orphaned nieces." Brisco's wife (née Sarah Rose) was Paul Revere's niece and Phillip Rose's sister.

Zachariah's own home, still standing across the street from the site of his general store and adjoining tin shop, was built in 1800, and his practice very likely began a few years before that time. His best toleware is said to have been an early accomplishment. The community of Stevens Plains prospered with Stevens' trade, but he withdrew gradually from tinsmithing to give his time to local affairs, becoming coroner of the Plain in 1823, and postmaster in 1833, after transferring his business to his sons, Samuel Butler and Alfred Stevens. The former had signed a six months note for six boxes of tin 13 x 19 3/4 inches, at $58.50, in 1830. The sale represented the entire stock of tin plate of which Zachariah Stevens "was at the time possessed." An item in *The Portland Argus* for April 11, 1842, gives the rest of the story: "Fire broke out this morning about two o'clock at Stevens Plains, in the blacksmith shop of Z. B. Stevens, and soon communicated to the tinware shop of his son Samuel B. Stevens. Both shops were consumed. Mr. S. B. Stevens lost his books, ware, tin plate, etc., amounting to $1500.00, insured $300.00. The fire extended to the shop of Rufus Dunham, block tin manufacturer, which was also destroyed with contents. Loss $1000.00 to 1200.00."

The poorer toleware in the collection still to be seen at Stevens' home has been attributed to his sons. The early, better ware has been accepted as Zachariah's own. They include:

- A small pin-cushion box of octagonal shape, with padded velvet top sewn thru tiny holes in the cover rim. Painted within a decorative frame is the name *E. Stevens,* i.e. Emmeline, Zachariah's daughter, born in 1811. The color background of this box is a rich ivory white, on which the rose pattern is painted in vermilion, red, green, and black. The method used is as on lace-edge trays: a vermilion circle is the basic foundation, and the detail of the rose is superimposed in pellucid tones. (Collection of Mrs. O. H. Perry, Stevens' granddaughter)
- A pair of flower holders, made for Zachariah's wife, Miriam Stevens; light golden asphaltum ground, decorated in black with toleware brush design, enclosing the initials *M. S.* Each holder is a double-cone in shape and stands about six inches high. The lower section is filled with lead. About one inch down from the top a circular disc of tin has been soldered, thru which there is a centered aperture about the size of a small steel knitting needle. It is probable that these holders were meant to hold sprays of artificial flowers. (Collection of Mrs. O. H. Perry)

The above three objects are the only initialed pieces owned by the Stevens' family. Other pieces include:

- A cake box, showing evidence of long use. The ground was once cream white, decorated with green, blue, yellow and vermilion; the lid bore conventional flowers; the front, a rural scene with house, hedge, and all, flanked by a variety of tall trees. (Collection of Mrs. O. H. Perry)

- A small box with sulphur yellow ground, decorated with blue, green, red and vermilion. (E. S. Fraser collection, found at Stevens' home by Charles L. Woodside)

- Two commercial boxes, black ground, painted; perhaps typical of later work done "for the trade." (Collection of Mrs. O. H. Perry)

- Deed or document box of Alfred Stevens, used when he was a tax collector, but the making of which is ascribed to his father. The box is fitted at one end with a small transverse compartment in which official papers were kept; front and ends ornamented with festoons of colored flowers; conventional brush stroke yellow border around cover. (Collection of Mrs. Mary Mountford)

- Trinket box, possibly a wedding present to Zachariah Stevens' daughter-in-law, ca. 1826; molded lid, slanting sides, and applied rolled molding at cover and base line; ivory-white ground with varicolored flowers.

- Box with sliding drawer, an early item, ca. 1795–1800, made perhaps when Stevens was still an apprentice, as a gift for his future wife, Miriam Berry, whom he married in 1798. Weeping willow on cover: soldered over the drawer on the inside, a tin platform shaped like an inverted V; in the center back of the platform is a small hole accommodating a plug which, when inserted, locks the drawer. At the left is a hollow large enough to store beads or other small trinkets; at the right is a similar till with hinged cover. Decoration of roses, star flowers, silver and gold leaf. (E. S. Fraser Collection)

- Pair of boxes, painted perhaps as a gift for Maria Frances at the time of her marriage to Walter B. Goodrich, tinsmith of Stevens Plains, in 1829; or painted perhaps in 1826 when Goodrich first came to The Plains. Construction possibly by Goodrich, but decoration characteristically Stevens. (E. S. Fraser Collection)

- Trinket box, with flower and leaf decoration. (E. S. Fraser Collection)

- Small spice, trinket or money boxes with tulip, rose and leaf designs, brush wriggled border. (Collection of Mrs. Arthur Oldham)

- A tiny book-shaped box decorated to match the pin-cushion box made for Emmeline Stevens. (Owned by Miss Annie Stevens, descendant of Zachariah's brother, William)
- A bread tray.
- A box, the frontal decoration of which continues over the ends. Probably a presentation piece.

Most, if not all, of Zachariah Stevens' toleware said to have been devised for presentation purposes have grounds of cream color. He probably spent more time and skill on gift pieces for his family than on his pieces "for the trade." The latter which usually have a black ground are difficult to identify, resembling the many similar items produced by tinsmiths thruout the country in his time. None of Zachariah Stevens' pieces seem to have been painted with the wide cream-white band behind a decorative border often found in Pennsylvania and Connecticut toleware.

Bibliography

Americana Annual - An Encyclopedia of Current Events, 1936. Americana Corporation, New York, Chicago.

(American Folk Art Gallery) - Children in American Folk Art 1725–1865. Exhibition of Children's Art, their Portraits and their Toys, April 13 to May 1, 1937. New York, The Downtown Gallery.

(Barber, Edwin Atlee) - Decorated Tinware, by E. A. B. In *Bulletin of the Pennsylvania Museum,* July 1916, v. 14, no. 55, p. 43–44.

Bell, Enid. Tin Craft as a Hobby. New York and London, Harper and Bros., 1935. 111 pp.

Bishop, James Leander. A History of American Manufactures from 1608 to 1860. 3 vols. 3rd ed. Phila., 1868.

Bradney, Joseph Alfred - A History of Monmouthshire from the Coming of the Normans into Wales down to the Present Time, v. 1, part II (A Hundred of Abergavenny). London, 1904–1933.

Cahill, Holger and Barr, Alfred H., Jr., Editors - Art in America, A Complete Survey. Harper and Bros., Reynal & Hitchcock, 1934. 162 pp.

Calver, W. L. - Children's toys found in Revolutionary Camps, in *New York Historical Society Bulletin,* January, 1921, vol. 4, p. 100–103.

Carrick, Alice Van Leer - Collector's Luck. Boston, Atlantic Monthly Press, 1919. (Chapter II - Stenciled Furniture, pp. 17–31)

Carrick, Alice Van Leer - Old Stenciled Furniture, in *Country Life in America,* vol. 36, pp. 60–62.

Cordell, H. M. - The Canting Lamp, In *Antiques,* June, 1935, vol. 27, no. 6, pp. 226–7.

(Dossie, Robert) - The Handmaid to the Arts, London. Printed for J. Nourse, MDCCLXIV (1764 [1758]), 2 vols.

Eberlein, Harold Donaldson and McClure, Abbot - The Practical Book of American Antiques. Garden City, New York, 1927. 390 pp.

Editor's Attic: Purveyors of Pap. In *Antiques,* Dec., 1924, vol. 6, no. 6, pp. 300–1.

Editor's Attic: From off the Eaves. In *Antiques,* Feb. 1925, vol. 7, p. 69.

Editor's Attic. In *Antiques,* March 1928, vol. 13, no. 3, pp. 197–198.

Editor's Attic. In *Antiques,* July 1932, vol. 22, no. 1, pp. 4–5.

Editor's Attic: The Toys of the 1850's. In *Antiques,* December, 1934, vol. 26, pp. 210–211.

Encyclopedie Roret (Manuels-Roret), Fink, F., Peintre et vernissage des metaux et du bois. (p. 109, process for tole).

Fraser, Esther Stevens - Zachariah Brackett Stevens. Founder of the Japanned-Tinware Industry in Maine. In *Antiques,* March, 1935, vol. 29, no. 3, pp. 98–102.

Gray, William G. - The Manufacture of Tin Plates and Terne Plates. In *Iron Age,* May 20, 1909, vol. 83, pp. 1598–1601.

Hamilton, Edwin T. - Tin-Can-Craft, Illustrations by G. Ruth Taylor, Photographs by Ralph Sommer. New York, Dodd Mead & Co., 1935. 508 pp.

Hayward, Arthur H. - Colonial Lighting. B. J. Brimmer & Co., Boston, 1923. 159 pp.

Hommel, Rudolf P. - New Light on the History of Tin Plating. In *Bucks County Historical Society Collection of Papers,* vol. 6, Allentown, Pa. pp. 356–360.

Hough, Walter. - U.S. National Museum Bulletin, 141. Washington, D.C., 1928.

Lathrop, William G. - The Brass Industry in the United States. Mount Carmel, Conn., 1926. 174 pp.

Lounsbery, Elizabeth - Tole, in *American Homes and Gardens,* vol. XI, no. 7, pp. 244–7, New York.

R. H. Macy & Co., Exhibition of Drawings from Index of American Design, W.P.A. Federal Art Project, concurrently with July "All American" issue of *House and Garden,* June 1–July 15, 1938.

Littré, É. - Dictionnaire de la Langue Francaise, Paris, Librarie Hachette et Cie, 1873.

Mercer, Henry C. - The Tools of The Nation Maker (1897), In *Bucks Cy* Historical Society Collection of Papers, vol. 2, 1909, p. 480.

Mercer, Henry C. - The Common Tinder-Box of Colonial Days, ibid. vol. 4, 1917, pp. 359–366.

Nelson, E. D. P. - In *American Collector,* July and August 1937, vol. 6, nos. 6 and 7.

Northend, Mary Harrod. Colonial Homes and their furnishings. Little Brown & Co., 1912. 252 pp.

Percival, Maciver - "A Treatise of Japaning," An Old English Lacquerer's Vade Mecum. In *The Connoisseur,* Sept. 1929, vol. 84, p. 153, London.

Perrett, Antoinette - A Notable Collection of Tôle from Beaufort, The home of Mr. Henry D. Sleeper, East Gloucester, Mass. In *The House Beautiful,* Feb. 1924, vol. LV, no. 11, pp. 137-140.

Rushford, Edward Allen - In *American Collector,* vol. 6, August, 1937.

(Rushford, Elyse S. and Rennselaer, Stephen Van), "based on notes by."—Sundry candle moulds. In *Antiques,* June 1937, vol. 31, no. 6.

Rushford, Elyse Salignac - Tiny Toys of Tin. In *Historical Collections of the Essex Institute.* January, 1930, vol. 66, pp. 155-160.

Rushlight Exhibition Catalog, 1935. Boston, The Rushlight Club.

Stalker, John and Parker, George - A Treatise of Japaning and Varnishing, Oxford, 1688.

Swan, Mabel M. - The Village Tinsmith. In *Antiques,* March 1928, vol. 13, no. 3, pp. 211-14, Boston Mass.

Walston, Lady F. - Tôle Peinte. In *The Connoisseur,* Nov. 1925, Vol. LXXIII, pp. 144-152, London.

Watlston, Lady F. - Concerning Tole Peinte. In *The Connoisseur,* April 1931, vol. LXXXVI No. 356, pp. 240-243, London.

Watkins, C. Malcolm - The Whale-Oil Burner: Its Invention and Development. In *Antiques,* April, 1935, vol. 27, no. 4, pp. 148-149.

Webber, John Whiting - Roswell Gleason. In *Antiques,* August, 1931, vol. 20, pp. 87-89.

White, Elizabeth - Lead and Tin in Art. In *International studio,* Dec. 1928, vol. 82, no. 343, pp. 193-198. New York

Woodside, Charles L. - Marked American Pewter. In *Antiques,* May 1926, vol. 9, no. 5, pp. 315-319.

Woodside, Charles L. - Early American Lamps. In *Antiques,* December, 1927, vol. 12, no. 6, pp. 497-9.

Woodside, Charles L. and Watkins, Woodside Lura - Three Maine Pewterers. In *Antiques,* July 1932, vol. 22, no. 1, pp. 8-10.

Wright, Richardson - Hawkers and Walkers in Early America. Philadelphia, J. B. Lippincott Company, 1927. 317 pp.

Prepared for The Index of American Design
Completed 1/9/39
by Louis Zukofsky

Editorial Notes

* Manuscript is uncertain.

† scallop-shaped] scalloped-shaped

IV. American Kitchenware, 1608–ca. 1875

1
The Setting

Antique American kitchenware supplied the needs of the kitchens it decorated. The kitchens present a specialized history. They reflect the rise of the economy of self-sustaining households, the division of labor in the communal Amana and Shaker societies, and the growth of American industry and design as communication moved westward.

In time there were various regional kinds of kitchens, satisfying the demands and traditions of different settlers. But the earliest kitchens of the Atlantic seaboard were the same for both North and South. The house of only one room could depend little on the uncultivated country outside its door, and the economy of the home found its entire setting in this one room. It was called the "fireroom" by some settlers, and the name pointed to the hearth as the center of its activities. Abroad, the hearthstone was taxed. Here it was free. As in Europe, however, the floor of the American kitchen was sanded.

Early attempts were made to furnish it. Carving was practiced by most settlers. Glass works were established in Virginia in 1608, iron works in 1620. Clay for potteries was found in Massachusetts in 1630. Tin is said to have been worked there about the same time, but the tin and the other metal industries did not assume full importance till well on in the eighteenth century. Around 1700, the kitchens of the common settlers were bare places. Sarah Kemble Knight's *Journal of a Journey from Boston to New York* described a typical cottage of southern New England in 1704: the one room contained no furniture but a bed, a glass bottle hanging at its head, an earthen cup, a small pewter basin, a board set up on sticks taking the place of a table, and a block or two instead of chairs.[1]

---

1. This item is not listed in Zukofsky's bibliography. The journal of Sarah Kemble Knight (1666–1727) was published posthumously in 1825 as *The Journals of Madam Knight and the Rev. Mr. Buckingham, from the original manuscripts written in 1704 and 1710;* sub-

The kitchens of well-to-do settlers were exceptions. John Dillingham's, at Ipswich, Massachusetts, in 1634, contained pot hooks, tongs, iron pots, kettles, skillets, ladles, a fire shovel, a gridiron, a trivet, a brass pot, a mortar, a frying pan, a tray, a case of bottles, two jugs, three pans and two baskets. The inventory does not say whether they were made in the colony or imported from England.

Even a wealthy settler's house had at first but one room and an entryway on the ground floor. A half-loft serving as an extra chamber or garret over the kitchen made an unusually large house. Towards the end of the century, however, another room was built on the side of the entry and fireplace. Later, a lean-to was constructed to adjoin the rear of the house, so that it consisted of three rooms including the central kitchen. The original kitchen, now sometimes called "the holl," served as a general living or sitting room where food was prepared and eaten and all household activities were carried on near the open fireplace. The green log pole of the seventeenth century, and the trammel-bar or crane of the eighteenth, fastened to wooden or iron crossbars, *rested in* the middle of the wide flue of the chimney measuring approximately eight by ten feet.

In Pennsylvania, the five-plate "jamb" stove, used by the German settlers about 1740, did not stand out in the room which it heated but had an opening for fuel in the wall of the room adjoining. The six-plate stove of ca. 1760 stood out into the room, but like the earlier five-plate stove was used only for heating. Franklin's fireplace of 1744 improved the draught. The fashion of cooking on a stove was introduced to some extent by the invention of Baron Stiegel's ten-plate wood stove in 1765. The Revolution, however, adversely affected its market in Pennsylvania as well as the other colonies. The stove did not generally begin to replace the fireplace till about 1830.

Other factors, besides the introduction of the cookstove, affected the domestic economy of the kitchens in the different colonies beginning with the latter half of the eighteenth century. One was the new kitchenware of tin manufactured chiefly in Connecticut and Maine and distributed thruout the Colonies by the Yankee peddler. Another was the ascendancy of the planta-

---

sequent editions were titled *The Private Journal of a Journey From Boston to New York in the Year 1704* (Albany, F. H. Little, 1865) and, the edition likely available to Zukofsky, *The Journal of Madam Knight* (New York, P. Smith, 1935).

tion in the South. Cheap tinware meant greater facilities for the individual householder in the towns and in the back settlements. The pioneer housewife who made soap and candles, cooked, spun and dyed, and even doctored her family with herbs and roots gathered from the woods, must have readily appreciated time-saving utensils that made her work lighter. The plantation mistress no doubt supplied her servants with the new labor-saving devices, but whether she considered them more than attractive curiosities of the plantation kitchen removed from the manor is questionable. The kitchen on the plantation was the special province of the slaves who worked there. The mistress's dining hall where the table was dressed showed only the best imported and domestic plate. The negroes who cooked food did not serve it. The Marquis Francois Jean de Chastelleux in his "Travels in North America in the Years 1780, 1781, 1782" has described the servants who waited at table on one Virginia plantation: "Young negroes from sixteen to twenty years old, with not an article of clothing, but a loose shirt, descending half way down their thighs, waiting at table where were ladies, without any apparent embarrassment on one side, or the slightest attempt at concealment on the other." The social distinction of the kitchen as a removed or attached *building* was characteristic of manorial holdings before the Revolution in both the North and South.

Contemporary American museums have reconstructed the kitchen of the common man of the same time: a large room built around the open fireplace, or located in an ell in houses that could afford a separate living room. To serve the home industries and the social life of quilting bees, shucking, harvest and Thanksgiving Day celebrations, the fireplace had to be enormous, in New England often ten feet deep. Settles were frequently found on both sides of it to accommodate guests staying overnight. The back log of the chimney was often pulled into the kitchen by a team of horses and swung into place by a crane with block and tackle. Records of patriotic and religious gatherings testify that the fireplace cooked for 500 or 600 people. Cooking, baking, heating, lighting, dairying, laundering, carving, dyeing, spinning, weaving, and preparing remedies for the sick were some of the activities of the kitchen. It required utensils for all of these processes—iron implements forged and cast by the country blacksmith, tin and brittania ware sold by travelling artisans and growing urban establishments, wares of wood, brass, copper, pewter, silver, pottery and glass.

The long list of articles, now housed in collections, forms an index of the detailed activites of the housewife.[2] For cooking, she had gridirons, frying pans, forks, turners, toasters, waffleirons, coffee roasters, differing from contemporary utensils in that they all had long handles enabling her to stay as far as possible from the blazing heat of the open fireplace. Her pots, gridirons, skillets, trivets and griddles had a different characteristic feature: three short legs on each of them so that their contents rested safely above the hot coals. Part way up the chimney hung the heavy swinging crane with chains suspending utensils at different levels over the fire. She used pothooks with wooden handles to lift the pots from the crane. At its end, the clock-jack revolved after being wound up, so that the meat was roasted uniformly. Other implements stood near the fireplace: perhaps a long-handled peel for raising loaves of bread into the bake oven; perhaps a warming pan which, filled with hot coals, took the chill out of the sheets of the bed on winter nights; perhaps a tin container with punched design, to let in the draught, for carrying hot coals from a neighbor's fire—in short, sundry devices for heating and cooking. The jamb-hook held the shovel and fire-tongs in place beside the hearthstone, and the firedogs and andirons held up the heavy backlog and kindling over its floor.

Towards the end of the eighteenth century the "Dutch oven," more properly called the *tin kitchen,* and the *brick arch* began to be used for family cooking. The tin kitchen made out of tin-plated sheet iron, square or cylindrical in shape, stood on four feet, and had one side open to the fireplace which furnished the heat. A long spit projecting into a crank handle at one end of the oven turned the roast to be cooked. It was basted conveniently thru a little door in the rear.

The brick arch, built near the fireplace or in an ell adjoining the kitchen, had an iron door thru which the kindling was placed. A concentric series of iron rings called "rims" in the iron top of the arch was removable, so that

2. Zukofsky's use of "index" here plays on the title of the project, setting into play a word that will frequently recur, and foreshadows the importance of the textual device itself, in later works: *Bottom: On Shakespeare, "A,"* and *Prepositions.* That objects might act as indices for the whole reflects not only the "ideology of the everyday" central to the Index of American Design, but also reflects Zukofsky's own Objectivist "aesthetic of the particular" (Nadel 113). See the following epigraphs to the *Bottom: On Shakespeare* Index: "For, by the way, I'll sort occasion, / As index to the story we late talk'd of" / *R. III*, II, ii, 148; "in . . . indexes, although small pricks / To their subsequent volumes, there is seen" / *T. & C.*, I, iii, 343; "what act, / That . . . thunders in the index"? / *H.*, III, iv, 52" (*Bottom* 445).

each of the openings over the fire fitted a pot, kettle, or spider (i.e. a flat pan for baking) of similar size. A *rimmer*, a device with a hook at one end, usually of hand-wrought iron, was used to lift the rims or lids. The spider baked a single loaf or biscuit over ashes placed on an iron lid of the arch, which at different times also heated brass and iron kettles containing clothes, indigo blue for dyes, and swill for live stock. Most of the early cooking utensils were of hand-wrought iron; the later ones of brass and copper—including a copper cake-mould.

Household equipment for preparing food included iron knives; spoons of wood, iron, horn and pewter; wooden ladles; rolling pins; pudding sticks for making "Hasty pudding"; bread troughs shaped like cradles and fitted with wooden temse [*sic*][3] in the hollows at each end; cracker stamps; cake turners; ivory pie markers; toddy-sticks; mortars and pestles; potato mashers, and wooden tubs. Outfits for making butter included the early "pump" churn, the "lever" or "wig-wag" type, and the "cradle" or rocker churn rocked like a cradle, which it resembled, to agitate the cream. Scoops of maple wood were employed to pat out the whey after removing the butter from the churn. Wooden dashers, scales, skimmers, prints or molds, nests of trays, boxes and tubs were additional butter making equipment.

To prepare cheese, the housewife used a wooden press with ropes and pulleys for squeezing the whey out of the curds. Bags filled with cheese were then placed in large openwork baskets made out of ash. A wooden "folla" further pressed down the cheese after it had been surrounded by a wooden hoop, part of which rested on a drain-board with a slot for catching the whey which had not drained off previously. Cheese cupboards kept the finished product.

The maple industry in the New England colonies was partly carried on in the kitchen, which during the proper season liberally displayed sap buckets, barrels and paddles.

In the seventeenth century, there were powdering tubs or troughs for salting meat, some of them thirty inches wide. The many ways of mincing and cutting meat, such as "smyting on gobbets," "chopping on gobbets" and "hewing" required different instruments such as mincing knives, saws, clev-

---

3. A sieve or strainer used in sifting, especially in the brewing process from the eleventh through sixteenth centuries, but still found in twentieth-century West Yorkshire dialect. An undetermined hand has placed a question mark in the margin.

ers, and hooks for hanging carcasses and joints. The eighteenth century witnessed a series of implements for grinding meat and for "shooting" it into skins by means of "sausage guns."

Labor saving devices for peeling, coring and quartering fruits remain family heirlooms till this day, in the form of apple parers and cherry seeders.

The utensils for preparing food are so many and their functions so varied that it is often hard to find a category for each separate implement. Considering various collections, the eye is impressed by their miscellaneousness. The names identify the uses: sugar-loaf cutter; cooker for small game; toasting fork; iron trivet for roasting birds; charcoal broiler with hinged lid; grooved broiler for collecting juices; skewer holder; grater; saltbox; noggin; mechanical bellows; plate warmer; mixing bowl; corn-sheller; and flour sifter.

A "wikker Flaskett" is listed among the choice possessions of one colonist, ca. 1675. It may very possibly have been used for storing and moving foodstuffs. Besides cups of wood, pewter and tin for measuring out meal, sugar, etc., the kitchen shelves displayed brown glazed pitchers and pie plates, and gray and tan earthenware jugs and jars for holding molasses, vinegar, pickles, cider, preserved fruit and mince meat. Stoneware objects for storing included yeast jugs, cooky-crocks and bean-pots; glass objects— crust bottles, "rhum" bottles twenty inches high and high-shouldered green bottles for keeping simples or medicinal extracts of plants.

Dinner plate does not come under a study of kitchenware, but since the early kitchen was also the dining room, wooden and pewter platters, plates, basins, porringers and tankards which actually served in the kitchen should be mentioned.

For laundering, the housewife employed: wooden wash tubs (one of apple wood, 33" high by 21" in diameter); scrubbing boards of wood chiselled and grooved "into the proper cordoury surface," dating back [to] the seventeenth century; handmade clothespins; in one case, even a handmade washing machine; sad irons with devices for preserving the heat; goffering, crimping, fluting and pleating irons. Keeping the kitchen clean required mops, brooms, and vermin traps.

Spinning and weaving were also done in the kitchen. The flax wheels were made here by cabinet makers. The more simply constructed wool wheels were often manufactured in the kitchen, where the wool was carded and placed on the spindle. Clock reels clicked off the skeins. The wooden weaving loom required accessory quills and bobbins made of elderberry.

Other wooden implements used in the preparation, spinning, winding and weaving of flax and wool included: a heavy brake for removing the woody core from the fibre of rippled and retted flax; a scutching and swingling [*sic*] block; knives for scraping broken flax and a hatchel for combing flax. A collection of flax wheels made ca. 1750 includes four low wheels, one of them a Saxon type; a rare chair-frame wheel; a tall wheel with two spindles placed below it; and a vertical type with the spindle just above the rim of the wheel.

The kitchen was also the scene of the printing of calico and wallpaper done by wooden blocks.

Lighting appurtenances of the kitchen included glass, iron, brass, pewter, tin and silver candlesticks—some with attached cone-shaped extinguishers, and a variety of snuffers, from the early scissors with short broad blades, to the later one blade type with oblong box for catching the snuff or charred part of the wick. The housewife made her own candles in candle-molds. She used a wooden rack with twelve arms, at the ends of which were suspended wooden discs with wooden handles and iron hooks on which she doubled and looped the lengths of the wicking. Then she dipped these alternately in the melted tallow and hung them up to cool, subsequently pouring the wax around them in the candle molds. Some of these were of tin and fastened in groups of two, four, six, etc.; other single molds were of pewter, twelve in a set fitting in a wooden rack. Tinder boxes, tinder pistols and, later, match holders were objects of every kitchen. Making the vegetable or animal oil in which the short wicks of the Betty lamp floated, and trimming the many different varieties of oil, lard and camphene lamps manufactured between ca. 1700 and 1840 were necessary tasks of the housewife.

Many other sundry tasks, in addition to those already considered, are indicated by the following furnishings which were part of old kitchens: rope-making machines; neck-yokes for carrying buckets; low cobblers' benches (one with two large drawers, another with more drawers and leather loops for holding tools, also a leather-covered backrest in which a locked cash box was kept); branding irons for initialing tools; and barrels holding lye for soap. All but the last appurtenance, which the housewife tended herself, recall a time when men were likely to be found working on something at home, and for their homes, side by side with their wives.[4]

---

4. The suggestion of an ideal domesticity contrasts preindustrial life with alienated labor. It resonates with the roughly contemporaneous "24" of *Anew* (*Collected Short Poetry* 89) and

The foregoing general survey of the domestic economy developed in American kitchens can be supplemented by detailed descriptions of different kitchens in several regions, at different times. The kitchens of descendants of the Dutch settlers in Flatbush (Brooklyn, N.Y.) during the eighteenth century, often had the fireplace with attached brick oven occupying nearly the entire space of the room. A blue or pink check valance known as a "schoorsten valletje" hung over the top of the fireplace, along its entire width. Dutch tidiness probably saw to it that a clean valance was put on every Saturday. Tin and pewter utensils hung on the walls. The kitchen dresser with blue or brown pottery, wooden bowls and pewter platters stood at one side of the fireplace, before which a tin kitchen was usually to be found. Likely objects around the room included wooden pails with burnished brass hoops and hard and soft waffle irons. Peter Goelet, at the Golden Key, Hanover Square, New York, advertised the latter for sale on March 16, 1772. The Dutch waffles, thin cakes or wafers, known as Izer cookies, were split in half and buttered before being served.

The spacious early kitchens of the New England countryside were often decorated with hanging ears of corn and dried meat. But the several looms and reels made them look just as much the home factories for weaving as for produce. A kitchen in the basement of a brick house in a New England seaport of ca. 1825–1840, while not entirely divorced from the economy of seventeenth- and eighteenth-century kitchens, showed many new developments. The ceiling was plastered to hide the beams; the walls were painted instead of being papered or left bare; and the fireplace was considerably reduced in width and depth. Wood was still used for fuel, as were lard and whale-oil for lighting. But the meat to be smoked now hung in brick and soapstone closets of an upper chamber or attic connected with the chimney. In another 25 years, the fireplace would be dispensed with as a means for both cooking and curing.

The kitchen itself was about twenty feet square, with windows recessed in thick walls. The panelled shutters were held closed by wooden bars half way up the casement. The bars were often supported on two windsor chairs, to

---

the celebrated familial locus to the writing life reflected in "It Was" (*Collected Fiction*) and frequently attributed to mid- and later "*A*". The poem "24," which begins, "The men in the kitchens," was written in 1939 according to Celia Zukofsky's "Year by Year Bibliography," *Zukofsky: Man and Poet*. (This index essay was completed in April 1939.)

suspend flannel bags containing calves-foot jelly which was strained while warm into yellow-ware bowls placed under them. The same bars similarly set up on chairs held the three-foot beam scale with scoop at one end and leaden weights on the other for weighing out butter, sugar and flour, as Thanksgiving gifts for the poor families of the town.

Supplies of hickory logs and kindling known as "cooper's chips" filled the kitchen woodbox. The fireplace was still furnished with small kettles, firedogs, hooks for hanging spits, pokers, tin-kitchen, skewers, gridirons, long handled spoons, etc. But there were also new objects: a three-gallon water kettle with long spout and faucet; a "cooper back log" containing a coil of piping supplying hot water to the tank and bathroom on the floor above the kitchen; a copper wash boiler on a firebox on one side of the fireplace; a ham boiler of tin containing two compartments, the upper one a detachable steamer for making puddings—the complete device set on another fire box on the other side of the fireplace; and a Rumford oven of iron, placed into the adjoining brickwork, with ventilators leading to the chimney flue regulating the temperature. The oven door, opened by a brass handle, disclosed an interior three feet deep, with a slatted iron shelf in the middle, which slid outside of the frame of the oven by means of rods with brass knobs. The shelf was used to bake bread, cake, or a full dozen pies at one time. Ca. 1840, the local fire and range with water-tank started to replace even these comparatively new devices.

The cold water supply of this particular kitchen was furnished by a main of logs, each bored with a three inch hole and fitting into each other, extending some miles beyond town and connected at right angles with the house-log standing upright beside the kitchen sink. The latter was usually placed near a window and had an extra spout leading out of doors. In cases where the town did not supply the water, it was kept in well-buckets near the sink. Dippers of gourds, tin and wood hung on the wall beside it.

Most New England kitchens of this time displayed a pine cupboard with two doors in the lower part opened by pull knobs, and button fasteners in the open shelves of the upper part. Wooden boxes containing spices, sugar, etc., were kept on the lower shelf of the upper part. Another shelf held everyday dishes. The better china was closeted in the living room. On the lower shelf, too, was the wooden box divided into two sections—one for steel knives, the other for forks—with a hole in the partition for [a] handle. Such boxes were still whittled and carved at home by the men during the evenings. Well-to-do families were provided with a "butt'ry" or buttery, to the right of the fireplace—i.e. a large pantry with a window at one end and shelves on the side walls, beginning halfway up the walls and reaching to the ceiling. When the kitchen became too hot in summer, the baking was done on a wide, lower shelf of the buttery. Underneath the shelves stood barrels, butter boxes, kegs and buckets. The regular pantry adjoining the buttery was also built with an open window and had shelves on the left wall. A chintz curtain concealed the milk pans, earthen jars, crocks and kitchen china.

Some houses had a butter room—a shed built two steps down from the kitchen, with white plastered walls and painted wooden floors. Prosperous householders owning ten or fifteen cows needed this extra convenience for keeping milk buckets, churns and cheese presses used in dairying. A cheese closet hung on the wall and was covered with cheese cloth to keep the cheese from spoiling. Butter and cheese were made at least twice a week in most households, tho owners of only two or three cows did their work in the kitchen itself, with the buttery offering sufficient storage room for their produce.

Additional facts regarding the domestic economy of American kitchens in the middle nineteenth century are found in contemporary texts on the subject. Miss (Eliza) Leslie's *The House Book,* 7th edition, Philadelphia, 1844, described many utensils and their uses, among them: *demijohns,* large bottles covered with basketwork, for holding vinegar, molasses, etc.; *refrigerators,* i.e., large wooden boxes, standing on feet, lined with tin or zinc and generally interlined with charcoal, complete with drain, receptacle at the bottom, and movable shelves; *filtering jars* for river water; and *safes,* which were movable closets, standing on feet, with doors and sides of wire net or perforated tin, and shelves inside, used for keeping cold meat, pie and other food left over from the table. The author recommended that the safe should stand in the pantry, since the kitchen was too warm for it.

Miss Catherine E. Beecher's "Treatise on Domestic Economy For the Use of Young Ladies at Home and at School," a revised edition of which was published in New York, in 1845, may have been based on Miss Leslie's earlier volume, but included other information. A chapter on *Fires and Lights* described the making of molds for candles. Another chapter on *starching, ironing* and *cleansing* dealt with articles to be provided for ironing, including: a settee or settle used as an ironing table; a bosom-board for ironing shirt bosoms; a skirt-board, for frock skirts; a press-board, for broadcloth; a fluting iron or patent Italian iron, for ruffles; and a crimping iron used for the same purpose, but more efficient. A chapter on the care of the *kitchen, cellar and storeroom* mentioned the following articles among others: a slop pail; a soap dish; a water pail; a large boiler for warm soft water to be kept well-covered and always over the fire; a hearth-broom; bellows; and a clock, "to secure regularity at meals." Other kitchenware included: tin tubs, painted on the outside, for washing and rinsing; a waiter on which dishes were drained; a fork for handling soap; brown earthen pans for milk and cooking; lighter tin pans, mentioned as "too cold for many purposes"; and tall earthen jars with covers for holding butter.

Miss Beecher cautioned against putting acids into red earthenware jars, since they destroyed the glaze, and recommended stoneware as more resist-ant. Her lists of various objects of different materials form a full index to the utensils still in use at the time. Under ironware, she listed: a nest of pots; a long iron fork to take out articles from boiling water; an iron hook to lift pots from the crane; large and small gridirons, with grooved bars and a trench to catch grease; a Dutch oven, also called a bake pan; skillets and a spider or flat skillet for frying; griddles; waffle irons; tin and iron bake- and bread-pans; ladles; skimmers; skewers; toasting irons; tea kettles; spice, pepper and coffee mills; carving knives; cleavers; saws; steelyards, chopping trays; apple-parers; sugar-nippers; iron spoons and flatirons. She recommended besides, iron kettles lined with porcelain, of German manufacture, for mak-ing preserves; brass kettles for boiling soap; and portable furnaces of iron and clay as very useful in summer.

Under tinware she mentioned: bread pans; large and small patty pans; cake pans with a center tube to insure perfect baking; pie dishes (of block tin); covered butter-kettles; kettles to hold berries; sauce pans; oil cans; lamp fillers; lanterns; candlesticks; candle boxes; funnels or tunnels; a re-flector for baking warm cakes; a tin kitchen; an apple-corer; an apple-roaster; egg-boilers; various scoops for sugar, flour and meal; a set of mugs; pint, quart and gallon dippers; scales and weights; pails painted on the out-side; milk and gravy strainers; collanders; dredging-boxes; pepper boxes; large and small graters; boxes for cheese, cake and bread with tight covers. Woodenware included: a mush stick; a meat beetle to pound tough meat; an egg beater; a nest of tubs; pails; bowls; sieves; a beetle for mashing potatoes; a spad or stick for stirring butter; a breadboard; a coffee-stick; a clothes stick; a ladle for working butter; a bread trough; flour buckets; boxes for meal, sugar, starch and indigo; ironing boards; clothes frames and clothes pins. She noted further the kitchen's need for basket ware, carpenters' tools, dust pan, brushes and brooms.

Thomas Webster's voluminous *Encyclopedia of Domestic Economy* (New York, 1845) described three unusual objects: a cast iron stand like a Duncan Phyfe table with a revolving wheel for a top, on which to place things before the fire to keep them hot; a "superior" warming-pan filled with boiling water instead of coals, to prevent suffocating fumes, scorching, etc; and a potato drainer with a grating below to carry away the water after they were washed.

Even children of that time were made conscious of domestic needs and activities, by means of juvenile handbooks. *The Kitchen,* no. 5 of a series entitled New Books and True Books For the Young (New York, ca. 1850?) contained illustrations of a pail made of staves bound with hoops, a steelyard, a sieve, a *tunnel* (i.e. funnel), scales and bellows, accompanied by expositions such as the following: "The steelyard ... To weigh butter and flour etc ... put hooked to the steelyard. Then the weight is hung at the other end. Hold the steelyard up by the upper hook, and then move the weight till it balances. Sometimes they weigh little babies with steelyards. They tie them in a cloth and put them into a basket."

The books on domestic economy treated here were all published in the Eastern states. The extent of their circulation probably included the frontier, tho not in great numbers. However, a list of objects used in a Minnesota frontier home, ca. 1855, indicates that the home industries of the Middle West resembled those of the East. Pewter, copper and brass utensils were used extensively, as were potato mashing boxes, rolling pins, chopping trays, dippers, waffle irons, ladles, skimmers, coffee mills, sauce pans, frying pans, patent enameled iron kettles and the common dasher butter churn, which could be purchased for $2.00. A Kendall churn, priced at $4.00, was considered an economic, labor-saving device.

The home industries of the Shaker and Amana Societies, at the height of development in 1850, necessarily differed from those of individual households affected by the numerous supplies manufactured in a competitive, open market. The collectively managed communities, more or less self-sufficient, stylized their products and consigned the separate branches of production to different parts of their "households." They carried on the division of labor in small areas in New York, Kentucky, and a few other isolated places, while the individual household was already dependent for manufactured products on the division of labor of privately owned factories, soon to be introduced to the more complicated economy of large scale industry. Yet despite the division of labor fostered by a simple communist economy, the tradition of craftsmanship persisted among the Shakers and Amanites. For in a society with a limited labor force, one individual was often called upon to do numerous tasks. In the individually managed households of the rest of the country, however, craftsmanship was fast becoming a mere pastime.[5]

The Shakers had no common kitchen, but carried on various kitchen activities in different rooms and workshops furnished to suit the special purposes. Thus the Shaker bake-room furnishings in "North House," New Lebanon, New York, 1818, included: a table of pine, wooden bowls, a wooden sconce with angled side to protect the flame from drafts, a ladle, cup etc., as well as a bread-cutting table. The latter had a square top in the corner or center of which was set a long knife with a wooden handle. The knife, swinging on a pivot enabled the operator to slice quickly the homemade loaves of Indian corn, wheat or unleavened bread. In other rooms, similar tables with heavy top boards, grooved around the edges, were used for cutting maple sugar. The wood-box and washstand,[6] which also served as a small case of drawers, both of pine and painted red, were relegated to sitting rooms or various workshops. Special weaving rooms were furnished with the necessary accessories. In wood-turning rooms mortars and pestles were made for the medicinal herb industry at New Gloucester, Maine. The ironing room in the wash house of Hancock Church was furnished with starch tables, tubs, benches, drying racks resembling miniature hayracks for carrying wet clothes, troughs, scrub-boards, pressing boards and a wash-mill invented at New Lebanon and patented in 1858 at Canterbury. An improved

5. The tradition of craftsmanship is here carefully defined as that which produces quality forms through a preindustrial labor mode, where the individual attended to the work—with obvious analogues to the situation of the poet. Here the division of labor necessarily leads to a decline in craftsmanship; Zukofsky's radio talk of June 7, 1937, proposes poetry as collective labor. The issue of labor is addressed specifically in *"A"*-8, *"A"*-9, and editor Barry Ahearn's *Pound/Zukofsky: Selected Letters of Ezra Pound and Louis Zukofsky*. See Alec Marsh (noted above) for a closer analysis of Marxist conceptions of labor.

6. Zukofsky read his poem "To my wash-stand" October 24, 1938, in New York City on radio station WQXR, prior to the completion of this Index essay. Composed in 1932, according to "Year by Year Bibliography of Louis Zukofsky," Celia Zukofsky (386).

mangle was also devised there about that time. A rectangular, bin-shaped table with heavy, turned and raked legs was used at New Lebanon for washing and soap making. Another kind of laundry table, on which buckets of starch were placed, was manufactured by members of the same community.

The Shakers also turned out the following objects mainly for their own use, but readily manufactured a number of them in commercial quantities for outside communities appreciating usefulness combined with extreme simplicity of design: spool stands; canes; pitcher and medicine-glass covers; table-boards for hot dishes; scrub-boards; foot warmers; clothespins; brush, broom and mop handles; sieves; pegs; floor racks for towels; sconces with bored holes that could be hung on pegs at graduated heights (in Ky.); tool racks; pipe racks; mixing bowls; wooden spoons; rolling pins; trenchers; vegetable "shutes"; knife handles; and various boxes. The latter included: wood-boxes, chip-boxes; pipe-boxes; hat boxes for hanging bretherns' hats; rectangular dust boxes with central handles flanked by two hinged lids, to collect the frequent emptyings of dustpans; vegetable, berry, candle and cutlery boxes; and oval boxes for storing, the manufacture of which Faith Andrews has described: "A broad thin band of maple was cut at one end, by means of a template, into 'lappers' or 'fingers'; the piece was then steamed, wrapped around an oval mold, and the projecting fingers secured by copper or wrought-iron rivets. Discs of pine were then fitted into the base and cover. First made about 1798, oval boxes are still manufactured at New Lebanon and Sabbathday Lake (Me.) Formerly they were sold in graduated sizes or 'nests,' and if equipped with handles were known as 'carriers.' When colors were used instead of varnish, the reds and yellows, and the rarer blues or greens were of the mellowest hue . . . yellow or orange spit-boxes were made the same way, sometimes with a rim at the top."

The Amana sect, an offshoot of the German Pietists and mystics of the sixteenth and seventeenth centuries, first settled on a tract of 5,000 acres of the Seneca Indian Reservation near Buffalo, New York, in 1843, and called their community Ebenezer. In 1929, the Amanites still occupied 2,400 acres on the Iowa River, in Iowa City. An outstanding characteristic of their furnishings is the usual absence of color except for their brilliant rag carpets. Their "kitchen houses" cook and serve food for the community. Their main industry was at one time clock-making, an occupation no doubt affected by the regularity of their community life. But they are known also for the earthenware which they manufactured at Ebenezer. John Fritz (1828–1913), the community potter, produced among many pieces, two valued objects: a yellow, corrugated, highly glazed jar and a small, covered firkin with a medium glaze on a brownish base. Other pieces ascribed to him and his associates include a large jar of reddish clay, unglazed, and a highly glazed, reddish-brown pitcher. The Amanites also manufactured a lantern for barns and sheds, used in large quantities, and the famous strawberry basket with loops for fastening to belt or apron. Even now each Amana community has its own basket maker. Other Amana products included: tobacco boxes of copper and pewter; a box of burled walnut lined with zinc; a pan and cup of seamless copper; pewter lard lamps made in Germany or Ebenezer (the molds in which these lamps were cast were brought over from Germany); and a copper teakettle, ca. 1875, marked, *Manufactured by the Amana Society, Homestead, Iowa.*

Proofread - OK
Louis Zukofsky
3/13/39

2

The Wares

Reference to the histories of the wood, glass, ceramic and metal industries in this country afford a means of relating an overwhelming number of disconnected facts regarding American kitchenware design. Considering the purely American angle, a survey of the main types of utensils, grouped according to materials, might begin with *Woodenware.*

The colonists first saw trees, not ores, and while they had to teach the Indians the use of iron and other metals, the Indians taught them a number of things about the use of wood. Governor Bradford (1590–1657) of Plymouth Colony recorded that the settlers took over the native way of sticking a clam shell into a split stick and that they used this instrument as a spoon. He also refers to Indian wooden bowls, trays and dishes. The settlers made Indian bowls, mortars, and dishes out of maple—burning out the false growth in the wood, like the natives. The other woods used for early New England woodenware were a white wood, probably poplar or linden, known as "dish-timber," walnut, pine, red cedar and laurel.

The Virginians used red cedar as early as 1650. The bulk of this wood came subsequently from Tennessee, but almost all the colonies grew red cedar. John Lawson, in 1714, testified to its popularity in North and South Carolina, where it was "reputed to be comparatively immune from attacks of marine borers, and . . . especially recommended for clothes, chests and wardrobes." Another contemporary man of letters called the cedar "the most useful timber in the land, lasting and strong," adding that "great quantities" had been "sent to England for wainscoting, staircases, drawers, chairs, etc." In 1782, Crevecoeur noted that the settlers at Nantucket "always . . . a piece of cedar in their hands . . . while talking . . . will make bungs or spoyes for their oil casks, or other useful articles." The Metropolitan Museum of Art now owns a tankard, keg, canteen, and piggin with painted decoration, all of red cedar and made by American colonists in the early eighteenth century.

Circa 1770, Portsmouth, New Hampshire was the principal place of export of pine timber and manufactory of pine furniture in the colonies. But it is safe to say that the colonies exported few kitchen woodenware utensils, if any at all, and that the main influence on the seventeenth and eighteenth century kitchen woodenware design in New England was English *treen*. Unlike the English pieces which were carefully carved and often mounted with precious metals, the American treen was extremely simple, following the models of the mother country only in the types of objects used. The trencher was the most common dish even among wealthy families. Square or oblong, of poplar or maple, it was whittled out by hand with a jackknife. One trencher usually served two children or husband and wife. A trencher for each member of a family was a sign of elegance. The dish was important enough as a mark of wealth to be listed in wills. Miles Standish bequeathed 12 wooden trenchers.

Besides the trencher, there were other wooden plates and trays of various sizes; the *noggin,* a low bowl with handles, with a content of approximately one gill[7]; and the *losset,* a type of flat dish. Treen not made with a jackknife, in the days before the iron lathe, was turned on a spring-pole lathe (a device dating back to 13th century Europe) and later finished by hand.

Spoons were made out of laurel known as spoonwood. Other familiar, early kitchen objects of wood included salt cellars; lather boxes for shaving; quassia cups out of Central American or Jamaican wood which tinctured the water left standing in them with bitters; collapsible cap stands for visitors'

---

7. "Gill" is a unit of measure, a volume equal to one-quarter pint.

bonnets, to prevent them from wrinkling; tobacco boxes; wooden mugs first bound with wooden withes in Indian style, and later with copper or pewter; piggins, or wooden pails with one long stave; and rundlets, or small barrels having a capacity of eighteen gallons.

New England woodenware was still used in 1815. In fact, its use was not generally replaced by metal wares till well on towards the middle of the nineteenth century. The period of its dominance began about 1750, lasted till the turn of the century, and saw the introduction of oak, ash and hickory, in addition to the woods already mentioned.

Crevecoeur said of the citizens of Nantucket, 1782, that they were all brought up to the trade of *coopers*. The term probably included *dry coopers* who made casks or barrels for holding dry goods, *wet coopers* who made casks for liquids, and *white coopers* who made pails, tubs and the like for domestic or dairy use.

The smaller staved pieces, such as buckets, were the white cooper's specialty. Few of these are extant since they were used for liquids and rotted fast. Of those that remain the sugar buckets are perhaps the least rare. But there were also water, well, sap buckets and milk piggins. The staves and bottoms of these were of pine—the staves slightly curved and tapered at the bottom, some more than others, and some elongated into handles wider at the top to prevent slipping. The handles were of oak or ash which is resilient. In some cases the hoops were made of hickory, like those of barrels. For the most part of pine, the earliest hoops were designed with locked laps, while the later ones were lapped over and nailed.

The water buckets had two lengthened staves into which a bail handle was pegged. The staves were useful in keeping the bucket raised from the ground when it was turned over to dry. One rare example, six inches high, of pine with hickory hoops lapped and tucked under, and an oak bail handle, bears on the bottom the inscription "made by E. Proctor when he was 10 years old in 1770."

The well buckets were made with oak staves and iron hoops to resist moisture. The sap bucket was a common bucket with two extended staves—one type with bail handle, another with a stick of ash or hickory run thru the stave holes and bound with leather ties serving as a handle. It was the common practice in the maple sugar industry to hang sap buckets on "spiles" (or spouts) driven into trees when the maple sap was running, and to carry them back on shoulder yokes to the sheds and kitchens.

The milk piggins of different sizes had single stave handles made in various shapes.

Rare examples of sugar buckets produced before the factory era show three types of hoops, two with locked joinings and one with lapped-over ends fastened with handmade nails. The largest sugar bucket was twenty-four inches high, the smallest eight inches, and a child's sugar bucket only four inches high. The sugar buckets originally had covers of pine. Sugar *boxes* were a variant of the buckets, shallow like butter boxes (*vide infra*), but smaller, with lapped hoops of oak or ash, handles of the same wood, and pine covers with rims of oak or ash. Such boxes frequently carried butter and eggs to market.

The tubs, made with extra-long staves and reinforced with wooden or iron hoops, were round or oval-shaped. They included hand and laundry tubs and others for household use. The butter tubs, tapered in shape and about two feet high, had their wooden hoop ends tucked under in the earliest models, and covers resembling those of the butter boxes. Their use was to store butter, packed with the help of a long paddle, in the buttery or cellar. Maple-sugar tubs, smaller than the butter tubs, were similarly constructed.

Water, rum, molasses and powder kegs and water canteens were also made by the white cooper. They resembled buckets in form, but had two heads like a drum. The kegs had lock-joined hoops and bungholes, fitted in the early pieces with wooden plugs driven in by a mallet. The later pieces had threaded plugs. The use of the canteen dates back to the early seventeenth century. It was a lapped container, shaped like a mouse trap, with two heads and a plug hole and was equipped with straps thru which a longer strap could be passed and thrown over the shoulder in carrying. The laps of some of the oldest canteens were sewn with shoe thread.

An important class of woodenware which recalls the staved pieces in several points of construction is represented by the pantry boxes, subdivided into two classes, "Colony" and Shaker. "Colony" boxes were not characterized by uniform craftsmanship. Hand-forged nails generally identify the homemade pieces, but cannot be relied on as a test for establishing the date of the boxes, since individual craftsmen may have often resorted to the use of old hand forged nails even during the factory era. The lapping varied, occurring near the end or the middle of the box as the case happened to be. The lap points were of different lengths, and stitched with shoe thread, fastened with wire or splint, or tucked into holes without the use of nails. In all such boxes the bottoms of pine, or occasionally of oak or ash, were fastened to the sides of maple, and the pine cover to the rims with wooden pegs used by shoemakers. The late-eighteenth-century "Colony" boxes had copper nails for fastening the laps, tho wooden pegs were also used in these factory-made pieces. The length of oval "Colony" boxes varied from two to seventeen inches; of round "Colony" boxes, from one and a half to twenty-four inches.

Oval and round Shaker boxes, first made ca. 1798, were of uniform make, as has already been noted in the first part of this essay. Each box had a definite number of pointed, lapped joinings, according to its size, and a lapped cover with one point. A box with a diameter of three inches had two points, the number of points increasing with the diameter so that the largest box with a diameter of eighteen inches had eight points. Copper nails or wrought-iron rivets secured the lap points, definitely placed, and fastened the bottom and top of pine to the maplewood sides. The oval boxes were made in sets of nine and, later, twelve, in graded sizes, and used for storing meal, sugar, spices and herbs. They were kept on the pantry shelf or in the cupboard—the sugar in the large boxes, the spices in the smaller.

Both the "Colony" and Shaker pantry boxes had the covers always lapped in the opposite direction to the laps of the bodies of the boxes. There is but one extant exception to this practice. The laps were usually pointed or tapered. Straight laps were rare. In the large boxes, the hand forged nails used for fastening were made with large heads. Late eighteenth- and early-nineteenth-century boxes often bore factory names on the covers.

To present-day connoisseurs, the later boxes do not have the same "feel" as the early ones, and they use this sense that comes only with experience in determining the dates of individual pieces. The grays, greens, dark greens, blues and reds with which the boxes were frequently painted are also an aid in judging dates. Thus the "wagon blue" used for boxes was also a favorite color for farm wagons in certain localities of the colonies. The red known as "turkey red" among the Indians was called "coffin red" by the colonial box-maker, because coffins were also painted with this color. It was made of a mixture of red clay, scaled milk, butter milk, whey or the whites of eggs, and an animal hoof dryer.

Nineteenth-century pill boxes were round or oval and made of pine, which a grindstone had reduced to the thinness of shell. The laps too fragile for nailing were sometimes glued. The covers and bottoms held to the rims by friction. The round pill boxes were one and a half inches in diameter, the oval ones two inches. Occasionally one machine-made nail was used to secure the lap of a round box and another such nail used in the cover lap. Wooden pegs held tops and bottoms in place in some of the pill boxes. They were never painted. Extant pieces retain their original labels with directions for cures.

Related to the pantry boxes were round, butter and cheese boxes. The diameters of the former ranged from one to two feet. The depth of each box was sufficient to hold a pound roll of butter standing on end. The boxes were made with straight laps or with staves and hoops. The earliest hoops had notched ends which tucked under. Late-eighteenth and early-nineteenth-century butter boxes were distinguished by elaborate lapping: one end of the lap tapered and notched, to prevent slipping, was inserted thru an elliptical hole in the other end, and a peg was used to fasten them. The hoops of later, nineteenth-century butter tubs were lapped and nailed—machine-made nails following earlier handmade ones and brads. Butter boxes with lapped sides were made of oak or ash, with bottoms and covers of pine, and rims of oak or ash around the covers. The butter boxes constructed of staves and hoops were made of the same woods: the pine staves, dowelled together, with bevels at one end, fitting around odorless, white pine bottoms, and the hoops of oak or ash, like the cover rims.

Round cheese boxes were shallow with diameters large enough to accommodate a cylinder of cheese. There are a few surviving examples of these boxes: one of maple with large hand-made nails holding the laps; another of very thick, heavy, oak, also with hand-made nails; and a third that may have been a factory product, judging from its small machine-made nails.

Other classes of kitchen woodenware included sieves, bowls, bread troughs, mortars, cheese drainers, cheese baskets, and miscellaneous pantry tools Horsehair sieves in frames of maple or pine were produced in sets, with diameters ranging from two to twelve inches, and were used to sift herbs and spices. One set of five served in a doctor's office. Larger sieves for sifting flour in making bread were made with copper nails fastening the hoops. Bolting cloth occasionally substituted for hair, and later pieces used fine wire. Round sieves sometimes had top and bottom lids. Oval sieves with two covers were probably rarities. Extant winnowing sieves, about one hundred and fifty years old, twenty to twenty four inches in diameter, used oak rims and black-ash splints for the sieve. They have been traced to Colonial and Shaker origin. Charcoal sieves made of splints, with ash rims round the top, had larger holes than the winnowing sieves.

The bowls were of a variety of shapes and sizes, the earliest pieces hollowed by hand or turned on a spring-pole lathe. The maple knot bowl, most common, was made from the burl growth on trees—the "Down East" term for this growth was "knurl." The bowls were almost immune to warping and did not crack readily. The little known salt-bowl, five to six inches in diameter, round, and turned on a lathe, was used, as the name indicates, on the kitchen table for the family salt.

Bread troughs, of all sizes, box-like in shape, with bottom, and four sides dovetailed or nailed, and a cover, were used for kneading dough. In the autumn, when the winter supply of food was generally prepared, they were also used as chopping bowls for the meats, fruits and vegetables minced and subsequently canned in jars and crocks.

The mortars included small birch types for spices; heavy types of chestnut, oak or lignum vitae, for crushing salt, sugar, herbs or corn meal; and a third type with a stubby pestle used for snuff. The pestles were often merely roots whittled into shapes appropriate for use.

Cheese drainers and baskets were necessary appurtenances of colonial household dairying. The crudest drainers were made with a perforated board for a bottom. One early type consisted of rounded sticks placed in a wooden frame, painted red. Another variety, that has been called the "Windsor" type, was constructed of round ash hoops, joined to a bottom of rounded slats. The cheese baskets, of a later date, were made of oak or ash splints woven in hexagonal design with wide hexagonal spaces. Of odd shapes, one to two feet in diameter, they served to hold the curds drained thru the cheese cloth. The baskets were set on racks over tubs which caught the dripping whey. The curds, tied in the retaining cloth, subsequently went thru the finishing processes. Extant objects resembling splint cheese baskets in construction are a funnel, an ox muzzle, a clam basket, and a Shaker basket used for carrying eggs.

The pantry tools were numerous, many of them made at home with a jackknife. There were *wet* scoops and *dry* scoops. One large Shaker scoop with double-barred handle, made of one piece eighteen inches long, was used for stirring apple butter. Other scoops had even more elaborate handles, but the majority were plain and for use. Butter paddles, of similar construction but flatter, were made of birch, maple, pine and beech. One example had a butter print carved into the end of the handle. Two unusual paddles were shaped like an artist's palette, and were perhaps more useful than the ordinary shaped paddles.

There were several types of rolling pins, the early ones without handles. A ribbed piece served to roll cookies. Other handy kitchen objects entirely of wood included spoons, forks, spatulae, toddy spoons, toddy stirrers, lemon sticks, dippers and mashers—all of various shapes and sizes. Objects with metal parts and wooden frames or handles included chopping knives, apple parers, spice and coffee mills, pie crimpers and graters. A grater for horseradish and carrots was a crudely formed, broad spatula, about twelve inches long, having a sheet of punch pattern tin curved and fastened over the lower wooden part with handmade nails. The back of this piece was inscribed with initials and the date *1794*. Two other graters of more recent make used machine-made nails.

The butter molds were of two main types: one, a single piece of wood for pounding—the stamp within a box shaped case holding a pound of butter; the other, a single stamp with a handle. The obverse and reverse sides of the stamps of two rare butter molds of the eighteenth century, brought to Ohio from Massachusetts, bore the carved initials "W. T." Another early Massachusetts butter mold of the same type was designed with a crown, rose and thistle, suggesting Scotch or English craftsmanship.

Long handled sticks were used for stirring Indian pudding; other long sticks, for stirring the dye pot; and a stick of sassafras wood for stirring lye, a product which was the result of making a soap "leach"—i.e. a mixture of fat and wood ashes placed in a perforated barrel thru which water percolated. Short sticks served to beat clothes, broad spatulae to turn over apples drying on racks, other decorated spatulae to stir food in pots. Toddy sticks stirred toddy, differing from *grog* in containing less spirits and more sugar, while *flip*, containing beer or cider but no water, was stirred with a hot iron called a loggerhead.

The list of wooden pantry tools seems almost endless, continuing with ladles, bread boards, sausage guns, funnels, herb skimmers, Indian eating scoops, sugar scoops, maple sugar and salt boxes, and clothespins.

All the pieces described or mentioned above came chiefly from the New England states and New York. Woodenware peddlers helped to distribute them about the turn of the eighteenth century. Boston, in 1799, sang a popular song called "Come Buy My Woodenware." Hingham, Massachusetts was noted for its cooper manufactures—tubs, hoops, nests of boxies [*sic*], washtubs, keelers and piggins. Timothy Gillette and Son established their woodenware factory at Henniker, New Hampshire, in 1817. The son turned a lathe by hand, while the father controlled the blades and peddled bowls, plates, skimmers, cups and saucers of ash around the vicinity. Sauquoit Valley in New York was distinguished by a poet, also a woodenware maker and peddler, who sold rolling pins and butter molds. The molds used by the Dutch colonists of the Hudson Valley and their descendants showed the craftsmanship of the homeland.

Among the woodenware accessories used by the Dutch housewives of New York, was the *lepel-bortie* or spoon rack used also by the Pennsylvania Germans with a variation of indigenous design. The Pennsylvania settlers from Germany in their turn had brought over the style of decoration practiced by them abroad. They applied a simplification of it to their wooden brush-and-comb holders hanging beside pumps in wash-sheds or out-kitchens of their homes; to their razor and shaving boxes, tankards for cider, pie markers, butter and cake molds, and numerous other kitchen utensils. Many of the Pennsylvania woodenware pieces were brought to Ohio and the other future states of the Northwest Territory during the migrations shortly after the Revolution. The Pennsylvanians did not find themselves alone in the still unsettled west. New Englanders and New Yorkers were also pioneering. Design spread accordingly, and eastern influences on early middle-western woodenware are readily traceable today. Spoons, butter prints and paddles of Illinois resemble Pennsylvania ones. A walnut butter mold, built in sections and bound with metal, in the container of which the butter was pounded and then stamped with a removable carved disk in the bottom of the mold, comes from an Amish settlement in Holmes County, Ohio, but was probably made in Pennsylvania. Turned maple sugar and salt boxes of Loraine County, Ohio, are similar to types made in New England, Pennsylvania and Maryland. Ohio butter molds of ca. 1830–40 with flower and leaf design follow the motifs of earlier Pennsylvania molds. And the following pieces were all brought to Ohio by Pennsylvania Germans: maplewood butter molds belonging to an Amish settlement, ca. 1830; a pinewood pie board used for mixing pastry, but which also served to close the flour barrel, ca. 1818; and a cooky [*sic*] box of maple, the top of which screws in, decorated with reddish brown paint and gilt stencil, found in a Mennonite settlement.

From the standpoint of carving, the spoon racks, cake and butter molds merit detailed discussion. Other carved pieces such as spinning wheels, which were as much a part of Colonial living rooms as of Colonial kitchens, and loom stools with slight carving and elaborately decorative painting, demanding the consideration of the expert in furniture, need be mentioned only in passing for the purposes of the present essay.

The carving in the spoon racks derived closely from the Frisian style of northeastern Holland, which in turn can be traced back to Scandinavian motifs. The dominant element is the spiral wheel, connected probably with primitive symbolism of the sun. The carving sometimes crude, sometimes careful, was done always with a V-shaped tool and resembled wall-carving and the work of hanging boxes. Wallace Nutting has described nine American racks:

1- undated, probably eighteenth century, with familiar spiral wheel and flowing band in bottom section—several coats of paint obscure the details—, found on the Jersey shore of the Hudson.

2- probably eighteenth century and from New Jersey or eastern Pennsylvania, with spiral wheel and stars.

3- dated 1745, with tulip, star wheel, diamond motifs, and suggestion of Gothic tracery,—found on the Jersey shore of the Hudson.

4- probably eighteenth century, of unknown origin, the upper section seems to portray the elevation of a Dutch panelled Kas. The rest of the design consists of elaborate but not easily classifiable tracery.

5- probably eighteenth century, from Washington's Headquarters at Morristown, N.J., distinctly Scandinavian suggestion, especially the finial.

6- dated 1775, found near Bethlehem, Pa., diamond, star wheel, double heart and tulip design.

7- probably eighteenth century, origin unknown, with subtle modelling in the rosettes. The rack bars are slotted in front, instead of being merely pierced; design of spirals and six pointed stars.

8- spoon rack and box, probably eighteenth-century Pennsylvania German, with twin figures of crestings, slotted bars; box below.

9- spoon rack and box, ribbed decoration at top suggests the conventional evergreen tree. The scratch carving is of the decadent period. Several types of this rack have been found along the Maine coast.

Most of the spoon racks have been traced to the Hollanders or Swedes of north New Jersey, along the Delaware. Dutch origin has been considered more probable. The rack bars used to display pewter spoons, and in every case the arrangement provided for twelve: three bars had four slots each, two bars had six slots each, etc. One exception is a long slot in each of two bars. The Dutch racks and similar articles illustrating Pennsylvania German motifs were probably hung up in kitchens. Like the New England chest with heart motif, the spoon racks were probably given by the bridegroom to the bride in token of his affection. The racks are an almost isolated example of elaborate carving related to culinary use. The wood used was poplar or "white-wood" (the western Connecticut name for poplar), semi-hard, close grained and featureless, so that it was well adapted for carving. Besides the carved racks, there were others, uncarved, with scrolled or molded sideboards, which always had a knife box at the base. The earliest racks (late seventeenth century) came without boxes, probably because they antedate the use of household knives and belong to a time when each individual brought his own clasp knife to the table. The boxes were intended for two-tined forks with horn handles, as well as knives. The spoon racks themselves passed out of fashion toward the close of the eighteenth century, about the time the modern fork came into use.

Marzipan or "martzebaume" molds, carved by Pennsylvania German craftsmen, served to shape the candy-like pastry with which the German settlers decorated their Christmas trees and celebrated the days before Twelfthnight over cider, brandy and wine. The recipe for these cakes consisted of almond paste or finely chopped kernels of apricot stones, plus wheat flour or fine corn meal, plus honey or sugar syrup. The compounded dough was rolled very thin and cut into the molds with well buttered or larded fingers. A pie wheel or scalloper—one Pennsylvania example was merely an old cent filed into scallops and attached to one end of a handle (the other end displayed a crescent-shaped head with serrated edges useful for piercing dough and letting the gases escape)—trimmed the edges of the marzipan to the size of the mold. The stiff cake was then taken out of the mold, baked in a brick oven or before an open fire, and finally decorated with vegetable colors. The tradition of the marzipan mold and cake goes back further than the immediate German and Alsatian craft heritage of the Pennsylvania Germans, to mystic rites of Christian and pagan Rome, ancient Greece, and Persia.

The woods used to make these molds included box, pear, apple, cherry, maple, walnut and pine. The Pennsylvania molds were oblong in shape, ranging in width and length from two by three inches to five by eight inches, and from three-quarters of an inch to one and one quarter inches in thickness. The majority were carved with a single pattern on one face only. Occasional examples exist of molds carved on both faces. The rarest exceptions were two designs on one face, and *double double* molds carved with two designs on each face. The only extant example of the latter, 5 1/2 by 5 5/8 inches, shows a flower and stork on one face, and a gamecock and peahen on reverse. The occasional use of marzipan molds for pressing clay tiles seems to have been purely casual and not at all commercial.

The designs were always carved in intaglio—never in relief—so that dough would take the impression and itself present a raised surface. The subjects included animals, Old and New Testament illustrations, a gallery of notable portraits, scenes from a military sketch book, and reproductions from a botany and a book of wonders. The collection of Carl Dreppard, including a wild hare, wild boar, tulip, sunflower, peahen, peacock, gamecock, and a stork carrying a baby in its beak,—all but one of them carved out of pearwood, and traced back to 1790,—probably represents the work of a single craftsman. One mold of maple shows a general on horseback. The Landiss Brothers collection (Landis Valley, Pennsylvania) possesses one mold portraying a royal gentleman, with wig, long vest, skirt-coat, ruffles, frills, sword and cane, of before 1750[. A]nother mold, the carving of which shows a soldier in uniform of 1830[,] resembl[es] a contemporary illustration in Huddy and Duval's U.S. Military Magazine[;] he carries a long rifle, bayonet fixed; behind him are two spears or lances crossed with a tomahawk, a drum with sticks stands at his left, and the flag of the United States is at his right.*

A double-sided mold, which was formerly owned by a Mennonite family in Pennsylvania, pictures on one side a tree of life with two childlike figures perched upon its limbs, reaching up to pluck the fruit; and on the obverse, two similar figures reaching up to a cross, above which on a scroll are the letters INRI in Roman capitals. Other molds, the designs of which are related to Christian symbolism, illustrate fish and the tulip, the symbol of immortality. Further subjects include a stork, swan, goose, duck, cock robin, a pelican feeding her young with blood from her breast, a gamecock, hen, pheasant, rabbit, reclining deer, horse, sheep, sheep and lamb, a horn of plenty, fuchsia, daisy, sunflower, moon and stars, a balloon, butterfly, three cherries on a twig, a wild board, pig, dog, and eagle and shield, a castle and crown, Conestoga wagon, clinging vine, lion, unicorn, etc. Dreppard advises collectors to "Reject all moulds under two by three inches in size and all multiple molds carrying designs measuring individually less than those dimensions;" and further warns "all who are interested not to purchase multiple blocks with from four to eight designs cut in them, each design measuring about one-and-one half by two inches." He believes that "these are molds of an altogther different variety, and are being imported from abroad." He refers evidently to the "Springale" mold, which was used to make small pastries for St. Nicholas day. The American Index of Design has reproduced two such molds of poplar, attributed to Pennsylvania German origin, both measuring 4 1/16" long, 2 15/16" wide and 7/16" thick. The four designs on one mold are a butterfly, ship, anchor and rabbit; and on the other, a bird, beehive, bow and arrow, and shield.

The Pennsylvania butter molds were made in oblong shapes like the marzipan molds, and also in round shapes—of the size of about a standard one pound print of butter. The designs show less originality than those of the marzipan molds and limit themselves to simple subjects such as a sheaf of wheat, a cow, flower, etc. Pennsylvania butter molds of ca. 1790–93, of cherry and poplar in circular shapes, illustrate pineapple and leaves, and star and leaves. Early-nineteenth-century molds of the same origin are carved with leaf and tulip designs; middle-nineteenth-century molds, with spread eagle and shield. As in the marzipan molds, the carving was done in intaglio.

The cake boards, which molded large cakes and as carvings showed more complicated artistry than the smaller marzipan molds, were made not only in Pennsylvania, but in most of the other states of the Union throughout the first half of the nineteenth century. The following pieces were among the most striking:

1- A mahogany board carved in intaglio with three firemen pulling a fire engine—L. 14 3/8", W. 8 1/8", Th. 7/8", ca. 1800.

2- A mahogany board carved in intaglio: within a circular border is the figure of a horse in front of a row of tents. The name, *W. Farrow,* is cut into the design—L. 14 3/4", W. 26 1/4", Th. 3/4", early nineteenth century.

3- A mahogany board with cleats at both ends. In the lower center is a broken column; at the left, a robed female representing Greece; at the right, a Turkish soldier attacking with a sword; two other female figures, America with eagle and shield and Britannia holding the name Byron on a scroll - L. 14 3/4", W. 26 1/4", Th. 3/4", early nineteenth century.

4- A board carved with heart shaped urn and rose and bird design, L. 15 3/8", W. 12 1/2", Th. 1 5/16", early nineteenth century.

5- A wood mahogany panel - General Lafayette on a horse, spread eagle, leaves, scrolls, etc. - L. 17 3/4", W. 30 1/8" - the work of Henry F. Cox, carver, 1834.

6- A maple board carved with a rooster on one face, middle nineteenth century.

Proofread

4/6/39

Louis Zukofsky

Glass

Though the glass works established at Jamestown in 1608 marked the beginning of American manufacturers, the glass industry did not develop to any considerable position in this country till after the Revolution. Ventures before that time yielded an output chiefly of window glass and bottles. For want of authenticated data, the following list of early glass enterprises can only serve to establish the possibility that some kitchen glass was manufactured by them as occasional pieces:

1621—the 2nd glass house, at Jamestown, Virginia.

1638 (?)—the first glass works in Mass., village of Germantown, Braintree.

1639—Glass works, at Salem. Proprietors: Ananias Concklin, Obadiah Holmes, Laurence Southwick.

1645–1661—Glass House Field, Salem, Mass., established by Concklin after the failure of the previous venture.

1650—Wistar's glass works, Allowaytown, Salem, Cy., N.J.

1654—Jan Smeedes, South William St. (between Wall and Pearl), New York.

1655—Evert Duyckingk, New York.

1683—Joshua Tiffery, Philadelphia.

1683—Glass house owned by the Free Society of Traders, Frankfort, Pa.

1707—Pennypacker, Schwenksville, Pa.

1732—*Glass House Farm,* on estate belonging to Sir Peter Warren, north of 34 Street, between 8th and 11th Avenues, New York.

1753–85—Works at New Windsor, Orange Cy., N.Y.

1754—Loderwick Bamper, Brooklyn.

1754–7—Glass House Company, New York.

1762–ca. 1780 (?)—"Baron" Heinrich Wilhelm Stiegel, Lancaster Cy., Pa.

Baron Stiegel's enterprise failed during the Revolution, when he was cut off from financial assistance in Europe. According to Lord Sheffield, in 1783, glass was very scarce during the war. Aware of the fact that the colonies had produced little glassware except bottles, he asserted that the want of flint in America would always be a great disadvantage to glass manufactures. He was proved wrong shortly afterward.

In 1785, a glass house was established at Gloucester, New Jersey. In 1788, other works were set up by John De Neufville at Dowesborough, near Albany, New York, and at Alexandria, Virginia. The latter firm employed 500 people and exported 10,000 pounds worth of materials about that time. Mr. Carroll, the representative from Maryland, reported in 1789 that a glass manufactory had been successfully established in his state.

A few accredited facts relating to early glass kitchenware come from about this time. Ca. 1790, one shipment of plain glass tumblers costing less than $1,000 is said to have been sold for $12,000 in the Isle of France. About the turn of the century, a manufactory at Hartford, Connecticut, finding window glass too expensive to make, turned to the production of "Junk" (black) bottles for cider, great quantities of which were exported to the West Indies. These "Junk" bottles, like nearly all the glassware of the eighteenth century, were probably inferior products, full of bubbles and other defects.

Besides black, the other vitrifiable color used was green, as in the glass saucer and milk bowl from New Jersey, rendered by the American Index of Design. Other eighteenth-century glassware was painted red, yellow or blue. Applied to transparent glass, these colors usually indicate the workmanship of Dutch craftsmen.

The expansion of the glass industry in the States was spurred by the American invention, in 1827, of blown three-mold glass, which brought such kitchen objects as salt cups, pitchers, sugar bowls, gemmel flasks, cruet bottles, milk bowls (in which milk was set away for cream to rise), etc., within the price range of the average buyer.

The American Index of Design has made drawings of the following glass kitchenware:

- A mortar and pestle, from New Jersey, late eighteenth century, of amber and green bottle glass, H. 4", diameter at base 2 5/8", top 4 3/8". (Collection of the Metropolitan Museum)
- A butter mold, ca. 1868, blue aquamarine glass pressed in a two-piece mold; intaglio design of sheaf of wheat and sprays; knob handle on back. Diameter, 4 3/8". (Nadelman Collection)

For the purposes of this essay, molded early-nineteenth-century bar bottles designed with busts of Washington, Lafayette, and other historical figures and events, may be omitted, since they did not always properly find their way into the kitchen.

Ceramics

A letter of Higginson describing Massachusetts in 1630 contains the first reference to American ceramics: "It is thought here is good clay to make Bricks and Tyles and Earthen-pots." In 1636, Governor Winthrop writing to his son, John, in Connecticut, mentioned clay which "the potter saith is very good." The crude earthenware in the form of simple crocks, cruches, bowls, jugs, mugs and butter pots produced in New England until the reign of the Georges was on the whole very scarce. Stone bottles were about the only form of stoneware. All these pieces were used in the kitchen.

The color glazes employed in these early pieces were red, black *and* green, and, in the first half of the eighteenth century, cobalt blue. The forms followed various European influences in the different colonies.

Authenticated earthenware kitchen objects of the late eighteenth and early nineteenth century derived from three main centers of the ceramic industry: New England, New York and Pennsylvania. The beginnings of decorated stoneware date also from about this time, and developed in the same places, tho production did not reach its high mark till the middle of the nineteenth century, with the rise of pottery factories in New York State and Bennington, Vermont.

Felt's *Customs of New England* mentions a "butter boat" of earthenware, used for holding butter sauce, made in 1770. New England brown glazed earthenware pieces of the time included cider jugs, molasses jugs, dye pots, milk pans, bean pots and yeast jugs. The New York earthenware, consisting of pieces for similar use, included also brown glazed pitchers and pie plates.

Pennsylvania's contribution was *Sgraffito* ware—slipware, in which the body of the piece was covered with clay of a creamy consistency afterwards cut into to produce the design. Though most of these pieces decorated with tulip, flower and bird designs were parlor ornaments, many of them served useful purposes in the domestic economy of the Pennsylvania German kitchen, notably as pie dishes, some of them now owned by descendants of the original settlers. Dr. Mercer mentions decorated pie dishes in the possesion of Sarah Riegel, living between upper Trincum Church and Revere, about two miles from Revere; another dish owned by Sarah Krause living near Cornelius Herstine's pottery on Peter Mills farm; and other pieces owned by Emiline Rapp at Erwina.

Stoneware from New England pantry shelves of ca. 1790–1825 included a vinegar jug with bird decoration, preserve jars, cider pitchers, churns, cooky crocks, bean pots, etc. The glazes were light blue, floating blue, mulberry, black and white. Banded china decoration was employed frequently.

New York stoneware of the same period used brown, old gray and tannish glazes. The objects included jugs and jars for molassses, vinegar, pickles, preserved fruit and mince meat. The stoneware of John Remmey and of J. Clarkson Crolius (1794–1815) of New York City was the most popular of this type of ware. Some extant jars are marked with the names of later potters of New York City, including: A. E. Smith & sons, 38 Peck Slip; Pruden and Olcott, 185 Duane Street; W. Smith, Greenwich, N.Y.; and T. G. Boone and Sons, Navy Street, Brooklyn. Other nineteenth-century jars made in New York State were stamped on the sides with the following marks: S. C. Brown, Huntington, L.I.; N. Clark, Jr. & Clark & Fox, of Athens; N. White & H. Nash of Utica; Wm. E. Warner, West Troy; M. Tyler, & Tyler & Dillon, Albany; White and Wood, Binghamton; Jacob Claire, Francis Bogardus, Lehman & Rieding—Poughkeepsie.

Renderings by the American Index of Design include the following pieces, giving a fairly representative idea of the distribution, dating, and craftsmanship of earthenware and stoneware kitchen utensils:

Earthenware

- Cheese pot, late eighteenth century, red earthenware, dark brown glaze, cylindrical, with rows of holes and incised lines, three legs and one handle. (Nadelman Collection)
- Sieve or colander, late eighteenth or early nineteenth century, red earthen-

ware, brown glaze on inside only, three legs and two handles, H. 4", diameter at top 11 1/2", diameter at base 7". (Nadelman Collection)

- Jelly mold, late eighteenth or early nineteenth century, Pennsylvania, glazed earthenware of brown clay, mold shaped to form scallops or flutes, H. 5 cm., diameter at top 11 cm. (Brooklyn Museum)

- Pie plate, late eighteenth or early nineteenth century, Pennsylvania, glazed earthenware of dark brown clay, decoration in brown stain forming a cross, H. 3.5 cm., diameter 18 cm.

- Another pie plate with waving lines in gray and black forming lozenges, notched rim.

- Another, deep dish in shape, painted decoration of green and brown in straight and curving lines.

- Roach trap, ca. 1840, Pennsylvania, red earthenware, shaped like an ant hill, hole near bottom, H. 3/4", diameter at top 3", at base 5 1/8".

- Jug for batter, 1847 (incised on front), probably by John Austin, dark brown glaze, decorated with five fish and two American flags, wreath around spout, wire handle bound with cord. H. 9", diameter at top 4 1/2", at base, 7". (Nadelman Collection)

Stoneware

- Jugs and crocks ca. 1815 - middle 19th century by C. Crolius, N.Y.

- Preserve jars, 1794–1815, C. Crolius, N.Y.

- Milk pan, first half of the nineteenth century, probably from Pennsylvania or Ohio, gray decorated with blue flower and leaf, H. 7", diameter at top 12", at base 9 1/2".

- Baking dish for sponge cake, early nineteenth century, H. 3", diameter at top 9 1/4", at base, 7 1/4". (Nadelman Collection)

- Jug for pancake batter, middle nineteenth century, stamped White's Pottery, Binghamton, N.Y., gray salt glaze outside, inside glaze brown, touches of blue at the spout, H. 8 1/4". (Metropolitan Museum)

- Sugar bowl of porcelain trimmed with pewter and copper, Ohio, 1850.

- Batter jugs with and without spouts, Pa., ca. 1860.

- Nineteenth century pitchers, flask, teapot, and water cooler.

- Churn, tan stoneware with coarse salt glaze, blue slip decoration, 1883–94, E. Norton & Co., Bennington, Vermont.

Ironware

A small iron kettle made at Saugus, Massachusetts ca. 1645, for "The Company of Undertakers for the Iron Works," of which Joseph Jenks was the master mechanic, is said to have been the first casting in the colonies. The fire and kitchen implements produced in the iron centers of Massachusetts, Rhode Island, Connecticut, New Jersey and Pennsylvania, in the seventeenth century, satisfied the demands of individual households whose domestic economy concentrated around the fireplace. The long list of kitchen ironware manufactured during this period has already been given in the first part of this essay. The eighteenth century and the first half of the nineteenth produced greater quantities of the original types of wares as a result of the increasing number of iron establishments throughout the original colonies and the frontier areas; witnessed the use of new wares affected by the introduction of the cook stove which gradually replaced the function of the fireplace; and finally [saw] the obsolescence of iron utensils when wares made out of other metals, especially tin, began to dominate the market because of their cheapness and better service. Two factors, however, prolonged the use of iron kitchen utensils during the nineteenth century: (1) the discovery of mineral coal in Western Pennsylvania, West Virginia, Tennessee, Alabama and the Northwest territory, which resulted in confining the iron industry using this product to these areas newly settled by emigrants rich in the ironwork traditions of the Atlantic coastal states, and (2) the persistence of Eastern craftsmen and their followers in Ohio in furthering a more complicated decorative design after the immediate need for the early, more functional wares had declined. Nevertheless, the recurrence of simple, functional design in later craftsmanship imitating an earlier tradition is not to be overlooked. The history of the complex development of this ironware design can best be studied by considering several types of fire and kitchen implements. Because of natural limitations of the working processes, the wrought iron pieces usually tended to simpler forms than the cast pieces.

Skewers - Swift's "Advice to Servants" defined the function of this implement, originally known as a skiver and made of dogwood: "Send up your meat well stuck with skewers, to make it look round and plump." They were used throughout the colonies to keep the roast in shape. Three examples of the last half of the eighteenth century were merely pieces of flat iron forged to a point at one end and into a closed scroll at the other. Steel skewers were quite common, ca. 1790. Two extant pieces of soft steel made in Newburyport, Massachusetts, measure 7" and 9 1/2" in length. Such pieces are often mistaken for paper cutters today.

Gridirons - [These] were made of wrought and cast iron, in various shapes. One rectangular piece measured 16 3/4" by 11 1/2"; a circular piece, 12 1/2" in diameter. Both of these date from the eighteenth century. A wrought iron Pennsylvania gridiron of the early nineteenth century had a barred construction to facilitate the running down of fat. Other gridirons were made with revolving tops.

Trivets - These came in various shapes—rectilinear, circular and triangular—forged or cast, and were often pierced with geometrical designs. The following pieces rendered in American Index:

- Late eighteenth century, pierced sheet brass top, wrought iron base, maple handle, H. 11 3/4", L. 15 1/4", W. 7 1/8 (Owner,[†] Mrs. Katherine Willis, Flushing, L.I.)
- Eighteenth century (?). Found in Conn., wrought iron, H. 1 3/8", L. 5 3/8", W. 5", Th. 3/32".
- Early 19th century, Cast iron, 3 legs, diameter 6 1/2", H. 1 1/4", Th. 1/4".
- Early 19th century, Pennsylvania German, cast iron, 4 legs.
- Early 19th century, Pennsylvania German, cast iron, scroll and heart design.
- Early 19th century, Pennsylvania German, cast iron, design of concentric circles and radiating flower and leaves.
- Middle 19th century, Pennsylvania German, cast iron, diameter 8", L. 13", H. 1 1/2", th. 1/4", heart designs, handle ending in circle.
- Late 19th century, Pa., cast iron, heart and scroll design.
- Late 19th century, Pa., cast iron, pierced lacy design.
- Pair of pot trivets, late eighteenth or early 19th century, wrought iron, found in Bridgehampton, L.I. Each trivet is made of flat iron bars forged into horizontal arcs tapered at both ends and bent downward at right angles forming two legs. A round rod forged to the center of each arc is also bent downward at a right angle, and, terminating in a closed scroll, forms a third leg. H. 7", app. W. 7 1/4".

- Trivet-toaster, late 18th century, English influence, wrought iron. A flat horizontal ring with a turned wood handle: supported upon three legs made of half-round iron braced by three flat bars radiating from the center. Two toast hooks upon a square handle are adjustable horizontally at the top of a round bar which adjusts vertically from one of the legs. H., not including toaster, 12 1/2"; diameter of ring 9 3/8". (Owner, Mrs. Katherine Willis, Flushing, L.I.)

Flatiron Holders - The most interesting of these pieces were of Pennsylvania German make, both wrought and cast. The cast flatiron holders usually allowed for more ornate forms than the hammered wrought iron pieces. One late-eighteenth-century wrought-iron model had a triangular frame with wooden handle, the three legs being merely extensions of the frame. This simple, functional design is again illustrated in an early-nineteenth-century piece, L. 13 cm., W. 10 cm., now owned by the Brooklyn Museum. Cast pieces of the early nineteenth century were variously designed with gargoyle figures for handles, heart shapes, scrolls, George Washington medallions, flowers and leaves, initialed centers, eagles, harps, etc. Middle and late-nineteenth-century pieces employed other complicated motifs, including masonic emblems, mottos, portraits, crowns and crosses, urns, and horseshoes in which form they were cast. Names of the foundries which cast them were often woven into the pattern, such as "Colebrook Iron Company" cast in relief in one object made in Pottstown, Pennsylvania and "Less and Drake, Newark, N.J., U.S." Names of craftsmen were often stamped underneath the object.[8] Cast iron Pennsylvania German pieces resembling wrought iron ones in simplicity of structure and design were also produced in small numbers, ca. 1875.

Other types of cooking utensils and fireplace objects are covered by the following representative pieces which have been drawn by artists of the American Index of Design:

- Wafer iron, L. 18c., wrought iron, two elliptical plates with long round handles flattened near the plates and riveted scissor fashion. Incised design chis-

8. This description would be equally apt for *"A,"* where the names of those involved in its casting are incorporated in the design (e.g., PZ, LZ, CZ, B-A-C-H). Unlike craft objects where the maker's identity might be in question, Zukofsky's poem includes initials as *realia,* metonyms of the everyday or social context out of which the poem grows. Compared with the values of literary authorship, such minimalist marking minimizes the contribution of the individual.

elled upon the inside face of each plate. L. 37 1/2"; L. of plates 8", W. 5", Th. 1/8". (Owner, Mrs. K. Willis, Flushing, L.I.)

- Fender plate-warmer, late-18th or early-19th-century Pennsylvania wrought iron. A flat oblong tray of sheet iron, wrought handle riveted at the center of its back edge, and four cleats riveted underneath. Two parallel round rods, connected by a transverse rod, bent up in front at right angles and forged into flat fender hooks. The parallel rods pass thru holes in the cleats permitting the tray to slide back and forth. Painted black. W. of tray 12 1/2", depth 9 3/8", overall H. 5 5/8". (Owner Julia E. Kuttner, N.Y.C.)

- Toast rack, early-19th-century Pennsylvania German wrought iron. Horizontal square bar bent downward at both ends forming two legs. Welded at a right angle to the center is a long flat handle under which a third leg is riveted. The rack, loosely riveted to the center so as to turn horizontally, is made of a sheet iron base thru which are riveted, near the front and back edges, two lateral groups of two concentric semicircular loops made of round rods. Painted black. W. of rack 13 1/4", depth 1 7/8", H. 3 3/4", overall depth 15 5/8". (Owner, Miss J. E. Kuttner, N.Y.C.)

- Muffin Pan, late-eighteenth-century cast iron. Horizontal cluster of seven hemispherical cups, six circling around a center one. Underneath, three feet; radiating horizontally from the top is a flat pierced handle. Overall length 11", diam. 7 5/8", H. 1 7/8", found in Geneva, N.Y.

Andirons: 17th and 18th century, wrought.

- Also cast iron, late 18th century, in form of "squatting ladies," H. 11 1/2". (Metropolitan Museum)

- Late 18th century, squat standing figure with pipe, cast, found in North Carolina. (Brooklyn Museum)

- Ca. 1775, cast, made from anchors owned by a sea captain of New Bedford, Mass. The black legs are wrought bars.

- Other andirons of the late 18th or late 19th century, of wrought iron from Conn. and Winchester, Va., and of cast iron from Bethlehem, Pa.

- Middle-18th-century andirons of wrought steel and iron with cast brass finials.

- Middle-19th-century andirons of cast iron with cast brass finials.

- Coffee grinder, ca. 1800, cast iron, L. 15 1/2", diam. of circular knife 6 3/8", in boat shaped container. (Nadelman Collection)

- Egg roaster, 17th century, cast iron, three egg shaped cups in oblong frame,

H. 2 5/8", W. 2 1/2", overall L. 13 1/2". Original owner, Theunis Van Houten who lived in "Nauraushan," near Orangeburg, Rockland Cy., N.Y., 1694.

- Tea kettle, hobnail type, ca. 1860–70, cast iron, lid and hollow brass handle probably not the original, H. 7 3/4", diam. 9".
- Maple sugar mold, cups in frame, cast iron, early 19th century, 16 1/2" x 8 7/8" x 1 3/16" x 1/8".
- Aspic mold, middle 19th century, cast iron, curved fish shape, L. 8", W 7 1/2", depth 2 1/4". (Collection American Folk Art Gallery, N.Y.C.)
- Coal scuttle, ca. 1840, sheet iron, a conical shape, placed in a horizontal position upon two applied cast iron arched legs, and truncated so as to form an elliptical opening which is a cast iron flange riveted around an opening in the transverse joining a flat bail handle. A small flat "U" handle riveted to the back, L. 20", H. 11 3/4", diam. at the back 10 1/2". (Owner, Mrs. K. Willis, Flushing, L.I.)

Cracker Tamps, used for stamping crackers, were initialed iron molds, of the late eighteenth century or later.

R. M. Knittle has written about the following *Ohio pieces* ca. 1790–1840:

- A pair of wrought iron firedogs with unusual base, central Ohio, 1790–1810.
- A heavy corn popper with pan and cover of solid iron and hollow handle accommodating a wooden haft, made in a German community in southwest Ohio.
- A waffle iron with long handles and box-like irons engraved with floral design, made in the Zoar community.
- A very decorative toaster forged in Miami Valley.
- A broiler with dripping saucer, said to come from Columbus, Ohio. The disk revolved to ensure even cooking; the drippings ran down the spiral grooves and along the handle into the saucer, from which they were used for basting.
- A wrought flatiron stand of simple functional design, from Central Ohio.
- A wrought plate stand from the Amish community, 19th century. The iron grille rested on four wooden feet.
- A crimpling iron and heater from eastern Ohio, seventeenth or eighteenth century type carried over into the nineteenth. The outer case supported on a stander was warmed by the insertion of a hot iron tongue, and then used for fluting the ruffles of bonnets and caps.

W. L. Washington has described a homemade machine for cutting mince meat, head cheese, etc.—of ca. 1790, found in Rockland County, New York. The machine is not to be confused with other machines used for grinding sausage meat. The cutting box contained a removable revolving cylinder 2 3/4" in diameter, pierced by twenty-one pieces of hand forged iron or steel arranged in spiral pattern 1 1/8" beyond the surface. These metal pegs presented a powerful set of pushing teeth forcing the meat against twenty-two blades thru which they rotated. The meat was cut into 1/4" cubes and carried laterally to an opening in the box opposite the handle and discharged. The box made of pine is 13" L., 7" H., 7" W., when closed by two ornamental hand forged hooks. It stands on hickory strips intended for fastening to a table with screws, and has an arm of hickory 15 1/2" long, with handle at the end. (W. L. Washington Collection of early American Mechanical Devices)

A similar meat cutting box is owned by the Museum of the Bucks County Historical Society in Pennsylvania.

Eleven *Apple Parers* have also been described by W. L. Washington. The purpose of these parers was to peel the skins of apples, with the least waste of fruit. All of them work on the principle of fixing the apple on a fork and rotating it against the keen edge of an adjustable knife. Swift rotating was secured by multiplying the speed of a small wheel by means of gears or belts which transmitted the power derived from a larger, hand-driven wheel. The knife was placed at the end of a long flexible arm whose position was capable of considerable variation. Later forms of these parers seem to have been designed to be operated on a table stand. These particular parers were all Pennsylvania German models, with the exception of one coming from Connecticut. The dates range from ca. 1750 to 1882. One machine was operated in reverse instead of forward (date 1750); another, driven by an overhead round pulley; the late, 1882 machine, entirely of iron, employed the worm screw principle. The wooden parts consist of white wood, hickory, oak, maple and pine. Parers were made throughout New England, especially in Vermont and New Hampshire. One New Hampshire parer of cast iron bears the patent mark of the 1850's.

Proofread
4/13/39
Louis Zukofsky

Pewter

C. M. Andrews' reference to "pewter dishes in large numbers, chiefly for servants' use, and *yellow metal spoons*" in New England kitchens, would seem to apply to the early eighteenth century, after the development of the three-room house. It is safe to say that there were few of these wares made of an alloy of tin and copper, cast in molds, in seventeenth-century Massachusetts, and that their forms were the simplest. The insufficiency of materials prohibited experiment. The classic period of American pewter, when it served as highly decorative dining-room tableware, is beyond the scope of this essay. But ca. 1640, when the kitchen was still the house, four pewterers practised their trade in Boston. Henry Shrimpton who died there in 1666, had made pewter ladles, skimmers, spoons, candlesticks, kettles and a colander. In the eighteenth century, Newport (R.I.), New York, and Philadelphia joined Boston as pewter producing centers. And very likely, wherever the early colonial kitchen continued to serve partly as a dining room, the pewter platters, plates, basins, porringers, tankards, pitchers, beakers and syrup jugs, many of them marked pieces of a later date, were used as kitchenware from time to time. One New England piemarker with a pewter wheel must certainly have served as a kitchen utensil. The same may be said of the late-eighteenth-century funnel (length 7", diameter 5 1/2") made by Frederick Basset (1740–1800) of 4 Burlington Slip (later 218 Pearl), New York; and perhaps, too, of a thirteen-inch platter made by Joseph Danforth (18th century). A porringer by Samuel Danforth of Providence, ca. 1824, and teapots by J. Danforth and Savage, made in Middletown, Connecticut after 1825, may have been heated in kitchens of their time, though they were probably used in dining halls.

The later britannia ware (a silver-white alloy of tin, copper, and antimony, and frequently also bismuth and zinc), which took the place of pewter, undoubtedly served as kitchenware as well as cheap tableware. Roswell Gleason (1799–1871) of Dorchester, Massachusetts, and James Harvey Putnam (1803–1855) of Malden, Massachusetts, were among its chief producers. When britannia ware was in turn replaced by kitchenware of other metals and porcelain, pewter kitchen utensils had passed out of general use. However, and occasional decorative piece, like a kitchen sugar bowl of porcelain trimmed with pewter and copper, made in Ohio in 1850, served to remind the second half of the nineteenth century of pewter's early popularity.

Silver

Only two silver implements may possibly be classed under the head of American kitchen utensils—the skewer and the brazier. Both were luxuries and rarities. The silver skewer occasionally replaced the steel or wooden skewer, after the meat was removed from the kitchen fire and dressed before being sent into the dining room for serving. The silver brazier, a short-legged, bowl-like object filled with burning charcoal, may occasionally have found its way to a kitchen table as a chafing dish which sustained the heat in a boiling kettle or pot. H. R. Wray has published illustrations of the following American skewers:

1 - 12 1/2" long, by Harwood, ca. 1805.

2 - 13" long, with three faked English hall-marks, and "W. S." - William Seal, Philadelphia, 1819.

3 - 11" long, steel and silver plate, crude Prince of Wales' plumes, no mark, from an old N.J. family, 1790.

4 - 7 1/4" long, marked with an American eagle's head and "T. B." - Thomas Bentley, Boston, 1796.

New England silver braziers include pieces by John Coney, Jacob Hurd and John Powtine. Early Philadelphia pieces were made by John De Nys and Philip Syng. A Boston Museum catalog of 1911 listed eight silver braziers, and probably no more than sixteen to twenty pieces were made in the colonies all told. John Coney of Boston (1655–1722) has been credited with five examples. A silver brazier by Jacob Hurd of the same city (1702–1758), formerly in the Garvan collection, sold for $2,800 in 1931.

Brass

The first attempt to cast brass in the colonies was made by John Winthrop, Jr. in his iron foundry at Lynn, Massachusetts, in 1644. However, till well on in the eighteenth century few American artisans worked in brass, and even as late as 1820 the American brass industry imported its labor and machinery from England.

The earliest brass kitchen utensils were very likely kettles and skillets, which like their contemporary seventeenth-century European models, were probably worked under hammer. Swedenborg's "Regnum Subterraneum

Sive Minerale de Cupro et Orichalco,"[9] published in 1734, contained an illustration of a set of rolls for rolling copper and brass sheet. But a number of brass articles including candlesticks, pots, staples, and andirons, mentioned in wills of colonists in 1736, were undoubtedly cast. Between 1725 and 1775, Caspar Wistar and his associates and successors in Philadelphia hammered out stills and kettles from brass and copper and cast some brass. According to Dyer, there were numerous brass founderies in Pennsylvania, during the last years of the eighteenth century, among them Forbes' furnace. Together, New England and Pennsylvania, about this time, produced the following utensils: brass kettles for making pickles (brass was used to insure a nice green); brass kettles with iron tripods; brass skimmers with long crook-necked iron handles; trivets of brass and iron; trivets entirely of brass with pierced, heart-shaped tops; iron bakers with brass knobs; warming pans with brass lids; and fender plate warmers of wrought iron with sliding brass trays. Fashion favored brass fireplace instruments, ca. 1750. Warming pan lids displayed unusual decorative skill in the scrolls, foliage and flower designs chased on their surface.

Nevertheless, Thomas Cooper's suggestion in *Some Information Respecting America* (Dublin, 1794) that a brass founder might find employment in this country indicates that the industry was still in its early stages. Spurred by Hamilton's *Report on Manufactures* (1791), the tariff on brass imports had been raised from five to fifteen percent. But the real impetus to brass manufactures was given in 1802, when Henry, Silas and Samuel Grilley (Grilleys?) and their partners, Abel and Leir Porter, began making buttons from sheet brass, at Waterbury, Conn. Fusing copper—secured in the purchase of old stills, kettles, and ship sheathing—with zinc, according to the process invented by Adams Emerson in England, in 1781, they obtained brass ingots. These were roughly rolled first in a Litchfield iron mill and then returned to Waterbury, where they were finished by being run between steel rolls, 2" in diameter, driven by horse power. Water power was used after 1808.

Brass lamps, however, made about this time continued to be hammered and cast. And, even by 1820, the maximum number of employees at the Waterbury plant did not exceed twenty. The report of an eastern Connecticut establishment for that year, noting that the casting of andirons was carried

---

9. See previous note on Swedenborg. *Regnum subterraneum sive minerale: De cupro et orichalco* is included in *Opera Philiosophica et mineralia* (1734).

on in connection with the manufacture of shirtings, indicated the lack of organization in the industry. In 1820, James Croft, an English brass maker, came to Waterbury and found employment with the Scoville Manufacturing Company where he introduced English machinery and processes. Ten years later Waterbury rolled brass was a factor in the American market and the industry developed rapidly from then on. With the invention of the spinning process by Hayden, an American, the American manufacturers took the lead over the English. Naugatuck Valley and Connecticut remained the chief centers of the brass industry.

Large scale industry, however, did not entirely replace the craftsman.[10] Pennsylvania pie markers with wheels of brass, and a flatiron holder of cast brass made by E. Zweibel in the same state, are still among the most interesting nineteenth-century pieces from the standpoint of design.

Copper

Copper kitchen utensils were rarer than brass, and in seventeenth-century New England consisted chiefly of kettles and pans. Andrews mentions copper stills of eighteenth-century Southern plantations.

Circa 1750, colonial kitchens displayed copper kettles which were hammered from sheet metal and lined with tin, as well as cast kettles. Copper chafing dishes hammered by hand, and lined with tin, with covers which were lifted by means of brass knobs, were popular at the time. Other copper wares included tin-lined dippers with curving trap handles, measures, coffee pots, and warming pans. On the lids of the latter the coppersmith imitated the motifs used on brass warming pans.

The Index of American Design has made drawings of a warming pan of sheet copper, diam. 10 1/2", ca. 1750–1800, Pennsylvania; and of an early-nineteenth-century sheet copper coffee pot, probably from New Jersey.

---

10. More than empathy for the craftsman or nostalgia for unalienated labor, subtle editorializations such as this recall the possibility for poetic craft in the 1930s. See the radio talk noted previously, the plans for a Worker's Anthology; *A Test of Poetry,* and judgments in Zukofsky's period essay "Sincerity and Objectification": ". . . the mind is attracted to the veracity of the particular craft, the validity of writing apprehending the most energetic constituents of possible objectivications. . . . Interested in craft, Reznikoff has not found it derogatory to his production to infuse his care for significant detail and precision into the excellent verbalisms of others" whereas the "'literary market' [is] not interested in sincerity as craft" (*Poetry* (1931): 275, 283, 284).

Tinware

The tin, kitchen pail was still unknown in the colonies in 1700, when the Huguenot Andrew Faneuil arrived from France, at Boston, to sell imported lanthorns, dishes, pans and kettles of tin at prices that only Governor Winthrop and a few wealthy southern planters could afford. Edmund Billington, whitesmith, working in Philadelphia, in 1718, may have made some American tinware, but there is no record to prove it. In 1738, William and Edward Patterson (*William and Edgar Pattison,* according to Wright), natives of County Tyrone, Ireland, settled at Berlin, Connecticut, and began practicing the trade of whitesmiths. About 1740, they imported sheets of the "best charcoal tin" packed in oak boxes, from England. They worked at home, cleaning these sheets of pure iron, two feet square and of the thickness of a sheet of paper, and plating them in cisterns of melted tin, and the first objects they produced were cooking utensils: tin dishes, pots and pans, beaten out with wooden mallets, on anvils. They kept the secret of their trade to themselves till 1760, when they first began training several apprentices. The Revolution cut short their supply of sheet iron, and it was not till the end of the war that they expanded their business with the help of tin peddlers, who carried tinker's tools with their wares and set up temporary tin establishments throughout the coastal states.

Ca. 1799, temporary and permanent tin establishments (there were at least five of the latter in Berlin, Conn.) manufactured the following kitchen utensils: candle boxes, candlesticks, candle molds, lanthorns, scones, sand shakers, foot-warmers, tea caddies, bread trays, and small tin boxes, most of them unpainted. The decoration—aside from scalloping and embossed or responsee work, respectively effected by pressing and hammering—was accomplished by etching designs on the surfaces of the wares or by pricking them into their surfaces. Different workmen, perhaps of different regions, very probably confined themselves to one method or the other. E. A. Barber surmises that the etched designs were "outlined by metal wheels with serrated edges, the figures afterwards filled in by hand with short strokes of the graver. These serrations and lines were cut through the thin film of tin which covered the sheet iron beneath. By this treatment the ornamentation appeared darker in tint than the bright of the surrounding ground, producing a pleasing effect without the use of applied coloring. A coffee pot (probably early nineteenth century) in the Pennsylvania Museum Collection is embellished in this manner with tulips, birds and waving bands of etched work." The other method of pricking the designs into the surface of the tin was carried out with a sharp metal point and prepared stencils used as guides. In the case of punched or pricked lanthorns and foot-warmers, the decorations served the practical end of radiating light and heat.

Among the early makers of tin coffee pots, lanthorns, stoves (tin kitchens) and funnels was Eli Parsons, originally from Connecticut and later Dedham, Massachusetts, who advertised his trade in the *Columbian Minerva*, a Dedham newspaper, in 1799 and 1800. Effecting a partnership with Calvin Whiting of the same city, in 1803, he expanded his business to include manufacture of japanned ware, sugar boxes of different sizes, bread boxes, graters, flour boxes, harts and rounds, gill cups, etc., in addition to the tinware already mentioned. In 1806, Whiting and Parsons invented a patent machine for working tin plate which immediately effected an increase in the quantity of tinware produced and considerably lowered its prices; though three years before this invention prices seem to have been very reasonable— a tin kitchen selling for $3.25 and a skimmer for $.17.

Cooking utensils sold by other tinsmiths at this time included: the bake kettle with three legs, handle, and tight cover, shaped like a shallow dish, which was covered with coals and placed before the open fireplace—another style had hooks which fastened to a coal grate; the pie heater, resembling the present day tincake cover, with half the side missing; the tin bonnet, resembling a bun warmer and used to heat pies and bake apples; and the plate warmer, in which plates were stacked in racks and kept warm in front of the fire.

Ca. 1839, Peck's machine for making tinware gave further impetus to the tin industry, which by 1850 became one of the most thriving enterprises in Massachusetts. Leading manufacturers who successfully adapted their products to the current public demand for low priced, machine manufacture included: Roswell Gleason (1799–1871, at Dorchester), Thomas Smith (1791–1876), and David B. Morey (1807–1882), both of Boston, Timothy Bailey (1785–1852) and James Harvey Putnam (1803–1855), partners at Malden.

The following kitchen objects made by anonymous craftsmen are representative of the types of devices for which tin was used, their distribution, date and design:

- A coffee pot, natural color, punched design, early nineteenth century, of Pennsylvania German make, now at the Metropolitan Museum.
- Another of the same period, also with punched design, and the lower part of its spout fluted.
- A nursing can or bottle, shaped like a coffee pot, with handle, horizontal spout, flat lid, made of wrought tin in Pennsylvania, nineteenth century.
- An egg cooker, attributed to Thomas Clark, silversmith of Hingham. (Now owned by W. W. Lunt)
- A reflector baking oven with spit, nineteenth century.
- A Springele mold of sheet tin, oblong, partly filled with clay in which are six intaglio designs (monkey, dog, goat, cow, kicking horse, bison) within squares made by double-line divisions—L. 4 3/8", W. 6 1/8". The Pennsylvania Germans who used this cake mold to make St. Nicholas Day cookies, ca. 1850, employed various other designs in similar molds—flowers, leaves, ladies, babies, bunnies, birds, etc.
- Tin candle sticks and candle boxes for an extra supply of candles, made to hang on the wall, New England, 1680.
- Candle holders of sheet tin, saucer type, New York, late seventeenth and early eighteenth century. (New York Historical Society)
- Tinder box, with candle socket, Pennsylvania, ca. 1740.
- Candle molds, some for single candles, others for as many as six to sixteen, used in all the colonies in the eighteenth century.
- Various sheet tin lamps and lanterns, ca. 1650–1850, used throughout the colonies.

The painted tin tea-pots, coffee-pots, mugs, canisters, fruit dishes, waiters, bread trays etc., known as *toleware,* produced by Pennsylvania German craftsmen and Zachariah Stevens of Westbrook, (now Stevens Plains) Maine ca. 1810–1875, were, as inexpensive imitations of japanned ware, intended for dining room rather than kitchen use.

Kitchenware of miscellaneous materials

A number of interesting objects that find no place in the foregoing classification of wood, glass, ceramic and metal wares included:

- Leather fire-buckets to fight fires, and fire-sacks for saving valuables. The earliest official mention of fire-buckets occurs in a Providence decree of 1754, requiring each householder to provide "two good leathern buckets" on penalty of being fined twenty pounds sterling. The fire-sacks, made of stout linen or canvas, four feet deep by two feet wide, bore the names of their owners. The general use of both articles probably dates much earlier than the middle of the eighteenth century.

- Bee finders' boxes and bellows for smoking bees into unconsciousness (beeswax was used to harden candles).

- A washing machine, ca. 1860, with crude wooden pump to squirt soap on the clothes.

- A hand operated vacuum cleaner, ca. 1880.

- Black birch brooms.

The last three items are at the South County Museum, R.I.

Bibliography

Andrews, Charles M. - Colonial Folkways, A Chronicle of American Life in the Reign of the Georges. New Haven, 1919.

Andrews, Edward Deming and Andrews, Faith. Shaker Furniture. New Haven, 1937.

Barck, Dorothy C. - The Society's American Household Exhibition, in *The New York Historical Society Quarterly Bulletin* vol. *xvii,* no. 2. April 1933, pp. 27–37.

B., J. E. - South County Museum (R.I.) in *The Chronicle of Early American Industries Association,* New York, Mar. 1939, vol. II, no. 8, p. 61.

Beecher, Miss Catherine E., A Treatise on Domestic Economy, For the Use of Young Ladies at Home and at School. Revised Edition. New York, Harper and Brothers, 1845.

Bishop, J. Leander - A History of American Manufactures from 1608–1860. 3 vols. 3rd edition revised and enlarged. Philadelphia, Edward Young and Co., 1868.

Blodgette, R. H. - *Communications,* in the *Chronicle of the Early American Industries.*

Boas, Ralph Philip and Burton, Katherine - Social Backgrounds of American Literature. Boston, Little Brown and Co., 1933.

Bonney, Annie Maria - Old Pots, Trammels and Trivets, in the "White House Built for Twins," in Scituate, Mass. In the *House Beautiful,* Boston, Dec. 1919, vol. XLVI, pp. 360–1, 399.

Bridgeport Brass Company - Seven Centuries of Brass Making. Bridgeport, Conn., 1920.

Burgess, Fred. W. - Chats on Household Curios. New York, Frederick A. Stokes Company 1914.

Burris, Evadine A. - Furnishing the Frontier Home, in *Minnesota History,* June 1934, vol. 15, no. 2, pp. 181–193.

Carrick, Alice Van Leer - Collector's Luck or A Repository of Pleasant and Profitable Discourses Descriptive of the Household Furniture and Ornaments of Olden Time. Boston, Atlantic Monthly Press, 1919.

Carrick, Alice Van Leer - Collector's Luck in the Kitchen, in *Country Life,* Garden City, N.Y. November 1929, vol. LVII, no. 1, pp. 42–43, 86–87.

Catalog of Antique Articles on Exhibition at Plummer Hall, Salem, December 1875. Printed for the Ladies Centennial Committee.

Catalog of a Loan Collection of Ancient and Historic Articles, Exhibited by the Daughters of the Revolution of the Commonwealth of Mass., Copley Hay. April 19–20–21 1897 Boston.

Chaffee, Grace E. - An Analysis of Sectarian Community Culture, with especial Reference to the Amana Society, in *Antiques,* New York, August 1929, vol. XVI, no. 2., pp. 114–118.

Chapin, Howard, M. - Fire-Sacks and Fire-Pockets, in *Antiques,* Boston, Mass., vol. 7, no. 3, pp. 128–129.

"The Colonial Kitchen," Household and Cooking Utensils of Bygone Days, in *The Antiquarian,* March 1924, vol. 2, no. 2, pp. 22–23.

The Colonial Kitchen, as Portrayed by a Collection of Antiques at the Baltimore Museum of Art by Mrs. Miles White, Jr., in *Good Furniture Magazine,* Grand Rapids, Mich., March 1924, vol. 22., p. 127–8.

Cordell, H. M. and Haigh, H. A. - The Henry Ford Collection at Dearborn, in *Michigan History Magazine,* Lansing 1925–1927, vol. 9, pp. 17–35, 338–356; v. 10, pp. 37–48, 384–399, 582–592; vol. 11, pp. 61–72, 581–603.

Cornelius, Charles Over - Early American Furniture. N.Y., The Century Co., 1926.

Cotterell, Howard, Herschel - The Evolution of the Trencher, in *Antiques,* New York, January 1930, vol. 17, no. 1, pp. 40–41.

Depew, Chauncey M. (Editor) - 1795–1895, One Hundred Years of American Commerce. 2 vols. New York, D.O. Haynes & Co., 1895.

Dow, George Francis - The Arts and Crafts in New England, 1704–1775. Topsfield, Mass., The Wayside Press, 1927.

Dow, George Francis - Domestic Life in New England in the seventeenth Century. Topsfield, Mass., The Perkins Press, 1925.

Dreppard, Carl W. - Oh, das Marzipan in *Antiques,* Dec. 1932, vol. 22, no. 6, pp. 218–220.

Dyer, Walter A. - American Iron, brass and Copper, in the *New York Sun,* Sat. March 29, 1930.

Dyer, Walter A. - Early American Craftsmen. New York, The Century Co., 1915.

Eberlein, Harold Donaldson and McClure Abbot - The Practical Book of American Antiques. Garden City, New York, 1927.

Evan-Thomas, Owen - Domestic Utensils of Wood, XVIth to XIXth century. London, 1932.

Faust, Albert Bernhardt - The German Element in the United States. 2 vols., N.Y., The Steuben Society of America, 1927.

Felt, Joseph B. - The Customs of New England. Boston, 1853.

Fish, Carl Russel - The Rise of the Common Man. N.Y., The Macmillan Co., 1927.

Gould, Mary Earle - Early New England Woodenware, in *Antiques,* New York, February 1937, vol. XXXI, no. 2, pp. 68–72.

Gould, Mary Earle - The Pantry Shelves of 1840, in *Old Time New England,* Boston, Mass., July 1935, vol. XXXI, no. 1.

Haberlandt, Dr. Arthur - About Cake and Butter Molds, Translated by A. S. Levetus, in *The Studio,* London, July 1923, vol. 86, no. 364, pp. 35–41.

Hamilton, Alexander - Report on the Subject of Manufactures, made in his capacity of Secretary of the Treasury, on the fifth of December 1791. Philadelphia, William Brown, 1827.

Hart, Albert Bushnell - American History Told by Contemporaries. Vol. 1. N.Y., The Macmillan Co., 1910.

Hazen, Edward - The Panorama of Professions and Trades; or Every Man's Book. Philadelphia, Uriah Hunt, 1836.

Index of American Design. Data Sheets, New York City, 1936–1939.

Jones, Francis Arthur - Art in Gridirons, in *International Studio* 1898, vol. 4, pp. 99–103.

K., H. E. (Keyes, Homer Easton) - Braziers as Collectibles, in *Antiques,* New York, September 1933, vol. XXIV, no. 3, pp. 106–107.

Keyes, Willard Emerson - Those Endearing Old Charms, the Taproom Furnishings of the Past, in *Antiques.* New York, January 1924, vol. V, no. 1, pp. 13–18.

The Kitchen. (New Books and True Books for the Young, no. 5.), New York, Samuel Raynor, no. 76 Bowery (n.d. - ca. 1850?).

Knittle, Rhea Mansfield - Early Ohio Ironwork, in *Antiques,* New York, July 1936, vol. 30, no. 1, pp. 20–21.

Landis, H. K. - Hex Marks as Talismans, in *Antiques,* October 1936, vol. 30, no. 4, pp. 156–157.

Langdon, William Chauncey - Everyday Things in American Life 1607–1776. New York, Charles Scribner's Sons, 1937.

Lathrop, William G. - The Brass Industry in the United States. Mount Carmel, Conn. 1926.

Lathrop, W. L. - Stove Plate from Batsto Furnace, New Jersey, in *Bucks County Historical Society Collection of Papers,* Easton, Pa., 1917, vol. IV, p 382-4.

Leslie, Miss (Eliza) - The House Book: or a Manual of Domestic Economy, 7th Edition. Philadelphia, Carey and Hart, 1844.

Lindsay, J. Seymour - Iron and Brass Implements of the English House. Illustrated by the author. Introduction by Ralph Edwards. London and Boston, The Medici Society, 1927.

Mercer, Henry Chapman - Ancient Carpenters' Tools, in *Old Time New England,* vol. 15, no. 4; vol. 16, nos. 1-4; vol. 17, no. 2, 4; vol. 18, no. 3; vol. 19, no. 1. Boston, July 1924-1928.

Mercer, Henry Chapman - Notes on Forgotten Trades, in *Bucks County Historical Society Collection of Papers,* Meadville, Pa., vol. V, pp. 207-211.

Miniter, Edith - When Women's Work Was Never Done. Illustrations from the Collection of Miss E. O. Beebe, in *Antiques,* New York, September 1926, vol. X, no. 3, pp. 205-208.

Miniter, Edith - When Treen Ware Was "The" Ware, in *Antiques,* New York, December 1930, vol. XVIII, no. 6, pp. 504-507.

Morison, Samuel Eliot and Commager, Henry Steele - The Growth of the American Republic. 2 vols. New York, 1937.

Myers, Gustavus - History of the Great American Fortunes. New York, 1936.

"New England Kitchen" (illust.), in *The Antiquarian,* New York, April 1926, vol. 6, no. 3, p. 29.

Nutting, Wallace - Carved Spoon Racks, in *Antiques,* June 1925, vol. 7, no. 6, pp. 312-315.

Nutting, Wallace - Furniture of the Pilgrim Century, 1620-1720. Framingham, Mass., Old America Co., 1924.

Nutting, Wallace - Pennsylvania Beautiful. Framingham, Mass., Old America Co., 1924.

Peirce, Josephine H. - Cooking Stoves, in The Chronicle of Early American Industries Association, New York, March 1939, vol. II, no. 8, p. 57.

Prime, Alfred Coxe - The Arts and Crafts of Philadelphia, Maryland and South Carolina. Series 1, 1721-1785; Series 2 1786-1800. The Walpole Society, 1929 and 1932.

Rawson, Marion Nicholl - Country Auction. New York, E.P. Dutton & Co., 1929.

Rawson, Marion Nicholl - Candle Days, The Story of Early American Arts and Implements. New York, The Century Co., 1927.

Raymond, W. Oakley - Early American Iron Utensils, in *The Antiquarian,* New York, April 1928, vol. 10, no. 3, pp. 59-61, 80.

Robinson, Jane Teller - The Kitchen of the Colonial Home, in *House and Garden*, New York, August 1924, vol. 46, pp. 78–79, 90.

Romaine, Lawrence B. - Basket Making, in *The Chronicle of Early American Industries Association*, March 1939, vol. II, no. 8, p. 57.

Sprague, William B. - A Private Collection of Early American Implements, in *Old-Time New England*, Boston, Mass., July 1933, vol. XXIV, no. 1, pp. 3–14.

Spruill, Julia Cherry - Southern Housewives before the Revolution, in *The North Carolina Historical Review*, N.C. Historical Commission, Raleigh, N.C., January–October 1936, vol. XIII, no. 1, pp. 25–46.

Stearns, Elinor - A Kitchen of 1825 in a Thriving New England Town, in *The Granite Monthly*, The Granite Monthly Company, Concord, N.H., August 1923, vol. 55, no. 8, pp. 390–4.

(Stebbins, L.) Eighty Years' Progress of the United States, by Eminent Literary Men. Published by L. Stebbins, Hartford, Conn., 1869.

Stillwell, John E. - Crolius Ware and Its Makers, in the *New York Historical Society Quarterly Bulletin*, New York, July 1926, vol. X, no. 2, pp. 52–56.

Swan, Mabel M. - Artisan Leaders of 1788, in *Antiques*, New York, March 1935, vol. 27, no. 3, pp. 90–91.

Vanderbilt, Gertrude Lefferts - The Social History of Flatbush and Manners and Customs of the Dutch Settlers in King's County. New York, D. Appleton and Co., 1899.

Van Vick, J. Cornelius - The Romance of Cabinet Woods - Gum and Cedar, in *Good Furniture Magazine*, Grand Rapids, Mich., September 1928, vol. 31, pp. 164–168.

Washington, W. Lanier - An Early Household Device, in *Antiques*, Boston, Mass., August 1925, vol. 8, no. 2, p. 89.

Washington, W. Lanier - Apple Parers, in *Antiques*, Boston, Mass., Nov. 1925, vol. 8, no. 5, pp. 282–285.

Watkins, Lura Woodside - Early Fire making Devices, in *Antiques*, Boston, Mass., March 1929, vol. XV, no. 3, pp. 209–211.

Webster, Thomas (assisted by the late Mrs. Parkes) - Encyclopedia of Domestic Economy, with Notes and Improvements by D. Meredith Reese. New York, Harper and Bros., 1845.

Woodhouse, Samuel W., Jr. - Colonial Craftsmen of Philadelphia, in *Art and Archaeology*, April 1926, vol. XXI, no. 4, pp. 182–6.

Wray, Henry Russell - Skewers - Neglected Antiques, in *International Studio*, New York, vol. 79, no. 323, April 1924.

Wright, Richardson - Hawkers and Walkers in Early America, Strolling Paddlers,

Preachers, Lawyers, Doctors, Players and Others, From the Beginning to the Civil War. J. B. Lippincott Company, Philadelphia, 1927.

Zukofsky, Louis - American Ironwork 1585–1856, Index of American Design, Federal Art Project, New York City, 1938.

Zukofsky, Louis - American Tin Ware, Index of American Design, Federal Art Project, New York City, 1938.

Louis Zukofsky

April 3, 1939

Apr 28/39

L. Z.

Editorial Notes

* before 1750. . . . right.] before 1750; another mold . . . of 1830; resembling a contemporary . . . Magazine, he carries . . . right

† Owner,] owned by

PART TWO

Radio Scripts and Research Notes

V. Radio Scripts

1

Broadcast No. 1: "The Henry Clay Figurehead"

Music: "The Wayworn Traveller"
(Fade)

Announcer: Station WNYC presents "The Human Side of Art," a series of radio broadcasts by the Index of American Design of the New York City WPA Art Project. Today's program is entitled, "The Henry Clay Figurehead," by Mr. Louis Zukofsky, who will be interviewed by Mr. _____.

Int.: - I am very happy to take part in the first of these broadcasts which feature the work of the Index of Design. The artists, research workers, and writers of the Index, a division of the New York City Art Project, are preparing for publication a monumental history of American handicrafts. The whole field of manual and decorative crafts in America will be summed up in colored and black and white plates together with written descriptions of the objects rendered.

The Index of American Design promises to be a new history of our country from the earliest days down to the present revival of handicrafts.

Today Mr. Zukofsky will tell us about the Henry Clay Figurehead. I take great pleasure in presenting Mr. Louis Zukofsky _____.

Mr. Zukofsky: -* In objects which men made and used, people live again. The touch of carving to the hand revivifies the hand that made it.[1] Old wood

---

1. This conceit of mutability has correlatives throughout "A" and in the prose as well—the endurance of craft, the human communion it potentiates, etc. Compare, for example, "The best way to find out about poetry is to read the poems. That way the reader becomes something of a poet himself: not because he 'contributes' to the poetry, but because he finds himself subject

[149]

and weathered polychrome once painted over it—the means of past industry.

Looking at a ship's figurehead of which the idea has been oversimplified only to appear as of today, we wonder how this *thing* could have faded so quickly from men's minds, forgetting that we probably had no opportunity to see it before.

For old things are lost, destroyed, stored away in attics and cellars, sold—accumulate the dust of antique shops and museum cases. Only an enterprise like "The Index of American Design" can bring them back to the people.

As pictures, yes, and as facts. They still exist, because they existed. And because rendering the truths they were to the people who made and used them becomes part of the factual material of the artist's drawing.

A drawing of a ship's figurehead becomes a guide not only to all ship's figureheads that preceded it, but a reason for creating sculpture in our time.[2] It ceases to be a museum piece or a collector's item as soon as the form and color of the drawing help to circulate its image among people. They *must* admire, and demand an effort from contemporary art that will yield a comparable pleasure to the living.

Int.: - Which reminds me, Mr. Zukofsky, did ships' figureheads have a use and if so, why were they discontinued?

Mr. Z.: - Yes, at least one authority on ship building claims that ships' figureheads were more than decorative. During the Renaissance they were no mean problem in marine engineering—calculated to balance the high prow over the waters. It is obvious why they went out of fashion, when low steel prows came into use. But perhaps there were no artists to work steel figures with the same genius as wood. Saint-Gauden's designs are said to have been

---

to its energy" (*Prepositions* 23), and "Measure, tacit is. / The dead hand shapes / An idea . . ." ("*A*"-12, 131).

2. The Index project ambition could be characterized as conserving the national patrimony (Nadel, "A Precision of Appeal," *Upper Limit Music* 113). For Zukofsky, conservation and reproduction consistently lead to renewed creation, from "Poem Beginning 'The'" through *Bottom* and "*A*"-22, as Zukofsky uses literature as occasion and source for his own poems (and takes a similarly "free" approach to translation as extension of original creative process). This orientation has its correlative in *A Test of Poetry:* "Folk art occurs with inevitable order as part of the growing history of a people. Its technique is the result of their lives, their enterprises. . . . *But* the *essential* technique of folk art (*not* the technique of rhyme scheme, four line stanzas, etc.)—its simplicity, its wholeness of emotional presentation—*can* serve as a guide to any detail of technique growing out of the living processes of any age" (70).

responsible for the figurehead on the stern of Admiral Dewey's flagship at Manila, the U.S.S. *Olympia,* launched in 1900. Subsequently, the Navy Department found no room on their ships for figureheads. The effect of officially dispensing with them became habit and the end of an art many ages old. With the exception of connoisseur yachtsmen, who can afford to commission artists, no one thinks of figureheads anymore in a practical sense.[3]

But as you know, Mr. _____ there are all kinds of uses. The practical sense of material intention has many guises. The Egyptians and the Phoenicians used figureheads to affirm the identity of the ship, to symbolize its personality and to entice the proper god as protector. On the prows of Chinese junks there were eyes to make the ship go. And if a ship can have eyes, why not let it have an ibis or a dragon head, or the head of a powerful animal, or the bust or the full figure of a hero, as ambassador to see it from the land to the open sea and back to safe harbor. The Romans used many busts and full figures. Which brings us to our Henry Clay figurehead.

Recalling Clay, Webster, Calhoun and the others in the old Senate Chamber, the historian Henry Adams[4] wrote: "Senators wore a blue dress coat or brass buttons; they were Romans." The cue to his meaning is in several other statements, to the effect, that when in good temper, the Senate resembled a pleasant political club. It was a Senator's attitude that mattered. The Clay figurehead is *all* attitude. A young face, as in the days of his Democratic leadership in Congress, when he advocated his "American System." A system of national progress with emphasis on the building of canals and highways, on internal improvements and a high protective tariff, it was in more than one sense a Roman system. But for the costume the Clay figurehead might be that of a Roman. True, the costume recalls the Kentucky days. But Kentuckians, says Adams again, acted on motive of personal dignity. So did Brutus. Henry Adams' grandfather, John Quincy, appreciated the fact

3. Through its pun on the modern, figurative sense of "figurehead" and the suggestiveness of the many "kinds of uses" that follows, this passage calls attention to the contemporary situation of a craft or art classed as without practical use and thus a luxury item for the privileged. The Index project and Zukofsky's poetics—"folk poetry . . . is not the property of the few 'arty,' but of everybody" (*A Test* 103)—resist this specialization, even if they grant that figureheads like poetry are "after all for interested people." In *"A"*-12, within a list headed "The kinds that were": one finds the reminder of "A ship's figurehead" (192).

4. An edited version of Zukofsky's Columbia master's degree essay "Henry Adams: A Criticism in Autobiography" (1924) appears in *Prepositions.* See Barry Ahearn's "The Adams Connection" (Carroll F. Terrell, ed., *Louis Zukofsky: Man and Poet* 113–27) for more.

that his Secretary of State, Mr. Clay, was a good, practical political manager, an honest and a loyal man, besides being a gentleman, but noted that he was defective in elementary knowledge and had a very undigested system of ethics. Look close at the Henry Clay figurehead. The attitude of the orator looks forward to the Presidency, for which he was nominated three times, twice against Jackson and once again against Polk—never to attain it.

Clay's disappointment is almost a clue to the origin of the figurehead. It may not have been a figurehead at all. Found near Poughkeepsie, it may have been the totem of a "Henry Clay Club" in that town, the birthplace of his running mate, Talmadge, in 1844. Attempting to beat Polk's campaign and sincerely desiring to avoid war with Mexico, Clay hedged that year on the annexation of Texas. He received a crushing defeat, losing the Northern vote and New York State in his fear of losing the South.

Int. - Then, how has this carving come to be known as the Henry Clay figurehead, Mr. Z?

Mr. Z.: - That is another story—tragic. Ludicrous at the same time. One summer day, July 28, 1852, sometime before the Steamboat Inspection Act had put an end to the outlandish racing of steamers on the Hudson, the steamer "Henry Clay" trying to outrun the "Armenia," known to be a faster boat, met with disaster. True, the "Henry Clay" had kept ahead of her rival most of the way down from Albany, but the Currier and Ives print records at what cost. So did Russell Smith who saw her wrecked from a window of his Riverdale estate. He tells us that "Down the stream with fearful rapidity came what seemed a mass of living fire! It was the steamer *Henry Clay*. Beneath her rolled the waters of the Hudson; above and around the forked flames darted forth; while at the same moment a hundred human voices rent the air with their shrieks." There is also a contemporary newspaper account, Mr. _____, which I would be happy to have your read for corroboration.

Int.: - Thank you, yes ". . . when near Yonkers, while three or four hundred human beings were little dreaming of danger, a black smoke was seen to issue from the center of the boat near the pipes. Almost immediately the pilot turned his craft and headed for the shore. The steamer struck head on; and as the fire broke out in the center, and the breeze blew off shore, those on the stern of the boat had either to leap into the water or perish in the flames. One of the passengers who had reached the shore, said, that as he turned he saw the flames envelop a fine lad, standing on the verge of the upper deck, seemingly uncertain whether to perish by fire or by water. The flames and thick

FIGURE 2. Henry Clay Figurehead

smoke seemed to wrap around him like a winding-sheet, till he disappeared and is now no more. Another gentleman informed us, that he saw a mother take an infant in her teeth by its clothes, to have the babe come on top when she rose to the surface, and approach the edge of the boat to leap into the water. By a sudden jerk of the boat the child fell from the grasp of the mother, and also disappeared. There were several other heartrending incidents connected with this sad affair."

I see! I believe I can answer the question I asked you, myself. Our Henry Clay figurehead could very well have been at the prow of this steamboat, its namesake, and survived the disaster. According to the newspaper account the fire broke out amidships, and the wind was blowing aft when the boat headed shoreward. The figurehead could thus have escaped being burnt.

Mr. Z.: - Exactly.

Int.: - I take it that the newspaper account I have just read was discovered by a research worker on the Index. Has he decided if our carving was really a figurehead, or simply a political totem?

Mr. Z.: - The historian may decide only when he as all the facts. We don't have them yet. The imagination may favor one or the other.[5] Let us look at the figurehead again. It stands on a shield-shaped base. The front face of the shield is composed of thirteen gilded stars in relief on a blue field. Below are four red vertical strips in relief on a white field. The figure's two button dress coat is shining black, deep blue in the light. The arm at the breast is the orator's, the arm of the *Great Pacificator.* The other arm at the side is necessarily of wood curving stiffly out from the body. Only a forefinger of the splayed hand touches the coat. This hand that fought two duels belongs to the man who employed every movement of his body with grace and skill, even in using his snuff box. Maybe that decorative button in the white shirt front, now weathered gold, is a stud pin of the days of Boss Thurlow Weed who refused him the nomination in 1840.[6] The wing collar holds the head high. Clay's eyes were gray, but the eyes of the figurehead appear to be blue. A fine head, and the full lips, smiling, seem to have forgotten Clay's fears of threats of disunion from the South and the grasping after public lands.

Imagine this figurehead thrown up on the beach when the steamboat "Henry Clay" is wrecked. The living Henry Clay had died only about a month before in Washington. The drowned bodies that evening are covered with green boughs. At one side of a gloomy arch over the railroad is the wreck, the bow still slow[ly][†] burning. Above the arch, twenty persons try to identify the dead. The surface of the Hudson is broken by the oars of a few men still dredging for bodies. A full moon dimly lights up the water and the hills, perhaps shines directly on the figurehead miraculously safe on the embankment. In the Hudson, are the bodies of Henry Jackson Downing, the most famous of our landscape architects, and of Maria Hawthorne, sister of

---

5. This alludes to a longstanding interest in the relation between fact and imagination or between the occupations of historian and poet. The essay "Henry Adams" (*Prepositions* 97–99) poses the same opposition (see Ahearn, "The Adams Connection," *Zukofsky: Man and Poet*); the later work (*"A"*-22 and *"A"*-23) subsumes historical facts within the poem seamlessly.

6. "Boss Thurlow Weed" may be a conflation of Thurlow Weed (1797–1882), a journalist and founder of the New York Whig Party, and the more infamous William Marcy "Boss" Tweed (1823–1878), a Democrat and grand sachem of New York's Tammany Hall. It was the Whig Party for which Henry Clay stood as presidential candidate in 1832 and 1844.

Nathaniel Hawthorne. His story "Drowne's Wooden Image" evoked a figurehead as unforgettable as the Henry Clay. The coincidences seem to demand that the carving be a ship's figurehead and not a totem. Those interested may wish to decide for themselves. The figure is at the Downtown Gallery. It stands fifty-three inches high overall. But in good sculpture it is the proportion that matters. This figurehead is the life-size Henry Clay.
Int.: - Thank you Mr. Zukofsky. Ladies and gentlemen, you have been listening to Mr. Louis Zukofsky who spoke on the "Henry Clay Figurehead" in the first of a series of broadcasts by the Index of Design of the New York City WPA Art Project. These programs are directed by Carl Miller.

If you wish to obtain a copy of today's broadcast, send your request in writing to the Department of Information, New York City WPA Art Project, 110 King Street.
Next week Mr. Zukofsky will speak on _____.

Nov 16 / 39

LOUIS ZUKOFSKY   EXAMINATION: SENIOR INFORMATION SPECIALIST
202 COLUMBIA HTS., BROOKLYN, NY‡   PRESS AND PUBLICATIONS

NEW YORK CITY WPA ART PROJECT
INDEX OF DESIGN

SERIES: THE HUMAN SIDE OF ART

2

Broadcast No. 2: "American Tinsmiths"

Writer: Louis Zukofsky
Director: Carl Miller

Music: "The Wayworn Traveler"
(fade)

Announcer: - Station WNYC presents "The Human Side of Art," a series of broadcasts by the Index of American Design of the New York City WPA Art Project. Today Mr. Louis Zukofsky is heard in the second program of this series in a talk on American Tinsmiths. And now I take great pleasure in introducing Mr. Louis Zukofsky.

Mr. Zukofsky: - Last week, in our talk on the Henry Clay figurehead we did not mention the carver. The reason is simple. We do not know anything about him, not even his name.

The names of early American craftsmen are few and far between. Their lives were isolated. But those who gather information for the Index of American Design are aware of the fact that lives devoted to building up industries against odds must have produced many personalities. We know a good deal, for example, about that successful maker of glass and ironwork, Henry William Stiegel, a German immigrant to Pennsylvania, who affected the title of "Baron." Self-styled "Baron" Stiegel died impoverished at the end of the Revolutionary War, but he was a great business man in his heyday. He went so far as to supply sugar planters and refiners with castings for the West India trade. He invented a wood-burning stove constructed of ten cast-iron plates, known by his name as the "Baron" Stiegel ten-plate wood stove. He introduced still another stove, as an improvement over Benjamin Franklin's open hearth. The "Baron" immortalized his features in one of his stove-plate castings stamped with a portrait called "The Hero"—"Baron" Stiegel himself, of course. The "Baron" seems to have been especially proud of his career as a manufacturer of stoves. Some of his extant stove-plates till show the legend—dimly, thru wear and rust:

> Baron Stiegel ist der Mann
> Der die ofen Machen Kann.

Translated into a Briticism, this German verse may read:

> Baron Stiegel is the cove
> Who can make an iron stove.

There were other personalities, perhaps more extreme than the "Baron." In a future program, we may have occasion to delve into the legend or truth of the existence of an early owner of Colebrook Furnace in Pennsylvania. There is an early poem about him, in which, returning from a fox-hunt, enraged by the falseness of his hounds, he drives them all with whip in hand into the blazing tunnelhead.

The majority of American craftsmen who worked in tin remain anonymous. There exist only the wares they made and some few traditions connected with these. Thus, some verses from an editorial in the *Boston Evening Post* of 1783, remind us that in colonial days people carried punched tin boxes filled with hot coals, from room to room, or house to house, to keep warm. These particular verses, however, record a religious objection to the use of these so-called footwarmers in churches. The censorious lines read:

> Extinct the sacred fire of love
> Our zeal grown cold and dead,
> In the house of God we fix a stove
> To warm us in their stead.

A scrap of paper, dated Boston, June 6, 1803, and signed Divan B. Yate, tin pedlar, to Major Whiting, rising tinsmith of the time, gives an idea of how the tin business was run. We quote: "Major Whiting, Sir, I have a distant relative a very clever fellow but as I have no tin here any more than I want myself if you have any tin sold if you will let him have a lead out of your shop I will be answerable for the same and in so doing you will oblige him and me and not disoblige yourself. I am yours, etc."

We have the facts of the careers of the brothers William and Edward Patterson, called also William and Edgar Pattison, in Richardson Wright's lively book, *Hawkers and Walkers in Early America.* Natives of County Tyrone, Ireland, the Pattersons or Pattisons, came to this country in 1738 and settled at Berlin, Connecticut, to practice the trade of whitesmiths—as they still call it in Great Britain—or as we say, tinsmiths. They began importing, from England, sheets of the "best charcoal tin" packed in oak boxes, about 1740. These were really sheets of pure iron, two feet square and of the thickness of a sheet of paper. The Pattersons worked at home first cleaning the sheets of their black oxide by immersing them in sulphuric acid. Afterwards they dipped them in cisterns of melted tin, to plate them. The first objects they made were cooking utensils—vessels beaten out on anvils, with wooden mallets. They sold their wares from house to house in Berlin and to the settlers of nearby communities.

The nineteenth-century poetess Emma Hart Willard later celebrated the launching of their enterprise in poetry which might readily inspire a talented writer of copy in a modern department store. Enthusiastically, Miss Willard wrote: (N.B. read in character)

> "Oh, what's that lordly dish so rare,
> That glitters forth in splendour's glare?

Tell us, Miss Norton, is it silver?
Is it from China or Brazil or . . . . ?"
Then all together on they ran.
Quote the good dame, "'Tis a tin pan,
The first made in the colony.
The maker, Pattison's jest by
From Ireland in the last ship o'er.
You all can buy. He'll soon make more!"

And the Patterson brothers did manufacture more tin plate than the local purchaser could buy. And they kept the secrets of their trade to themselves until 1760, when they first began training several apprentices. The Revolution, however, cut short their supply of sheet tin until the close of the hostilities. After that, the business of William and Edward Patterson continued to expand with the help of the tin peddler, better known as the Yankee peddler.

He was an institution—the original Yankee peddler. He was not a mere house to house canvasser, but the forerunner of modern business enterprise, an important means of interstate communications and for the inland distribution of goods. At first, he travelled on foot or on horseback, his dishes and other wares packed in two tin trunks weighing about fifty pounds each, slung over his back or over the back of his horse. About 1790, his journeys became less burdensome. Carts with high box tops, in which his wares were placed on shelves and on racks, were substituted for his back. His sales territory, no longer limited to Berlin, Farmington, and other nearby towns in Connecticut, became country-wide. Timothy Dwight records meeting Yankee peddlers in places as far apart as Cape Cod and Detroit, Canada and Kentucky. The Yankee peddler is known to have made and paid his way to St. Louis and New Orleans. Scheduled trips covered two main routes—a northern and southern.

Since five tinsmiths working at Berlin, Connecticut, could supply enough wares for 25 peddlers on the road, about that many would leave in the late summer or fall for the South, and stop at the important manufacturing centers of Richmond, Charleston and Savannah, thru the winter. The peddlers carried their tinkers' tools with them, in addition to their wares, in case their patrons required repairs on old utensils. If necessary, the peddlers would even accommodate themselves to local demand, and manufacture to order on location. During these winter stops they would now and then exchange a share of their profits with an agent of the Connecticut tin manufacturer who gave them new supplies for the spring and summer routes taking them back north. On their return journey they travelled by water if possible, and gathered in New York. Not forgetting that a used wagon was as good as an old horse, it was there they sold their teams and wagons, and returned on foot or horseback to Connecticut. By that time it was summer again.

The peddlers who took the northern route started out early in the spring, made their way to Albany, then to the important Bay State ports, and up, as far as Montreal. Temporary tin factories were set up during the summer months in most of these centers.

A good deal of the Yankee peddler's trade was barter. Long before the turn of the eighteenth century, he had exchanged iron pots for potasheries for linen, and so on down the line, to suit his immediate bargain. Now at the dawn of the nineteenth century, he could get almost anything for his lanthorns, sconces, sand shakers, footwarmers, tea caddies, bread trays, tin boxes painted and unpainted, candlesticks and candle moulds. But Hugh Peters' Connecticut poem can tell you more about that than we can. He called it "A Yankee Lyric," and I shall try to read it in character:

A Yankee Lyric

There is, in famous Yankee-land
A class of men ycleped tin-peddlers
A shrewd, sarcastic band
of busy meddlers;
They scour the country through and through,
Vending their wares, tin pots, tin pans,
Tin ovens, dippers, wash-bowls, cans,
Tin whistles, kettles, or to boil or stew,
Tin dullenders, tin nutmeg graters.
Tin warming-platters for your fish and 'taters!

In short
If you will look within
His cart,
And gaze upon the tin

> which glitters there,
> So bright and fair,
> There is no danger of defying
> You to go off without buying.
>
> One of these cunning, keen-eyed gentry
> Stopped at a tavern in the country
> Just before night,
> And called for bitters for himself, of course
> And fodder for his horse:
> This done, our worthy wight
> Informed the landlord that his purse was low,
> Quite empty, I assume, sir, and so
> I wish you'd take your pay
> In something in my way.

Let us interrupt here at the expense of breaking into the suspense of the narrative. We have already mentioned candle molds today. In those days people cast their own candles in molds. A landlord was well stocked with these no doubt. He needed a constant supply of candles for his guests. And it is quite unnecessary for us to say that candle molds were used for no other purpose than to make candles. But the landlord of our poem tried to be smart:

> Now Boniface supposed himself a wag—
> And when he saw that he was sucked,
> Wasn't dispirited, but plucked
> Up courage and his trousers too!
> Quoth he t'himself, I am not apt to brag
> 'Tis true
> But I can stick a feather in my cap
> By making fun of this same Yankee chap.
> "Well, my good friend,
> That we may end
> This troublesome affair,
> I'll take my pay in ware,
> Provided that you've got what suits
> My inclination."

"No doubt of that," the peddler cried,
Sans hesitation.
"Well, bring us in a pair of good tin boots!"

But, alas, our landlord was not smart enough for our Yankee peddler:

"Tin boots," our Jonathan espied
His landlord's shanks
And giving his good genius thanks
For the suggestion,
Ran out, returned, and then—"By goles!
Yes, here's a pair of candle-moulds!
They'll fit you without question!"

Announcer: - Thank you Mr. Zukofsky. You have been listening to Mr. Louis Zukofsky who spoke on "American Tinsmiths," the second in this series of broadcasts by the Index of Design of the New York City WPA Art Project. These programs are directed by Carl Miller.

If you wish to obtain a copy of Mr. Zukofsky's talk, send your request in writing to the Department of Information, New York City WPA Art Project, 110 King Street. Next week Mr. Zukofsky will speak on _____.§

3
A Pair of New York Water Pitchers**

Cue, Theme Song, Announcer, Miller, as on previous programs

Miller: - Today, Mr. Z. will tell us about a pair of silver water pitchers made in New York State, about 1817.

Mr. Z.: - There is something in the act of drinking water, for the thirsty, which at all times takes on the character of a sacrament. This feeling should be especially keen in the case of a pair of water pitchers - the subject of our talk today. The originals of the plate made by The Index of American Design, may still be seen at the New York Historical Society. They are of silver and engraved with a scene which represents the freeing of the slaves in New York State.[7]

7. A substantial passage was cut from the autograph, presumably by Zukofsky himself: "As objects to pour water and drink from you can see they are a visible sign of an inward and spir-

Our water pitchers symbolize a struggle. Or rather, presented by the Manumission Society of the State of New York to Joseph Curtis, as a testimonial of his efforts towards obtaining the passage by the New York State Legislature of the Manumission Act of March 31st, 1817, they are dedicated to the triumph of that struggle. The South was not the only partner in the Confederation whose revolutionary statesman hated slavery and yet kept slaves. All thru the Revolution, the estate of Morrisania owned by Governor Morris, as well as other estates in New York City, were manorial holdings, plantations which did not grow cotton, of course, but which were run by slaves.
Miller: - I believe slavery existed in New York even before the English, didn't it, Mr. Z.?
Mr. Z.: - Yes, Mr. Miller. The Dutch introduced slavery into New Netherland. But, at that, they brought the slaves over in ships captured as prizes from their enemies. The boweries or plantations of the West India Company occasionally employed Negroes, but generally they were not of much use to the Dutch traders. They were practical business men and auctioned off the slaves they did not need, or exchanged them for beef and pork. Otherwise, their slaves, history tells us, received good treatment. Manumission was not rare, as attested by land patents of the time.

The English conquerors of New Netherland firmly instituted slavery in New York. Enough slaves were brought into the colony so that the colored population equalled the white in New York City, by 1712. The economic evils which slavery engendered here brought on the so called Negro Plot, a horror of incendiarism and bloodshed inspired by the worst white elements, which New Yorkers today are happy to forget with other unfortunate annals of over 200 years ago.

But we must not forget also that the law then was harder on black and white alike. The criminal laws of 1776 in the free colony of New York still

---

itual grace. Somehow they remind one of that touching episode in the life of King David, when battling the Philistines in Bethlehem, he longs for a drink of the water of the well by the gate of that city. When three of his mighty men broke thru the host of the Philistines, and drew the water out of the well and brought it to him, he would [not] drink it. Pouring it out to the Lord, instead, he said "Be it far from me that I should do this; is not this the blood of the men that went in jeopardy of their lives?"

Compare "A"-8: "This water you almost got killed for, / Said David, do you expect me to drink it?" (93). Somewhat earlier, "Thanks to the Dictionary" references David's exploits. Thanks to Mark Scroggins for drawing attention to this.

followed the unjust code of the mother country. Sixteen crimes, among them, arson, forgery, robbery and housebreaking, received the death penalty for the first offence.[8] John Jay's first term as governor saw the death penalty limited to murder, treason and stealing from churches.[9]

With such reforms, the movement in New York State towards complete manumission kept pace, and acted as the forerunner of abolitionism. An act of 1781 provided that Negroes who enlisted in the Revolutionary army be given freedom at the end of three years. An act of 1785 prohibited the importation of slaves. The following year, the law gave freedom to the slaves of forfeited Tory estates.

In 1788, the slave code was completely revised. The purchase of slaves for export was forbidden under penalty of £100. Slaves were allowed trial by jury in capital cases. Masters were permitted to set free without bond any able bodied slave under fifty. However, the number of slaves in New York City, in 1790, was still 21,324. The Act of March 29, 1799, providing that male children born of slaves after July 4th of that year be freed at the age of twenty-eight, and female children likewise at the age of twenty-five, would secure only gradual abolition.

Miller: - Your words "would secure only gradual abolition," Mr. Z. leads me to suspect that it was right then and there that the Manumission Society which later presented our water pitchers to Joseph Curtis, considered it proper to begin its efforts in earnest.

Mr. Z.: - Well, Mr. Miller, you anticipate the conscience of the members of the society by about a decade. The Manumission Society of the State of New York was not incorporated until 1808, when there were still 15,000 slaves in New York. It had to extend its life in 1824. It was not until 1841 that property rights in slaves brought into the state by travellers or tempo-

---

8. The following text has been deleted from the autograph but is legible: "A number of felonies demanded the death penalty on a second offence. English law in New York remained unrevised during the Revolution, but was administered with less severity. By ..." Apparently in Zukofsky's hand, this and several subsequent ommissions convey an overt politics or editorializing tone.

9. This text deleted from the autograph: "Still, the jails were overcrowded, men and women were often placed in the same cells. The prisoners were permitted to gamble, and the wardens sold them drinks at a profit. Insolvent debtors made up a considerable percent of these prisoners. But New York was one of the first states to reform the law in this respect. An act of 1784 provided for the release of a debtor if credtors representing three-fourths of his debt petitioned for his freedom."

rary residents ceased to be recognized and all slave ownership was prohibited. Curiously enough, most of the slaves in New York had been owned by Federalists, members of the party of financial aristocracy. Yet its leaders Jay and Hamilton advocated manumission. The fact is slavery was not profitable in New York, except to the artisan who feared Negro competition in the craft industries. The aristocracy could afford to be benevolent, especially when free Negroes voted for their former masters' party.

Miller: - I don't suppose, Mr. Z., that all these facts are shown in the engraved scene on our water pitchers.

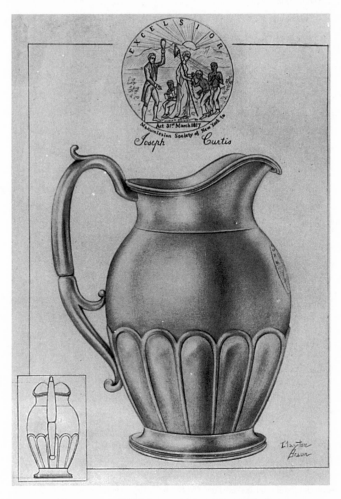

FIGURE 3. N.Y. Manumission Water Pitcher

Mr. Z.: - Not all. Yet the scene sums them up adequately. At the top of the circle we see the device EXCELSIOR over a sun rising over mountains and the rays spread down into the foreground, a level tract of land. Here, a female figure bearing the standard of Liberty unshackles a slave boy somewhat stooped before her. Another shackled boy stands knock-kneed, and with the palms of his hands together, raised, ready to be freed, behind him. Sheltered behind Liberty, sits a Negro lad, his hair well-combed, reading from a book in a contemplative attitude—his eyes looking out over the book. To the side of him, with the familiar, inspiring gesture of one arm forward, palm turned upward, as if to say "behold," and the other arm high, holding a light, stands the immediate liberator in coattails. Perhaps his model was Joseph Curtis, to whom the water pitchers were presented. In any case, after the material events of history, the symbolic scene is touching only because it is tranquil.

Joel Sayre of Southampton, L.I., who lived from 1778 to 1818, made these large silver pitchers with barrel shaped sides, short necks, wide mouths, and stylized repoussé petals from the base to the center of the body meeting the engraved scene. He had successive establishments at 437 Pearl Street, New York City in 1802, at Maiden Lane, New York City, from 1805 to 1811, and in Cairo, New York in 1818.

Now another aspect of slavery, concerning not Joel Sayre directly, but a member of the Sayre family before him, disturbs the composure of our silver water pitchers. History has minimized the evils of this brand of slavery by giving it another name—indenture. History tells us that servitude under indenture was neither lifelong [n]or hereditary, that the term of servitude lasted only a number of years, and that the basis on which it was instituted was contractual, at least in form. The indenture or contract as such was not important in itself. It was a legal form, like a lease signed today. Many indentured servants went thru their term of service without the formal legal papers. Indenture was really a means by which the growing mercantilism of the seventeenth and eighteenth centuries employed government sanction to transfer labor to undeveloped colonies.[10] The difficulty of securing a per-

10. This passage deleted from the autograph: "Advocating the theory that wealth consists not in labor and its products, but in the quantity of hard gold and silver in a country, mercantalism encouraged mining and importation of these metals by the state and the exportation of goods as well as people who make them. It sought to increase national rather than common individual interests, and as such especially influenced the legislative policy of Great Britain. The first extensive use of indenture, as of modern slavery, occured in the British colonies."

manent labor force in the British colonies, so that the mother country might be enriched by the money resulting from its industry was easily solved by the difficulties of the labor situation at home. Here, according to a seventeenth-century text, there was "such penurie and want, as (great numbers of peoples) could be contented to hazard their lives, and to serve the years for meat, drink and apparel only, without wages, in hope thereby to amend their estates." Most of the colonial indentured servants were the Scotch poor who had migrated to North Ireland where they had fared no better than at home. Thousands of these poor agreed to serve for transportation. They made the perilous crossing in the hope of finding relatives or friends to redeem them so they might set up in business or as craftsmen for themselves. For the most part they did not find such friends, and served not one year, but usually four or five. The average term of service in New York State was about seven years, and children served longer.[11]

Those who suffered the trials of indenture were ultimately not social outcasts. Its terms approached apprenticeship rather than slavery. But nearly fifty percent of the white immigrants to the colonies came over by the legal means of indenture, many of their own free will so-called, but many because they had been kidnapped, or in the term of those days *spirited* away or robbed of their money and placed in irons by the ship captains during their voyage. Indenture did not fully die out in this country till well on in the 1830s. Slavery replaced it in the South.

The treatment of indentured servants varied widely and produced varying results. Good masters often allowed their daughters to marry their servants, or, in any case, made good mechanics, laborers and peasants out of them. At the end of their term of servitude they went off with their "freedom dues," "apparel," or an axe or two hoes and a year's supply of corn. Sometimes they were rewarded with fifty acres of land. Bad masters who took advantage of the prerogatives of the *indenture,* carried out their right to inflict—we quote "moderate corporal punishment" and prevented their servants from engaging in trade or marrying without their consent. Those who dared became fugitives. The newspapers of those days are filled with advertisements requesting the return of runaway indentured servants.

Paul Sayre, born probably at Southampton, Long Island, like Joel Sayre,

11. This passage deleted from the autograph: "The supply of indentured servants was increased by immigrants from the German Palatinate in the eighteenth century."

but very likely sixteen years earlier, was such a runaway advertised for in the *Connecticut Courant and Weekly Intelligencer* of Hartford, May 9, 1780. We say "probably" and "very likely" because the advertisement tells us very generally that Paul Sayre was a native of Long Island. But he was a goldsmith, and earlier Sayres were among the original settlers of Southampton, and their family name may, again very probably, have been derived from the word *assayer*—i.e. originally, the Sayres were probably *assayers* of gold and silver in the royal mint. Furthermore, the genealogy of the Sayre family records a Paul Sayre, born at Southampton, Oct 22, 1760, who married in 1784, and was a silversmith by profession and a member of the church in 1800. The crafts of goldsmithing and silversmithing were usually practiced together. Or, perhaps, Paul Sayre, silversmith, if he is the same as our young runaway goldsmith's apprentice, learned silversmithing later in life. If he is the same, he is one of the indentured servants whom fortune favored. We find him married only four years after his escape. It would be a fair guess to conjecture that the cause of his running away was the fact that he eloped. For the sake of a story one might play with this guess. In any case, the runaway could not very well have been the father of Joel Sayre, the maker of our manumission water pitchers, who was born in 1778, six years before Paul Sayre's marriage. He may, however, have been an uncle or a first cousin of the silversmith who, in 1817, commemorated the freeing of the slaves in New York State, in the engraved scene already described. Whatever Paul Sayre's relationship to Joel was, he was a Sayre, and the shadow of servitude modified his early career, as it modified the later career of Joel Sayre. The advertisement in the Connecticut paper seeking Paul's return is complete but quick, living with the breathlessness of the chase itself. It reads: " Runaway from the subscriber, on the evening of the 23rd instant, an apprentice boy, named Paul Sayre, a native of Long Island, by trade a goldsmith, about nineteen years of age, about five feet, seven or eight inches high, a thick set fellow, flat nose, light eyes, thick lips, somewhat pitted with small pox, has short, straight dark hair. Had on and carried with him a broadcloth blue coat, jacket and breeches, a light-brown short coat, with open sleeves, a jacket about the same colour, a blue great coat, a pair of brown broadcloth breeches, a large castor hat almost new, two pair of shoes, a pair of open work silver shoe buckles and sundry other articles of clothing.†† Whoever will take up said apprentice, and return him to his master, or confine him so that he shall get him again, shall have One Hundred Dollars Continental

Money Reward and all necessary charges paid by James Tiley." Then, there follows an N.B. Note well: "It is supposed that he will endeavor to go on to Long Island. All masters of vessels are forbid carrying him off, or harbouring or concealing him at their peril. Apr. 24, 1780."

Well, where else would indentured servant Paul Sayre wish to run to, but to his native Southampton, where he would be free. Having considered our manumission, silver water-pitchers, and knowing now that the Continental money offered as reward for Paul Sayre's return was in time not worth the trouble of trapping him, we hope that Paul Sayre escaped to that freedom which his later namesake visualized for another race.

Louis Zukofsky
Nov. 7 / 39

NEW YORK CITY WPA ART PROJECT

INDEX OF DESIGN

SERIES: THE HUMAN SIDE OF ART

4

Broadcast No 4: Binnacle Figure—1851

Music: "The Wayworn Traveller"
(Fade)

Announcer: - Station WNYC presents "The Human Side of Art," a series of broadcasts by the Index of American Design of the New York City WPA Art Project. This is the fourth program of the series with by Mr. Louis Zukofsky, who will be interviewed by Mr. _____.

Interviewer: - I take great pleasure in presenting Mr. L. Z.

Mr. Z.: - Thank you, Mr. M_____, and may I present you with this dodger?

Interviewer: - *Thank you* but what did you call it?

Mr. Z.: - A dodger, or handbill, a throwaway.

Int.: - Well, is it something people dodge, or accept and then throw away?

Mr. Z.: - That depends on people's curiosity. On the Index of American Design we don't throw away such things, even if it is an advertisement. We're pleasantly surprised, and since there's an address on it—T. S. And J. D. Negus, Nautical Instruments, 69 Pearl Street, New York City—we go over to where it comes from and bother them for more surprises.

Int.: - Sixty-nine Pearl Street? That's downtown somewhere?

Mr. Z.: - Yes, in the heart of the shipping district, and on the very site of Peter Stuyvesant's Government House, near where his barge used to lie at anchor in the river ready for a pleasure trip at a moment's notice. It's downtown, Mr. _____, where one is always likely to trip over some old object of New York history, or for that matter history that isn't always confined to our part of the world. Downtown, you come across a ship's figurehead that travelled the seven seas, or an old tobacconist sign, or whatever carving used as a sign for whatever old shop. 69 Pearl Street is downtown, which is both the shipping and financial district and which still can bring forth an old sea dog, who will just as soon as not buttonhole a financier and tell him a story.

Int.: - True enough, Mr. Z., I'm sure one can meet with more than one seadog there and even a few cigar-store Indians. They always give me a kick, and I'm especially fond of a group of three figures, I once came across in a book; —I believe it was an English Tobacconist sign representing a Dutchman, a Scotchman and a sailor, explained by a rhyme which read—

> We three are engaged in one cause
> I snuffs, I smokes, and I chaws![12]

But I don't suppose the nautical instrument makers who issued this handbill would be advertised by a tobacconist sign? I'd say the sailor on this handbill or throwaway, which you people don't throw away but study, is a ship's figurehead. However, this thing in his hands makes it different. I know what it's used for: to hold a compass. But since I'm only a landsman, I can't remember its name just now.

Mr. Z.: - Yes, it's a stand or case for a ship's compass. It's a binnacle, and is placed usually before the steering wheel. It's an instrument of navigation, not of spirit force like a ship's figurehead which, according to the legends of some sea dogs may or may not affect the course that a ship takes. After the landsman hears the sea dog's story which has animated a ship's figurehead with a life that is more than ligneous, a figurehead still remains an ornament,

---

12. Inclusion of such doggerel recalls Zukofsky's engagement with similar forms, though most examples in his poems precede or supersede this work (e.g., "It's a gay li-fe" 43; "15: I'm a mosquito" 121 *Complete Short Poetry*.)

a decoration, at best a fine piece of sculpture. But a binnacle, with its lamps, hood, quadrantal spheres, magnet-chamber, compass-chamber, and window which admits light to the latter is a thing of science. There is nothing occult about it, and it must reflect on the scientific accuracy of its makers. This particular binnacle head and compass, which the sailor shown on the handbill is holding, was made by T. S. and J. D. Negus, the present owners of the figure. And it's not a figurehead, but a binnacle figure. He's a piece of very interesting sculpture alright, but he was made to hold up the binnacle. He's a sailor whose job was not to let the fancy roam, but to be practical about this particular task. See how his hands, the worked hands of a seaman, with their closed fingers, fit carefully around the binnacle. It rests partly on his chest, so that his head is perforce tilted back on his thick neck. He looks a bit romantically heroic that way, yet he has a round, full face like a practical young Benjamin Franklin, hair combed back from the forehead and falling down to the neck but brushed away from the ears. The words MIND YOUR HELM are painted in black on the front brim of his regulation, turned-up sailor hat. And the helm, as you know, is the steering apparatus of the vessel.

But the job of holding up the binnacle is not left entirely to his extended hands and distended chest. The main weight of the binnacle rests on his raised left knee, so that he must support himself standing on his right leg with his left foot on the top of a water barrel made of oak staves and iron hoops. The entire weight of the figure, water barrel, and binnacle is placed on a heavy elliptical base of teakwood. The sailor carved in the round is also of teakwood.

Int.: - Is that an imported wood, Mr. Z.?

Mr. Z.: - Yes, the teak is a large East-Indian tree, the durable timber of which is highly valued in ship building. The whole effect of the carved sailor of teakwood, teak base, and water barrel of oak staves and iron hoops is somehow to incarnate one past epoch of American industry—a time when the trades of cooper, making casks and barrels, the shipbuilder, carver and sailor were intimately related. This binnacle figure, to me, recalls St. John de Crevecoeur's *Letters of an American Farmer,* in which he describes Nantucket of about 1782. In Nantucket, he wrote, men carve wood, all are brought up to the trade of coopers, there is always "a piece of cedar in their hands" and "while talking" they "will make bungs or spoyes for their oil casks, or other useful articles." Our binnacle figure must have passed the Nantucket lightship at least once in the days of fast racing clipper ships, before he came to be used as a shop sign for nautical instruments.

Int.: - Then he is a shop sign, after all, Mr. Z.? I'll have to go down to Pearl Street, one of these days and take a look at him myself. Meanwhile, would you mind telling us more about him? I don't mean to buttonhole you as a sea dog, but maybe there's a story which makes our binnacle figure just more than a sign.

Mr. Z.: - He has been a shop sign. But I should complete my description of him. He's fifty-nine inches tall. He was made by a figure carver employed at Westervelt Yard, East River, New York City, in 1851, for the clipper ship *N. B. Palmer,* built in the same year by Low Brothers. I am not sure that Westervelt Yard is the same as Low's Wharf listed in Stoke's "Iconography of Manhattan Island," as on the East side of Old Slip. But if it is not, the two shipping yards must have been pretty close. Finally, carved out of wood, our sailor is not one of those dead, pseudo-classic plaster casts.

Int.: - Has he been painted, Mr. Z.? It's polychrome which always makes wood sculpture seem especially alive.

Mr. Z.: - Yes, he's painted, that is, first he was coated with gesso and then painted from sailor hat to shoes. His hat is white. His shirt is dark navy blue. His wrinkled duck breeches are white. Two rings at the bottom of the binnacle hang like large earrings on either side of his bent left knee holding it. These rings are part of the binnacle structure, of course, not decoration. His duck breeches break well over his black sailor shoes. Aside from this expected costume, his face is flesh color, his hair is brown, his eyes are deep ultramarine. The eyes give the sea dog his story.

Int.: - Did he travel much—I mean the binnacle sailor.

L. Z.: - Our sailor didn't travel very much—in fact, I should say not over several months, but his eyes did. Especially at night and on dark days in heavy fogs. The eyes looked from port to starboard, when a sailor happened to be looking from the stern towards the bow. And they glanced up at the sky especially when a sailor was minding his helm.

Int: - ‡‡Was it a case of delirium tremens on the part of the sailors of the clipper ship *N. B. Palmer?*

Mr. Z.: - No, they were sober mostly as sailors always are in their jobs. Stern discipline was unquestionably necessary on the high seas, then as now, and especially in those times of expanding American trade, when ships were making speed records with their cargos on the way to and back from the far ports of the world. You will probably remember that, in 1852, the year after the N. B. Palmer was built, Commodore Matthew Perry opened Japan to commerce. But our story is, after one trip to China for tea, this binnacle figure was removed from the *N. B. Palmer,* because the sailors insisted that his eyes would move, especially at night, and distract their attention from the compass or whatever they were doing or watching.

Int: - Well, how do you mean?

Mr. Z.: - I don't know, but just what I said, that's the story. It may seem all the more strange when I add the fact that our research workers have found that the *N. B. Palmer* was lost at sea. It was this fact that made us question how the binnacle figure could have survived at all. When we asked the descendants of the original firm of T. S. and J. D. Negus, they told us how the figure was removed previous to the disappearance of the *N. B. Palmer,* because of the sailors' preoccupation with the eyes.§§ Of course, they were, as I said, deep ultramarine eyes, the kind that would glint in any case, mercurial and bulging somewhat under arch eyebrows, and that may have produced the effect of rolling from side to side.

Int.: - Yes, he evidently was a bit arch, our binnacle sailor. Would you say any of the lights of the ship had something to do with the peculiarity of his eyes?

Mr. Z.: - Maybe the light falling on them from the mast.

Int.: - How about the binnacle lamps?

Mr. Z.: - Possibly. They were two oil lamps which slid, port and starboard, into the upper hemispherical hood of the binnacle. This had a glazed elliptical opening in the part thru which the compass was read as it swung inside a lower hemispherical bowl. But I should say the lamps were constructed so as to illuminate the compass directly, not to reflect up to the eyes of the figure. Anyway, after its one trip on the *N. B. Palmer,* it served for many years as a shop sign, and no passerby ever again saw its eyes move.

Int.: - Where is the binnacle figure of the sailor now?

Mr. Z.: - Inside the nautical instrument shop, still holding the original brass binnacle. But you wouldn't know that it's brass today. It's been painted with aluminum paint after eighty-eight years.

Louis Zukofsky

Dec. ~~12~~/ 39

18 (turned in)

NEW YORK CITY WPA ART PROJECT

INDEX OF DESIGN

SERIES: THE HUMAN SIDE OF ART

5

Broadcast No. 5: "Wide Awake" Lantern and Eagle

Music: "The Wayworn Traveller"
(Fade)

Announcer - Station WNYC presents "The Human Side of Art," a series of broadcasts by the Index of American Design of the New York City, WPA Art Project. This is the fifth program of the series, with Mr. Louis Zukofsky, who will be interviewed by _____. Mr. _____.

Interviewer: - I take great pleasure in presenting Mr. L. Z.

Mr. Z.: - Artists of the Index of American Design have made renderings of a swinging square lantern and a swinging torch in the form of an eagle, both of which were probably carried on poles in the torchlight parades of Abraham Lincoln's presidential campaign of 1860. The originals of the drawings are interesting objects in themselves, but they have additional significance as items in the history of lighting devices. Furthermore, tho electricity has replaced the fuels which they burned and they have remained unlit for many years now, they still have the virtue of being able to light up social currents of a past which the electric light by contrast has placed in the shadows.[13]

One supposes that the idea of the torchlight procession is, in the history of gregarious civilizations, almost as old as the idea of the torch. For wherever people gather for conviviality or a common purpose, wherever crowds are on the move, so to speak, and there is night, there is also illumination.

Our colonial forbears originally stuck a candle on a spike. That was the essential idea of the old rushlight holders subsequently made in various shapes, cast or forged by the country smith. The spike was replaced by the socket, in which the candle could be fixed more conveniently. Lanterns came into popular use about 1700, with the development of lard and fluid fuels. The invention of new lighting devices from about 1830 to 1860 marked the heyday of other fuels, such as whale oil, camphene and kero-

13. Figurative editorializing on "light" recalls the refrain "light lights in air" of the contemporaneous *"A"*-8.

sene. The torchlight processions thru our American history made use of all of these fuels and lighting devices in whatever convenient forms for a parade. It would be hard to say exactly when the first one took place. The picturesque firemen's torchlight procession goes back at least a hundred years. It was probably not the forerunner but the contemporary of the political torchlight parade. And together they marched, bringing events into urban and civil life, displaying devices, attracting slogans and people, celebrating civic improvements with joy, and the strife of hard-won elections down into the early years of this century. We still have our Firemen's Night, our electioneering and Election Day celebrations, but usually without the old lanterns and torches. It would be a shame to use the old ones and risk harm to them—for with time they have attained another use. They now serve to date the old parades.

Int.: - How precisely do they do that, Mr. Z.? For example, you said a while ago that the lantern and torch which you will discuss today go back to Lincoln's 1860 campaign. How do we know that? And what distinguishes them from earlier examples, if any are still extant.

Mr. Z.: - Well, one early lantern with nail-punched decorations, rendered by the Index of American Design, carries the words "Old Hickory Forever." We know that these words were a slogan of Andrew Jackson's Campaign of 1828. It is very likely that this lantern was used in a torchlight procession. The lanterns used in General Harrison's campaign of 1840 bear devices similarly appropriate, and portraits of the presidential candidate. We know also for a fact that Harrison's campaign began an upsurge of torchlight processions. Intensification of political issues caused that. Our swinging square lantern and torch mark almost the end of the struggles of abolitionism. We know that similar lanterns and torches were carried by the *Wide Awakes* in the torchlight processions of 1860. So it is fair to assume that our lantern and torch are a *Wide Awake* lantern and torch.

Int.: - Yes, but what or who were the *Wide Awakes*?

Mr. Z.: - They were an outgrowth of the abolition movement. On Feb. 25, 1860, Cassius M. Clay, noted abolitionist from the South came to Hartford, Conn., to spur the Republicans to greater efforts for the cause. He was greeted by a torchlight parade of young party members—their lanterns gay and their torches flaming. But they were careful enough to wear caps and long black capes of oil cloth to protect their heads and clothes from the dripping oil.

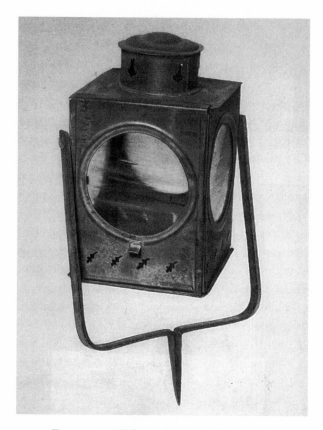

FIGURE 4. "Wide Awake" Lantern (square)

Int.: - Curious, one often wonders why political organizations choose such outlandish costumes. Aside from mass effect, the Wide Awakes at least had an immediate practical reason.

Mr. Z.: - Yes, but the costumes took, as always. The immediate consequence of this small Republican demonstration was the organization of the Hartford Wide Awakes, limited at first to fifty members under the leadership of James S. Chalker. But Mr. Chalker not only had in mind the rallying of young Hartford to Lincoln's cause. He knew how to get them and how to advertise. I quote from one of his current newspaper notices:

> Wide Awakes Attention
> Organize and Close up your ranks
> Young men say you will

The undersigned will furnish the original Hartford uniform consisting of Full Cape, first class glazed cap, Pitkin's celebrated patent torch and Wide Awake Eagle, at a lower rate than any other manufacturer.—Address James S. Chalker, Commandant Hartford *Wide Awakes, Hartford, Conn.*

As manufacturer of uniforms, Mr. Chalker won over some 500 converts by the end of the presidential campaign. They journeyed long distances to swell the rallying cries of torchlight paraders in other cities, marching for Lincoln. Wide Awake organizations sprouted throughout the country. Almost everywhere, the young men paraded with flags, torches and lanterns, and their glazed black caps were usually ornamented by a large brass eagle in front—the symbol which their eagle torches repeated.

The torch drawn by the artist in the Index of American Design is a fine example. It is made of tinned sheet iron into a kerosene receptacle in the form of a spread eagle in the half-round. That is, two sides of tinned sheet iron were fashioned on a template or stamped with dies in identical left and right modeling and soldered together along the edges. A brass, cylindrical wick support is screwed into the top edge of each wing. The entire eagle swings in an iron wire bracket looped at each side of the body under the [fit] of the wings and descending to an applied pole socket of tinned sheet iron. This eagle torch, 12 1/4" high and 9" wide, is now in the permanent collection of the New York Historical Society.

The "Wide Awake" lanterns are rarer finds than the torches. The lanterns are perhaps more interesting to the general collector of lighting devices, and easier to date, since a good number of them carry lettering or decorations, or both. Patriotic emblems, party symbols, names of candidates and clubs were painted on the circular window glasses of these square lanterns, some of which had colored panes, usually one red, one blue, and two white. The white panes were often decorated with etched designs. Other lanterns had two transparent glasses and two colored; still others had painted and decorated colored glasses, occasionally including green and purple.

The square lanterns used in Lincoln's campaigns were of two main types, as the torches, and known as stationary and swing. Both types were borne on the top of wooden poles. Our square lantern of today's talk, found in New England, and owned by Helena Penrose and J. H. Edgette, New York City, is one of the swing type. It is 8 3/4" high, 5" wide and 5" deep. Like the Eagle torch, it is made of tinned sheet iron, the most convenient substance to

FIGURE 5. "Wide Awake" Torch

handle of all [those available in the making of] early American lighting devices. The rectangular shape has circular glass panes above horizontal bands of oak leaf piercings in the four sides, one of which is a door sliding upwards. A cylindrical turret with a pierced design around its vertical sides is applied to the flat top. The lantern swings from opposite corners within a forked wrought-iron bracket forged at the bottom, center, into a pricket which was originally placed into the end of a wooden pole. All the oak leaf piercings I have mentioned helped the light to come thru, but the candle socket originally soldered to the flat bottom is now missing.

Int.: - Tell me, Mr. Z., were there organizations in the torchlight processions in Lincoln's campaigns other than the *Wide Awakes* and did they have other uniforms, insignia and lighting devices?

Mr. Z.: - Yes, there were other organizations. It was the historic season of ardor and exuberance in the annals of American torchlight parades. First, there were the Hamlin Guards of Portland, Maine, —all of them timber-drivers, all of them 6'4" in stockinged feet. To top themselves off, they wore huge bearskin hats over a foot in height, and each of them carried a huge axe, rallying around Lincoln. Then, there were the Bell and Everett Guards, with their torches and lanterns surmounted with tinkling bells. Then, there were the many other Republican Clubs: the Lincoln cadets, the Horse Guards, the Rail Splitters, the Maulers, the Giant Killers and the Union Zouaves.

The ranking officers of these organizations were often mounted. The costumes, as the names of the organizations have probably suggested to you, were by no means only black or drab. There were military uniforms of blue and gray with red trimmings. The costumes of the Union Zouaves followed the Oriental brilliance of the French Zouaves of Algeria. The caps of the marchers were usually of a color contrasting with the uniforms, and embellished with large eagles. Inverness capes were popular. Sleeveless, silver-enameled cloaks wrapped the lieutenants, and capes of gold cloth the captains.

As for lighting devices, in one torchlight procession, each man carried a flambeau which emitted eleven streams of fire. There were flickering torches and torch banners, chinese lanterns and transparent lanterns. Many of the latter had the pictures of the presidential candidate in color pasted or illuminated on the glass windowpanes. Huge transparencies, as they were called at the time, were constructed on wagons, lit up from within. The transparencies made of a framework of wood drawn on with cloth were also decorated with the portraits and names of the candidates. Volcano wagons emitted sparks intermittently from replica volcanoes. Small cannon, field pieces and fireworks, added to the detonations. Expected lighted tapers and kerosene lamps in the houses and hotels along the line of march reflected the gaiety of the young men marching for abolitionism.

The most spectacular feature of these torchlight parades was probably the lighting-up ceremony. For the *Wide Awakes,* like all the other groups of marching young men who were soon to fight a bitter civil war, assembled for the procession with all lights out. There they united in the night till at a given signal a cannon boomed. Only then, as a contemporary newspaper account tells us, did "a grand conflagration of torches, lanterns and lamps burst forth in bewildering light." It is in all this light that we must imagine the *Wide Awake* lantern and eagle torch talked about today.

Louis Zukofsky
Dec. 29 / 39

SERIES: THE HUMAN SIDE OF ART

6

Broadcast No. 6: Duncan Phyfe

Music: The Wayworn Traveller
(fade)

Announcer: Station WNYC presents "The Human Side of Art," a series of broadcasts by the Index of American Design of the New York City WPA Art Project. This is the sixth program of the series, with Mr. Louis Zukofsky, on behalf of the Index of American Design, speaking on the plates in black-and-white and color, on which the Index artists and researchists are working towards a definitive history of manual and decorative crafts in America. Today Mr. Z_____ will be interviewed by Mr._____. Mr._____.

Int.: - Thank you. Which of the many renderings by the Index of American Design form the subject of our talk today, Mr. Z._____?

Mr. Z.: - Today, Mr. _____, we have as many as eleven plates, all illustrating the furniture of the cabinet maker, Duncan Phyfe, at the height of his career in New York City, during the first three decades of our republic. The pieces are two end tables, a sewing table, a washstand, a sofa, three side chairs, a wing chair and two armchairs. They are not too great a number to talk about in the short time we have, when we consider that their style and intention are those of one man. There are similarities of construction. The subtle variations are in the decorative elements. But for one side chair, the frame and back rails of which are of cherry and one back rail of ash, the wood used in all these pieces is mahogany, evidently chosen for its hardness, fine grain, and reddish color. In the late eighteenth and early nineteenth centuries, making chairs was a specialized branch of the furniture crafts, different from cabinet making. Duncan Phyfe practiced both, but his entire attention seems to have been focused on furniture nearest related to the making of chairs. His main output embraced chairs, sofas and tables. These were the pieces his time and environment wanted. Having answered the question as to why Duncan Phyfe made certain furniture, we must now ask the question, for whom did he make it.

Int.: - Before you answer that, Mr. Z., would you mind telling me if Duncan Phyfe worked on all of his pieces himself?

Mr. Z.: - No, not all of Phyfe's furniture was made by his own hands. Authorities judge that only the pieces dated before 1825 were made by Phyfe himself. That is why all the Index plates illustrating his work are of that period. In the later years of his career, Phyfe employed over one hundred journeyman cabinet makers, wood-turners and carvers, and most likely did little, if any, work himself, tho he probably continued to draw his own designs. Thomas H. Ormsbee, in his "Early American Furniture Makers," tell[s] us, however, that two rough pencil sketches of chairs by Phyfe "illustrate the odd fact that [he] was a wretched draftsman. These sketches of his typical delicately executed lyre-back chairs were bunglingly done and lacking in perspective. With cabinet tools he was a master of line, but not so with paper and pencil."

Int.: - Curious. I understand, Mr. Z., that the furniture produced by the Duncan Phyfe workshop towards the end of his life, and done in the so-called later American-Empire and black walnut "Butcher" manner, was inferior in design to the work which the Index plates have rendered. Would you suppose, the fact that Duncan Phyfe was a poor draftsmen [*sic*] affected mistakes in the reading of his later designs on the part of his help. That is, you have already told us Duncan Phyfe did not execute his later design. If they were poor drawings, perhaps his cabinet makers did not grasp their master's intentions.

Mr. Z.: - Possibly. That's an interesting conjecture, but I do not know how we can verify it. On the other hand, we can safely say that Phyfe's rise as a business-man indicates that like all successful craftsmen, he must have held his thumb at the pulse of public taste. Phyfe is said to have hated the cumbersome pieces of furniture he had to make in his later years, but when he died he was worth nearly half a million dollars. When we remember that the population of New York City, only 60,489 in 1800 increased to 168,000 in 1825, and that the value of merchandising passing thru that port grew from 14 to 34 millions in a quarter of a century, —we can readily see that Phyfe began his career for a much more limited, and necessarily more specialized, public, than the one he was to end it for.

C. O. Cornelius, in his book on Phyfe, tells us that, in the qualities of the furniture which Phyfe made for the people of New York may be seen the results of various influences which distinguished the period not only in the city but along the whole seaboard. The demand for fine craftsmanship and materials, when Phyfe was making his best work and making it himself, arose directly from the increasing wealth of the population and the artistic appreciation they possessed. The economic revival after the War of 1812 was rapid; the unanimity of taste, the result of the growth of a compact metropolitan society. Its widening horizon, continues Cornelius, was shown in the European flavor of its taste, partially English in response to inherent British preferences, but French in many elements of form where fashion dictated intellectual content in the design.

The furniture of Phyfe's early Federal period was made to the specifications of the gentlemen of taste of that time. Phyfe's later work went to the burgher, whose taste was not refined but expensive, —showy, but neither original or creative. During the early Federal period, the emigrés of the French Revolution effected the taste of the American arts directly, tho in isolate instances. During the reign of the Emperor Napoleon between 1804 and 1815, the nobility of his court and the rising nouveau riche in America did not know each other too well, but in another fifteen years or so the style of the Empire furniture was to have its effect on the thriving middle-class American who had just got around to a so-called classic revival of heavy archaeological knickknacks.

All these varied trends of style, the outgrowth of developing economic orders, explain Duncan Phyfe's changing from the influences of Hepplewhite and Sheraton to Directoire and Sharaton, from these to the later American-Empire style and the final style of the black walnut furniture. His changing clientele demanded it. We must now outline Duncan Phyfe's career to show how these factors worked out in his life.

He was born, not in New York City, but in Loch Fannich in the northern highlands of Scotland, in 1768. He came form the Mackenzie clan who may have been shepherds, and spent the first fifteen years of his life with them in the rather desolate Scotch country. The family—Gabel Phyfe, his wife and six or eight children—immigrated to America in 1783 or 1784, the time when the successful end of the Revolutionary War opened up new opportunities for industry and trade. Two of the Phyfe children died during the hard voyage over. The family landed in New York but did not stop here, going immediately to Albany. In this growing town, Duncan, the second son, served his apprenticeship with an unknown cabinet maker or perhaps a coach maker, since the Scotch immigrants of Albany were doing very well then as coach makers.

From a study of the manuscript book of the enumerator who took the census of 1790 for Albany, Ormsbee, in his biographical matter on Phyfe, concludes that certain erasures were made to conform to a recent death in the family, probably that of Duncan's father. An entry shows that only two boys under sixteen were still at home, but none of the daughters. The Phyfe family was breaking up, and since in 1790, Duncan was 22 years of age, and according to the census not in Albany, he may have already returned to New York. Ormsbee's biographical sketch of Phyfe continues: "The first (New York) city directory of 1786 does not mention him, but the second of 1792 lists both Duncan and his brother John. Also this entry proves the family tradition that the name was originally spelled F-i-f-e. Brother John was a Carman living on Dey Street, and Duncan is listed as "joiner, 2 Broad Street." By the time the third directory was compiled Duncan Phyfe's days of discouragement and hard times are past. He is not any longer thinking of giving up and going back to Albany. Instead, he is the protégé of Mrs. Langdon, daughter of John Jacob Astor, the fur prince of New York. Now [that is, in 1794] he is listed as *'P-h-y-f-e, Duncan, cabinet-maker, 3 Broad Street'*.

"Family tradition has it that a schoolmaster suggested this change in spelling as a means of distinguishing the family from any other Fifes (F-i-f-e-s) that might come over from Scotland. Possibly this is so, but since brother John, the carman, clung to the old spelling of their name until 1800, when he is listed as John Phyfe [P-H-Y-F-E], coachman, we suspect that Duncan saw in this distinctive spelling a business advantage not to be overlooked by the man who was fast becoming the favored cabinet maker and furniture designer of New York. From 1800 on, all the Phyfes used the new spelling until 1828 when Martha, widow of William Phyfe, half reverted to the old style and spelled it F-y-f-e." And this is the story of the Phyfes changing their name as Ormsbee tells it. The researchists of the Index of American Design, in compiling their lists of American craftsmen, have further verified Ormsbee's facts by studying the New York City directories year by year down to the end of Phyfe's life in 1854.

Int.: - I notice that, in 1792, when Duncan spelled his name F-I-F-E that he had himself listed as *joiner,* but that when he changed the F-I- to P-H-Y he was listed as cabinet maker. Would you say, Mr. Z., that his adoption of the more distinctive name for his profession, like the more distinctive spelling of his name, was assumed with a view entirely towards business advantage?

L. Z.: - Well, Phyfe's biographers suspect that it was. But as I see it, the important aspect of his change of name and title of his profession represents a real change in the life around our cabinet maker. The fact is the designation of joiner no longer fitted the times. By 1806 his craft-standing *was,* as Phyfe's age called it, that of a cabinet maker. That year he moved his shop and home from Broad Street to adjoining buildings at 34 and 35 Partition Street, renamed Fulton Street for Robert Fulton in 1817. In 1811, Phyfe bought number 33 Partition Street, so that he now owned three buildings on the same side of the street—his workshop, showroom and warehouse, all designed in the fashionable Georgian manner. Shortly after, he purchased a house across the street from his shops, which was his residence until his death. From 1806 on, when Phyfe enlarged his business, his clientele consisted mainly of the wealthy and the distinguished. He received orders from the well-to-do of Philadelphia, Albany, New Jersey, the Hudson Valley estates, as well as from the rich of New York City. They demanded dining-room and drawing-room suites and it was dining-room and drawing-room pieces that he made for them for the most part, tho he occasionally accommodated them by furnishing kitchen accessories such as ironing and pastry boards, clothes horses, and servants' beds, and doing repairs. A man who sold mahogany chairs at $22 each, a sofa at $122, a Piere table at $265, a pair of card tables for $130 and charged $19.00 for packing this shipment to Charles N. Bancker of Philadelphia certainly merited the designation of cabinet maker according to the standards of his times.

I doubt if Phyfe was pretentious in changing his name. One can't be too sure, but his signature written in an old book now owned by Phyfe's great grandson F. Percy Vail shows the *h* in the late spelling of his name is rather shaky. The rest of the signature seems more certain of itself. Perhaps Duncan Phyfe never got used to the new spelling.

One thing is certain in his best years he was a distinguished and sincere craftsman. He imported the finest Santo Domingo and Cuban mahogany, his biographers tell us. And further: "West Indian exporters referred to their best timbers as Duncan Phyfe logs . . . He is said to have paid as high as $1000 a piece for them. The veneering which he used was cut under his supervision and applied with Peter Cooper's best glue."

He never advertised his trade, except for the listing in small type in the directories of New York City. He tended to his business and was solicitous about the welfare of his family. His brother Lochlin worked with him all his life and made several trips to England to select the ornamental brass for the Phyfe furniture. In 1837, his firm name was Duncan Phyfe + Sons; three years later, Duncan Phyfe and Son. He retired from business in 1846, selling his stock at auction, but continued to make presentation pieces for his family—always at the bench in his own shop—in the backyard of his home, for the remainder of his life. The notice of his death in the *Times* was brief: "In this city on Wednesday (i.e. Aug 16, 1854) Duncan Phyfe in the 86th year of his age." His will remembered his poor relations generously. It is doubtful whether most of the public remembered him then. The most public moment in his career seems to have passed quietly in 1825, when all New York turned out to celebrate the completion of the Erie Canal, in a dazzling parade led by trades and professions. Tho Phyfe is credited with having made the cedar boxes for the medals struck off for this event and the wooden casket for the bottles of water from Lake Erie sent to Lafayette, our cabinet maker did not march in this parade.

All his life he refused to sit for a daguerreotype, so that posterity owns no portrait of him. For that we must look again at the Index plates illustrating the characteristic reeded legs, wing*** trimmings, stamped brass handles, brass tipped with leaf carvings, dies carved with Prince of Wales feathers and other distinguishing marks of his furniture. The portrait of the craftsman he was is always apparent in the balance achieved between the vertical and horizontal members of his best pieces—between the lightness of their vertical lines and the contrasting heavier architectural lines of the horizontal.[14] And the symbol of his career is almost summed up in the horizontal curves of his table tops, chairs, seats and sofas—as Cornelius has noted, curves so slight as to escape detection, not geometrical curves, but free hand lines based on the geometrical. His best art, like his time, was given over to order and freedom, simultaneously as it were. Phyfe's furniture reflects the virtues of his life and age.[15]

Louis Zukofsky, Jan 11, 1940.

---

14. This compares with Zukofsky's later sense of 'the work' as sufficient autobiography, and anticipates the claims that will subsequently be made for his long poem *"A"*.

15. Zukofsky's admiration for Phyfe's work evidently exceeded the scope of his Index work. In a passage that apparently documents a domestic scene from the Zukofsky residence, *"A"*-12 describes a collage with an image of "'Duncan Phyfe's house, workshop and store'—" (239–40); it expressly analogizes Phyfe's workshop to the Zukofsky workshop "On the third floor / Of our Brooklyn brownstone."

SERIES: THE HUMAN SIDE OF ART

7
Broadcast No 7: Carpenters of New Amsterdam

Music: The Wayworn Traveller
(fade)

Announcer: Station WNYC presents "The Human Side of Art," a series of broadcasts by the Index of American Design of the New York City WPA Art Project. This is the seventh program of the series, with Mr. Louis Zukofsky, on behalf of the Index of American Design, speaking on the plates in black-and-white and color, on which the Index artists and researchists are working towards a definitive history of manual and decorative crafts in America. Today, Mr. Z_____ will be interviewed by Mr. _____. Mr._____.

Int.: - Thank you. Which of the many renderings by the Index of American Design form the subject of your talk today, Mr. Z.?

Mr. Z.: - Today, we have four plates, Mr. _____, each of them representing a *Kas* or cupboard done in the Dutch colonial style. Three of these pieces were made in the early eighteenth century. The remaining one is earlier, going back to 1675. We do not know where the eighteenth-century pieces were made. Presumably in New York. The cupboard of 1675 comes from Connecticut, the English joiners of which were then producing furniture along distinctly American lines, especially in the form of chests. When we compare our Connecticut Dutch cupboard with a chest, the earliest piece of American furniture of established origin, made by the English joiner, Nicholas Disbowe, we note certain resemblances of essential structure as well as ornament.

The construction is rectangular, determined it would seem by the simple way of life in the seventeenth-century colony, which did not yet require elaborate furniture. That the joiners had few tools may be guessed from the spare use of moldings, the little variety of turning, the general simplicity of the decoration attempted, and the solid effect of the pieces as a whole. The detail in both pieces is subsidiary to good proportion and the fitting of the parts.[16] It follows the architectural motifs of seventeenth-century European

---

16. This passage deleted from autograph: "All the early pieces of whatever origin are simplified versions of European pieces."

furniture, as in the panelling. It imitates the tulip and sunflower motifs which the English themselves took over from the Low Countries. And yet these pieces are American. Take our Connecticut cupboard, made out of pine and whitewood of the native soil. The tradition of the early American joiner, who is at the same time a carpenter doing the woodwork in houses, is already established. He must use the wood he *has;* hard wood to withstand greatest wear, soft wood where it is suitable or hidden. And the effect of the surface can be original—or American. The whitewood and pine produce lighter color effects, and these take paint differently. Our Connecticut cupboard, which has no open shelves but is entirely closed with a door, is painted with a conventional floral pattern on the top, sides, and end panels of the front. The painted side panels of oak show stylized leaves, rosettes, tulips, pine cones and fern. The center front panel, which forms the door attached by iron *H* hinges, is decorated with freely rendered trees—perhaps pines—some tall, some short. Their trunks are almost parallel uprights growing above each other so that the panel is divided vertically into three very similar scenes. The grain of the wood and the strokes of the paint give an atmospheric effect of cloud and wind somehow recalling New England landscapes in vignettes—tho the entire panel effects some of the characteristics of a Japanese screen.

Int.: - I take it, Mr. Z_____ that the Connecticut joiner who made this cupboard while attempting to be original yielded to his recollections of Oriental design then influencing the European continent?

Mr. Z.: - Very likely. But the other three cupboards shown in the plates are different, more characteristically Dutch colonial.

Int.: - Yes, I see, for one thing they are not entirely enclosed. They have open shelves, and drawers.

Mr. Z.: - Exactly. The open shelf cupboard was not used originally in the English colonies. The cupboard made by English joiners in America was intended mainly for storage. In the seventeenth century, the English settlers had little plate to show. But, the settlers of New Amsterdam displayed, beside their famous Dutch silver, porcelain and stoneware, the manufacture of which, spurred by Oriental importations, was considerably developed in Holland. This cupboard with the two open shelves, then, was probably made by a Dutch carpenter. Or rather, since it is an eighteenth-century piece, it was made by one who came strongly under the influence of Dutch carpenters. Perhaps he was a descendant of an early Dutch carpenter of New

Amsterdam. You may remember that trades were inherited in those days. In any case, this cupboard with two shelves, made of pine and oak painted in grizaille and with ornamental birds, fruits and flower wreaths, very much resembles in style this other of pine, painted gray-blue, with white floral design, molded cornice-ball feet, and two drawers below the cupboard compartment, now housed in the Van Cortlandt mansion in this city. The fourth cupboard made circa 1730 is a close relation, with its rectangular construction emphasized by two doors with molded panels, and pilasters at ends and center. This, too, probably stood in a Dutch mansion as elegant and as well-to-do as Van Cortlandt's.

All three of our eighteenth-century cupboards subsume in a sense the history of the development of this piece of furniture in the colonies. If we take these cupboards apart so to speak, we can very well see how authorities have traced the evolution of the cupboard, from a table for the display of cups and other vessels, to a piece of furniture with shelves, a closet and drawers, in the Dutch mansions of New York, to the familiar item of eighteenth-century New England kitchens—the pine cupboard with two lower doors opened by pull knobs, and with button fasteners in the open shelves of the upper part. So you see the original Dutch style went a long way. We can now only imagine what the seventeenth-century New Amsterdam cupboards looked like.

Interviewer: - But surely there still exists an early New Amsterdam cupboard, or Kas as you have called it, like our Connecticut piece of 1675?

Mr. Z.: - Well, perhaps there is one still to be found. But they do exist in the early inventories of goods owned by New Yorkers. One list of 1690 names a "Holland cupboard furnished with earthenware and purslin"—that is, porcelain—worth £15 pounds. But you see that, too, was after the fall of New Amsterdam.

Int.: - Too bad. I am led to suppose that since we know so little directly about the seventeenth-century "Holland cupboard" of New Amsterdam, that we must know next to nothing about their makers. I should imagine that they were an interesting lot, if their constitutions, tempers, and minds were as foursquare, and as solid and as stolid, so to speak, as their cupboards.

Mr. Z.: - I am glad to say that your regrets in this matter are unwarranted, Mr. _____. In fact, we know a good deal about the carpenters of New Amsterdam, and their characters were not always respectable or stolid.

Int.: - And how do we know that, Mr. Z.?

Mr. Z.: - Mr. Scott Williamson of the Index of American Design, who supervises its research on [furniture,] is responsible for the Index's lists of local craftsmen, [and] has looked up our Dutch carpenters in the early court records. In these he found the names of fourteen; also that they were not simply carpenters, but, at different times, glaziers, upholsterers, masons, shipbuilders, cabinet makers, chair makers, joiners, metal workers, merchants, dealers in real estate, policemen and politicians. Most of them never paid or collected their debts without a law suit. And, furthermore, most of them were given to drink! Mr. Scott Williamson's researches fully confirm an early traveller's description of New Amsterdam as "a city consisting most entirely of taverns and ale houses." That's rather a remarkable fact when we consider that New Amsterdam of 1653 had a population of only 1,120. It's a fact but hard to reconcile with the traditional picture of the industrious, sober Dutch burgher. Even in his choice of an occupation, the burgher seems to have drifted. One carpenter, Jan Cornelissen by name, not in Mr. Williamson's list of fourteen, seems to have been fed up by his trade and left Rensserlaerwyk upon hearing that the first teacher of New Amsterdam, Adam Roelandsen had quit his job after being charged with drunkenness. This was about 1639. Jan Cornelissen went down the Hudson to Manhattan where he taught school for ten years. In Albany, Jan's reputation had not been too good. He would lie drunk for weeks at a time. One need hardly repeat the charge that he was lazy. Perhaps his character improved in Manhattan, but our suspicion is that our city of ale houses must have been more tolerant of Jan's weak points. We were metropolitan in attitude even in those days.

To go back to Mr. Williamson's list: Frederick Arentsen was a turner, and *he* got into trouble. This is what the court record says of him: "The Schout (i.e. the Sheriff) complains of some misconduct and disrespect toward this W(orthy) Court, and the President complains and says, that the deft. has delivered in a very unreasonable a/c to the city. Deft. excuses himself. The W. Court condemns the deft. for his disobedience toward the Court in a fine of fl. 25 (florins), for the benefit of the poor, with costs, and the deft. shall make sufficient bowls for the use of the city, for which he shall receive as much as he was payed in the fort."

Int.: - I take it, Mr. Z., that the court record establishes the facts that Arentsen must have done construction work, probably carpenter's work, on the fort in New Amsterdam, and that he also turned wooden bowls.

Mr. Z.: - I believe you are justified in drawing these conclusions from the record, Mr._____. To continue: Frederick Flipsen, carpenter, was accused of drinking brandy at the taphouse on the Sabbath, "while the first preaching was going on," and has induced Steenwick's Negro (who had likewise been absorbing Andres Johginsen's brandy) to play the jewsharp and [...] ††† Flipsen's morals didn't improve. In 1662, he tries to collect some brewing equipment in payment for a debt. And later, he took possession of a widow's petticoat as security for another account.

Jan Hendricksen, carpenter, quarrelled over farm lands in Midwout, now Flatbush, and was accused of overcharging for his woodwork when he demanded no less than three beaverskins in payment.

Abram Jacobson, carpenter, attempted to appropriate a stray sow, but the court awarded her to the local deacon, who, by the way, had no proper claim to her.

Carpenter Albert Jansen, 1658, "requests as he is about to build a small house, and his lot is Too little, that an adjoining lot be granted him." He goes to court on another occasion and claims "he made for Mr. Stickley two pillows, two cushions and a bench, on which they sleep, and one bedstead for which he should have 500 pounds of tobacco."

FIGURE 6. Dutch Kas

Int.: - Quite a pipe-load for one man to smoke! But perhaps Mynheir Jansen bartered some of that tobacco for wood. Why, Mr. Z., did Jansen's client sleep on a bench?

Mr. Z.: - That was a special kind of bench, Mr._____. Alice Morse Earle in "Colonial Days in Old New York" describes it as a very common form of bedstead, scarcely more than a bench to hold the bedding, and built into the house in an alcove, or recess. Thus, the contract for the ferry-master's house built in Brooklyn in 1665 specified for the wainscoting of the whole length of the east side of the house, and in the recess two bedsteads (betste was the Dutch word), one in the front room and one in the inside room, with a pantry at the end of the bedstead." The alcove *betste* resembled a cupboard and was closed behind doors, when not used. Another form of Dutch bedstead was the *sloep-banck* or *slow-bunk,* one type of which was simply a wooden box furnished with feather-bed, undersheet and blanket cover. Another type resembled the bed-in-a-wall of our modern studio apartments, which set up vertically on hinges when unoccupied. Many Dutch fireplaces had these *sloep-bancke* or benches enclosed in alcoves on either side of them.

Int.: - I see, they were a quick means for our Dutch carpenters to get over a katzenjammer. Pull a bed out of a closet, set it up horizontally, and fall asleep by the fireplace. What were some of our other carpenters like?

Mr. Z.: - They were all creatures out of a saga, Mr. _____. Frans Jansen was accused of breaking windows in the company of Abel Hardenbroeck and others, and of making a noise in the street. He denied the charges, but admitted being in their company alright. He was accused, another time, of creating an uproar and "a great insolence in the street" along with some soldiers. Again he acknowledges his company, but as for breaking windows, his testimony says "he did not even know where those live whose windows were broken," which, granting his condition, must have been true enough. He ended his career proper as a professional beer-carrier.

Thomas Lambertzen was accused by his fellow-craftsman Frederick Flipsen for breaking the Sabbath. You will remember that Flipsen had broken it himself. Otherwise Lambertzen held to the letter of the law, seeing to it that his wife who had nursed another woman's child was paid in salt mackerel.

Pieter Pieterzen was in debt for drink, while David Wessels was always suing or being sued for debts.

The story of Cornelis Willemsen is touching. Willemsen could not pay one Jansen for his woodworking tools, yet would not give them up. The bailiff called on him, only to find him out. He had gone off with Stoffel Educart's boat and Joseph Waldron's son. Sailed away, and behind him he had left "at Joseph Waldron's one bed and appurtenances as a bolster with two pillows, one quilt, two sheets, one pillow case, one gun, a grindstone, one chest with old rags of no value." The court record continues: "At Geirtje Hoppe's, widow of Andries Hoppe, was found an octagon[al] little table and an old workbench. With Dom. Drisus is remaining . . . the sum of fl. 60 in Zeairan (wampum, that is, Indian shell work) which he earned there in wages. Joseph Waldron went to other colonies to look for his son, but returned without him. The last entry of this case reads: ". . . request of Joseph Waldron, wherein he asks to be allowed to sell the goods in his house belonging to the fugitive Cornelis Willemsen, carpenter . . ."

Int.: - That was indeed a very moving story. Why, Mr. Z _____, do you suppose the lives of these carpenters were so harassed? Was it the lure of so many taverns which weakened them?

Mr. Z.: - Perhaps, but I hardly think so. Drink, seems to me, to have been an outlet for them, the consequence of a struggle. And the struggle evolved, I should say, out of the very conditions of building a colony in the new land. Our carpenters looked for material things in payment for their work: brewing equipment, a widow's petticoat, beaver skins, tobacco, salt mackerel, a boat to sail away in, and leave it all. Maybe bartering with the Indians was distasteful to them after the red men became civilized as to the nature of a bargain. Carpenter Cornelis Willemsen at least did not bother to collect his wages in wampum before running off from New Amsterdam.

Perhaps the addiction of the Dutch carpenters of New Amsterdam to drink is explained by a request of Wonter Van Turller, Director-General, appointed in 1632. He writes, Aug. 14, 1636, to the directors of the colony at Amsterdam: "It would in our opinion be advisable if the carpenters who are already here or are still to be sent, were put on a daily wage, in order that the Company might employ them according to their capacity. It would in that case be necessary to pay them every week, in order to stimulate their interest and inclination to work."

Constantly suing and being sued for debt, our carpenters, we may justifiably suspect, were never put on the daily wage their Director-General had requested. Without an assured income from day to day, it must have been hard for our joiners and wood-turners to keep their minds on the making of cupboards, bedsteads, and bowls. But if our suspicions are too much in our carpenters' favor, then the cupboards and bedsteads which they made, and which we have described, were indeed nobler works than their makers in their unemployed hours saw fit to do.[17]

Louis Zukofsky

Jan 24 1940

SERIES: THE HUMAN SIDE OF ART

8

Broadcast No 8: Remmey and Crolius Stoneware

Music: The Wayworn Traveller

(fade)

Announcer: Station WNYC presents "The Human Side of Art," a series of broadcasts by the Index of American Design, a division of the New York City WPA Art Project. The Index of American Design is engaged in preparing a graphic survey of American decorative arts and crafts from the earliest Colonial days to the beginnings of large-scale production. Research in the historical background and manufacture of American costume, ceramics, glassware, furniture, metal work, woodcarving and textiles, supplements the thousands of paintings of objects vividly rendered by the artists on this project. This is the eighth program of the series in which Mr. Louis Zukofsky of the research staff will be interviewed by Mr. _____. Mr._____.

Interviewer: - Thank you. What, specifically, Mr. Z., are these objects of pottery shown in the plates you have brought for our discussion today?

Mr. Z.: - This is a group of stoneware, including, as you see, jugs, jars, pitchers, vases, an inkwell and a butter churn.

Int.: - They are certainly a varied collection. I should say that they represent a concise review of our early domestic economy in themselves.

Mr. Z.: - Exactly. This group of stoneware is an excellent illustration of one of the purposes of the Index of American Design in rendering a faithful picture of the early industrial and domestic life of our country. These house-

---

17. The social emphasis in the treatment of the carpenters' lifestyle appears relatively progressive, as if the unemployment and social unease of the late 1930s causes Zukofsky to superimpose some of those concerns on history.

hold objects were once intimately bound up with the lives of people who often turned them out in their own homes. You will remember that in those days when householders also made their own candles, soap and clothes, that the home was in more than one sense a small industrial establishment.[18] Stoneware vessels, along with other vessels of iron and tin, were extremely popular in the United States, when aluminum was still unknown. Some of this stoneware is over 150 years old.

Int.: - That's a ripe age, indeed. What is stoneware, Mr. Z.? What is its composition that has preserved these objects for us, over so long a time?

Mr. Z.: - Stoneware is one form of earthenware—that is clay turned on a wheel, molded and hardened. Like earthenware, its composition is coarse-grained and opaque. But unlike the commonest earthenware, stoneware is glazed. So that if you take a chip off the surface of stoneware and compare it with a chip of common earthenware, you will notice that the stoneware is less porous than the earthenware, and also that it's less opaque. This characteristic of stoneware—of taking on a quality of translucence, which we find in fine porcelain—is due to the fact that stoneware is fired in the kiln to harden at a higher temperature than earthenware.

Now, if you look at these drawings, you will see that the surfaces of some of these stoneware objects are rougher than others. That's the potter's hand, and the processes of turning and molding are visible in the grains and shape of his objects. As for the figured decorations, trade marks and signatures, mostly in deep blue, which you see on this stoneware—all that was applied after the objects were turned and molded, but before they were fired. Some of the decoration is, as you see, brushed on loosely; some of it is incised, that is, the still unhardened clay was gouged out and the decoration applied, into the surface. That again shows the different wishes of each potter's hand.[19]

Int.: - Is the blue figured decoration part of the glaze, Mr. Z.?

Mr. Z.: - Yes. As a matter of fact, when first applied the color of our finished decoration may not have been this rich blue at all. It may have been a drab gray, or some other undistinguished shade. That's not mere paint which our potter applied to decorate his pots, but a special consistency—a mineral—

18. This evocation of the home as a productive space has echoes in the Index writings included in this volume and throughout "*A*," in theme as well as the situation of its production.

19. The potter's hand achieves a poetic quality evoking the poem as a record of life lived, autobiographical and timeless in that manner. The theme recurs in "*A*," as in these lines from "*A*"-12: "Measure, tacit is. / The dead hand shapes / An idea . . ." (131).

which turned into beautiful deep blue when fused with the clay in the fire. It took a great deal of experience, much trial and effort, considerable technical knowledge and imagination for our stoneware craftsmen to get the right temperature of the fire which would turn their clay and applied minerals into the colors and glazes they wanted.

Int.: - When did they first begin, Mr. Z.__

Mr. Z.: - About 1730. The authority for that date is the first Clarkson Crolius, one of our most important stoneware manufacturers, who lived from 1773 to 1843.

Int.: - That's rather late, isn't it?

Mr. Z.: - Quite late, especially when we consider that iron utensils were made in New England from the very beginning. There are, true enough, extant inventories of objects in seventeenth century households of Massachusetts which list stone bottles. But these are rare, and the manufacture of this crude stoneware must have been quite haphazard. I should venture to guess that it was almost the casual whim of craftsmen whose main product was earthenware. Even that was very scarce. No, New England was not to begin with the center of stoneware manufacture that it was later with the coming of the Bennington potteries into the picture.‡‡‡ It was in New York that American stoneware was first produced, and right here in our own city. The Dutch and their descendants here had the advantage of a longer tradition of ceramics in their prized Delftware over their English and English colonial imitators. First hand knowledge of this tradition, shown in the Delftware brought over by Dutch immigrants, must have spurred the local manufacture of stoneware considerably. As I said a little while ago, we started in 1730, and the authority for it is the first Clarkson Crolius. He writes as an old man, one year before his death: "The first stoneware kiln or furnace was built in (1730) in this city." In 1842, it was still standing. Crolius tells us further that, "The lower part or arches are under the foundation of the house on the 5th lot from the corner of Center and Reade Streets; the house is seventeen feet wide. It was first called Corselius Pottery; what was called Potters Pump, celebrated for the purity of its water, was taken into the large well now used by the Manhattan Company for City purposes; it was at the foot of the hill called Potters Hill."

Int.: - Does most of the stoneware shown in the Index plates which you have brought here today come from this pottery, Mr. Z__?

Mr. Z.: - A good deal of it, and the remainder comes from the kilns of the

Remmey family which originally had an establishment on the hill . . . near the pottery already mentioned by Clarkson Crolius. Of course, research by the Staff of the Index of American Design has discovered many other potteries known thruout New York State which are generally unknown. But I have selected the stoneware manufactories of Crolius and Remmey for today's discussion for two reasons: first, local interest, and, secondly, because the combined and closely related efforts of these two families of stoneware makers represent an output which shows a continuous tradition branching, and like their family trees, from 1730 till well past the Civil War.

For example, the pottery which Clarkson Crolius says was originally called the Corselius pottery, stood on the site of the lake reservoir known as Little Collect Pond, now for many years filled in by the square back of our Municipal Building, where I am now giving this broadcast.[20] Now it happens that Mr. Corselius, according to tradition, was the father-in-law of both the first Crolius and the first Remmey in the stoneware business in this city. Whether his sons-in-law subsequently took over his establishment, or whether they benefited directly in some ways by his previous business experience is not known for certain. They may have been partners at one time. Again, we don't know. But this we do know, where we are broadcasting is very near the site of the earliest stoneware potteries in the United States.

Int.: - That's a coincidence alright. I almost see a double exposure shot in the movies, our Municipal Building superimposed startlingly over the old

20. Attention to New York geographic lore reflects Zukofsky's personal interest as much as those of a local radio broadcast audience. Emphasis on street names, with the implication that such mappings reveal New York's historical strata, is evident to a lesser extent in the body of the Index essays. Compare with the essay "For Wallace Stevens" in which Zukofsky explains the contingency of poet reading poet as an "impersonal friendship" that transcends time and notions of influence; he then imagines this closeness in literal terms: "For all I know a few years later we may have walked—I forget where Stevens lived in New York, I think it was 9th Street near Fifth Avenue—and walked the same streets, past each other unknown" (*Prepositions* 28); remembering Whitman he writes in *"A"*-12: ". . . Leaves of Grass / In their first printer's shop, / The house it was in still stands / On Cranberry Street / That I walk nights / I go to teach / In the Eagle building, of old / Brooklyn, freighted with the lost / Years and winds of Whitman's editorials—" (228).

21. This bears a resemblance to a conception in Henry Adams's *Education* that Barry Ahearn describes as the dream "of time as a series of layered transparencies" through which events of historical past are superimposed, losing the distinctions of temporal sequence (*Zukofsky: Man and Poet* 127). Transposed to the aural domain, a similar image of historical contingency

stoneware potteries.[21] Well—why Mr. Z. do we have so much faith in the accuracy of Clarkson Crolius' statement on the origin of his pottery?

Mr. Z.: - For one thing, no authorities have denied it. And, if for no other reason, we will see when we presently look at his work, that he must have been sincerely interested in the tradition of the craftsmen he followed.[22] Also, the few facts we know about him show him to have been a serious character, the kind who would attempt to be very accurate about details of local history, at one and the same time a manufacturer and a political figure in a rapidly growing community. In 1802, he was on the building commission of the new City Hall. On May 13, 1811, as Grand Sachem of the Tammany Society, he delivered an address celebrating the twenty-second anniversary of that society and the laying of the cornerstone of the "Great Wigwam" or the first Tammany Hall. In 1820, he was on a committee of the Common Council considering the manufacture of porcelain by paupers and criminals of the city.

Int.: - I see, he knew enough and cared enough about local affairs involving his business to want to leave a true record of them. By the way, did the city ever go thru with the committee's program for the manufacture of porcelain by prisoners in its jails?

Mr. Z.: - I am not sure. If it did it wasn't very good porcelain. Most of our American porcelain, except for very late examples, imitated the European. As a matter of fact, its dealers usually tried to pass it off as such, leaving it unmarked, so that innocent buyers thought they were getting fashionable importations. Our stoneware dealer did not have to fake his wares. It was serviceable in the old days, and seems beautiful to us today even when placed alongside the more aristocratic porcelain.

But we were speaking a little while ago of the city's interest in the manufacture of ceramics. It may interest you that one of the four earliest potteries

---

appears in "*A*"-23: "... the gifts / of time where those who / never met together may hear / this other time sound *one*" (539). It also recalls the description of the opening montage of Charlie Chaplin's "Modern Times" in Zukofsky's 1936 essay of the same title, a sequence that Zukofsky lauds as "the cinematic equivalent of material thoughtfulness" (*Prepositions* 60). Mark Scroggins was kind enough to note this latter connection.

22. The logic here, that good craftsmanship is kindred to sincerity of character, finds application in Zukofsky's own poetry and criticism. See previous note to American Kitchenware and Zukofsky's essay "Sincerity and Objectification" (*Poetry*, February 1931).

on the hill once nearby was owned by the City. In the Minutes of the Common Council for October 30, 1730 we find this reference: (p 99) "Order'd that Alderman Filkin, Alderman Bogart and Alderman Mesier, Messrs Roosevelt and Randell or the Major part of them to be a Committee to treat with Mr. Henry Van Vlack Concerning the Rent of the Pott Bakers House Belonging to the Corporation near the Negroes Burying Place."

Int.: - Potters Hill with its four potteries, the Crolius and Remmey establishments competing with the city's, near the Negro cemetery, all overlooking the waters of Collect Pond, must have been a rather outlandish place in those early days?

Mr. Z.: - Why, yes, it was on the city's outskirts. Few people came there except those who were interested in the stoneware trade, and maybe lovers. There is this unusual incident connected with the place. On January 2, 1800, four days after the disappearance of the beautiful Young Juliana Elmore Sands, her body was found in the well of the Manhattan Company.

Int.: - Which Crolius occupied Potters Hill at the time?

Mr. Z.: - Clarkson I, but I am sure he had nothing to do with this tragic incident, tho' it may have hastened the removal of his business to Cross Street two years later, in 1802.

Int.: - How many Crolius potters were there in all, Mr. Z__, and where were their establishments located?

Mr. Z.: - There were sixteen Crolius potters in all and it would take too much of our time to enumerate them and their various addresses as given in the early city directories. From about 1795 to 1845, they were located all over lower Manhattan, what is now the East Side, on the Bowery, Broadway, Little Ann Street, Division, Allen, Eldridge, Chrystie, Beckman, Cherry, Reed, Boyard Streets etc. etc.

Int.: - And how many Remmeys were stoneware manufacturers?

Mr. Z.: - Five, and they were always near the Crolius potters on the hill on adjacent streets—with one exception. This was the unfortunate Henry Remmey, son of John II, who was forced to leave New York in 1811. In 1803, he had been appointed to the position of Superintendent of City Scavengers— street cleaners we call them today—and when three [years] later the office was abolished, he was found guilty of appropriating city funds. He begged, "on account of the distressed state of his family," to be excused from repaying the money which he had collected during his term of office. But the Council refused. He is said to have gone off to Philadelphia and to have started another pottery which is still in existence under the name of Richard C. Crolius + Son. How the pottery of *Henry Remmey* became *Richard C. Crolius and Son,* our research has been unable to verify, since the original Remmey pottery does not appear in the early directories and histories of Philadelphia. However, if the alleged story of Henry Remmey's setting up business in that city is true, his ultimate tie up with a Crolius is in character. The members of the several Generations of Remmey and Crolius potters were always in the trade side by side, and perhaps as partners. And the similarities of their stoneware parallel§§§ this tradition.

If the stoneware shown on our Index plates could speak, like Omar Khayyám's pots, they would say[23] "'Who *is* the Potter, pray, and who the Pot?' It doesn't matter really which Crolius or Remmey made us. The tradition is unbroken. If the Crolius and Remmey families are still remembered it is in the glaze, the blue floral brush work, in the incised painted blue and their bird motifs. O yes," this stoneware would say, "we were made at different times, by different hands. Sometimes instead of an ear handle, there is none. Or instead of a gray glaze, there is a gray-brown glaze. Or instead of a decoration of daisies and leaves, signed *New York, Feb. 17, 1798, flowered by Clarkson Crolius,* it is another kind of flower and leaves brushed loosely on a pebbly surface by Richard Clinton Remmey in Philadelphia, in 1865; or an ingenious eagle with shield on breast, arrows in talons, six stars above and leaves, of an earlier Remmey. But, for all that, we are not so different one from another. Taken together you see in us the continuous work of Remmey and Crolius, stoneware makers, giving these states a permanent ceramic art for over 150 years."

Louis Zukofsky

Feb 8 / 40

Revised Feb. 21 / 40

23. Omar Khayyám (1050?–1123), was a Persian poet and mathematician. Zukoskfy refers to *The Rubáiyat of Omar Khayyám,* translated by Fitzgerald, and includes an excerpt as exhibit "I: 17b" in *A Test of Poetry* (30–31).

9

**Research for Broadcast No. 9, "The Human Side of Art."
The Caswell Carpet**

Accession No. 38-157, American Wing, Metropolitan Museum of Art, N.Y.C.

The so-called Caswell carpet was embroidered by Zeruah Higley Guernsey, during two years or more preceding 1835 in Castleton, Vermont. The carpet consists of rectangular pieces, not quite square, each a complete design. Each piece was worked on a tambour frame in double Kensington or chain stitch over a coarse homespun ground. The wool used for embroidering was grown, spun and dyed at home. Tradition is that Zeruah did all the work from the shearing of the wool to the decoration. Her father is said to have been a maker of spinning wheels and of machines kindred to them, and to have made the wooden needle with which his daughter wrought the colored work.

The coloring of the designs is mostly pink, rose and deep bottle green. Blue, yellow and white are subsidiary. The background which now shows up as deep brown, as result of wear, fading, and having been pieced together at different times, was originally black. There are seventy-eight pieces of these designs, each in various colors, as stated, against a black ground, and the designs are *absolutely original* and no two of them alike. Included are flowers, leaves, a rooster, butterflies, birds, cats, fruits, ferns, puppies, and a man and woman. These last, dressed in costume of ca. 1835, have been suggested, by interpreters romantically inclined, as the couple who, Zeruah, in the anticipation of her handiwork, foresaw as the ultimate possessors of her carpet—that is, herself and her future husband. Others see in the couple Adam and Eve in the garden of Eden, as imagined by a Vermonter of Puritan extraction in the early nineteenth century. "Apparently Zeruah had qualms as to her success in depicting the pair, for after her carpet had been completed she kept the lady and her sevain covered with another design sewed tightly over them." (M. G. Higley)

The original owner's initials and date of completion are at the top of the carpet:

Z H G 1835 (attempt at facsimile)[24]

24. The autograph manuscript gives the impression of three script capitals.

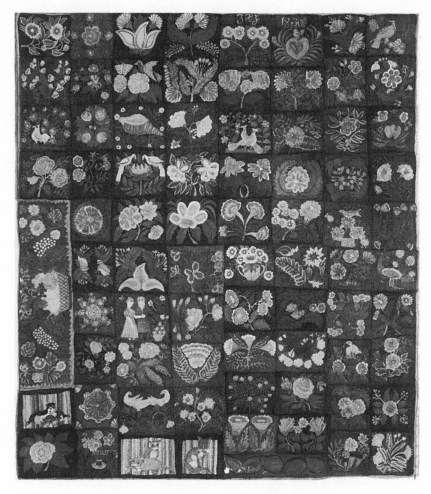

FIGURE 7. Caswell Carpet

Two other rectangles have the initials "F. B." and "L. F. M." worked into the design. These initials are the signatures of two young Indians of the Potawatmi[25] tribe who were students in the Castleton Medical College. They were virtually the guests of the town while taking the course, and townspeople, including Zeruah, took turns in giving them a home. "F. B." stands for Francis Baron.

25. Potawatomi: A Native American people living about the western Great Lakes through the nineteenth century, later displaced to the Midwest and Canada; it is also the name for the Algonquian language they spoke.

In addition to the seventy-eight pieces of carpet already mentioned, Zeruah also embroidered a panel which fitted onto one side of the carpet and over the hearth in seasons when there was no fire. This extra panel could be lightly stitched in place.—Thus:

[Illustration, probably in Zukofsky's hand]
Additional detail that one may note in a description of the carpet:
The ground material probably linen or burlap.
The colored embroidery wrought over it probably with a crochet needle, is *not* raised from the black ground.
The flowers are probably roses, poppies and thistle.
There are strawberries and blueberries, fairly realistic. Two of the cats appear to be siamese. The large blue and white cat occupying one rectangle was probably inspired by the family cat, tho its stiffness and color suggest the porcelain cats of Staffordshire ware or imitation American cottage ornaments. The tradition is that the family cat once stopped over the cat in the carpet, glared back and spat at her rival.
The fruit baskets, conch, and abstract composition of vase and shell may have been suggested by architectural and furniture motifs of the period. The floral urn may be related to similar designs in velvet painting.
The birds include cuckoos, and peacocks, notably the latter, in pairs. Tho the forms of these birds are absolutely original, the conception of showing them in pairs occurred also in woven coverlets of the time.
"Adam and Eve" may be compared to similar figures in samples of that day.
Zeruah's colors are "neither true to nature or to fancy . . . their value in the fine gradations of tint. She kept the carpet in her seldom used parlor" (M. G. Higley)
Size: approx. 12 by 13 1/2 feet.

The carpet's importance in the history of embroidered rugs has been summed up by the Editor of *Antiques* (vol. II, 6) ". . . aside from interest as *tour de force* of early 19th c. handiwork . . . the Caswell carpet constitutes a textile document of no inconsiderable importance . . . The stitch . . . in essence the ancient oriental chain stitch . . . the standard stitch for embroidered carpets of Spain, and used in conjunction with other stitches for embroidered English carpets . . . This industrious needlewoman (Zeruah H. Guernsey) conducted her work according to tradition already some centuries old when she conceived the idea of beautifying the floor of her father's best parlor . . . No doubt her desire was to emulate imported or professionally woven floor coverings.

"Zeruah invented her own designs . . . reminded of 18th c. forms and methods, yet sensitive to the new . . . of the 19th. For the most part dominated by the earlier period, every motive highly stylized . . . each bit of pattern worked with careful reference to its contours and to the play and sparkle of each element against the dark background. This feeling for outline or—perhaps better—silhouette is a manifestation characteristic of almost all European design previous to the 19th c. In the 19th c., on the contrary, we find naturalism taking place of stylization and mass effect substituted for emphasis upon contour . . . However, she occasionally yields to naturalism as in the depiction of the tumbling puppies and kitten and blue cat. In each of the latter three the background is devoid of perspective but it unmistakably represents a simple rag carpet (of a striped pattern). The normal carpeting of Zeruah's house we may, therefore, safely infer to have been the woven rag strip . . . She probably had never yet heard of a hooked rug or if she had she might have been satisfied with the easier technique of hooking rather than the traditionally sanctified method of embroidery. The hooked rug was soon to appear to answer demands of women folk with less patience than Zeruah . . . Thus, perhaps the embroidered carpet serves as a kind of forerunner of the hooked rug—the latter a type of carpeting which offered the advantage of comparatively speedy production and of adequate durability; a type, further, which, as rags from manufactured clothes became plentiful and homegrown yarn grew relatively scarce, afforded interesting utilization for materials which had become plentiful and cheap."

• • •

"Zeruah (née Higley Guernsey) Caswell, daughter of Esther (Higley) Guernsey, was born Oct. 31, 1805 . . . only survivor of her generation, now a resident of Castleton, Vt., where the main part of her life has been spent. Now (1895) 90 years . . . a woman of strong character and rare ability . . . beloved by kindred and friends she still superintends her household affairs, and retains her memory and lively faculties to a very remarkable degree. . . . Married Memri Caswell of Middleton, Vt. Mar. 5, 1846.

"In connection with her young days . . . the first Sunday school held in Castleton . . . 1819 . . . on "Frisby Hill" . . . in a little old-fashioned, unpainted schoolhouse. Mrs. Caswell, who was one of the youngest children, well remembered how the young teacher knelt upon the bare floor to ask

God's blessing ... the lesson given the scholars was the first ten verses of the first chapter in Genesis, to be perfectly learned and repeated to Miss Merrill at the close of the hour. (p. 264–5, M. C. Johnson).

Among Mrs. Caswell's ancestors were Brewster Higley II, follower of George Whitefield and Deacon of Simsberry Church, Castleton, Vt., and her grandfather, Brewster Higley III, also deacon, who had fought with Col. Ethan Allen at Fort Ticonderoga. As for the lineage of Mrs. Caswell's father (v.s. page 1): the name of Guernsey as a family name first appears in the New Haven colony at Milford, Conn. in 1639. Since there is no record of the family in England, it is assumed that they probably had lived there under another name before migrating to Guernsey (one of the English Channel Islands) where they acquired the name they were to use later in America. Pronounce the name like the name of the island, tho in New Haven Colony—i.e. in Yankee or Conn. dialect—it was pronounced *Garnsey*. The Guernseys were Puritans, who migrated to Vermont and were among the first settlers of Castleton in that state.

Solomon Gouernsey (sic) is supposed to have been the first merchant. He built and occupied the house which stood where the Bomoseen House (social center) now stands. A. W. Hyde (ca. 1806 or earlier) succeeded him in the same building.

James K. Guernsey graduated at Dartmouth ca. 1812.

Wm. C. Guernsey was a trustee of the Rutland Grammar School, 1865. The town of Castleton, Vt. is in the center of Rutland Cy., miles miles west of Rutland, thirteen East of Whitehall, N.Y. and sixty-five miles north of Albany. It contains thirty-six square miles, in the summer resort section near Lake Bomoseen. Its charter was granted to Samuel Brown of Stockbridge, Massachusetts by Gov. Wentworth of New Hampshire, September 22, 1761. Previously, the French and Indian wars had made settlement impossible, but the conquest of Canada by the English removed the obstacles to the fertile valley in which Castleton was founded. Most of the settlers came from the state of Connecticut on horseback, bringing their household effects. The early occupations of Castleton included tanning, shoemaking, hat manufacturing, carpentry and joinery. The town was the mobilization center of the Green Mountain Boys before the attack on Ticonderoga. The present population is 1,794 and the chief industries slate quarrying and dairying. Castleton, Vermont is also the seat of a state normal school.

Bibliography

Higley, Mary Gerrish. The Caswell Carpet. *Antiques,* vol IX June 1926 pp. 396–398.

A Note on Embroidered Carpets (by the Editor of *Antiques*), vol IX June 1926; pp. 398–402.

Editors Attic and Frontispiece, Embroidered Carpet 86" x 58", owned by Mrs. Payne Whitney, Made by Lucelta Smart, ca 1820, near Rumney, N.H. - *Antiques,* vol xiii no. 4, April 1928.

Johnson, M. C., The Higleys and their Ancestry: an old colonial family, N.Y. 1896.

Guernsey, Rocellus Sheridan. Origin of the family name of Guernsey and Garnsey in "Round Lake Season," Sept 21, 1895.

Steel, J. History of Castleton, Vt. pp. 501–547, Miss Hemenways' Historical Gazetteer, vol III, 1877.

Index Data Sheet, Plates and Photographs.

Feb. 29 / 40

Louis Zukofsky

10

Research for Broadcast No. 10, "The Human Side of Art"
Friendship Quilts

Index Plates TE–177 and TE–81

TE–177:

Appliqué quilt 1846–7. Original owner Rev. John Smart, minister of First United Presbyterian Church, 1838–50. Inherited by his son, Rev. John Smart, Cambridge, N.Y.

This quilt was designed by the ladies of Rev. Smart's parish at Baltimore, Md., and presented as a gift to him. It is composed of twenty-five appliqué squares and border[ed] in plain red and figured green cottons, with pink, yellow and white also used on time yellowed muslin. In two central blocks many colors appear. In some blocks the appliqué is embroidered. The design represents for the most part flowers and leaves—abstract floral motives as well as realistic poppies and rosettes (?) in woven baskets. The border is wreathed with *S-shaped* stems and fringed with red and white balls. The quilt, slightly stained, unwashed, measures 113 by 113 inches. The present owner is Mrs. Lois Harris (dealer), Cambridge, New York.

The names of the parishioners embroidered on gilt include: "Mrs. King; Mrs. Emerson; Jane Cooper December 8, 1846; Eliza Cooper December 8, 1846 Baltimore, Maryland; Mar 18, 1847, Mrs. Eliz. McCren; A. Milliken, etc. (see TE-177 Data Sheet). Each appliqué square has a name, and three of the squares are dated, showing that at least two of them were made at different times. Note that Jane Cooper and Eliza Cooper dated their squares on the same day. Perhaps these two ladies were related.

From the standpoint of local history, this appliqué quilt can lead to a mine of information about the parishioners of the First United Presbyterian Church of Baltimore, 1846–7. But it would take months to follow up the clues offered merely in the names. The research becomes all the more difficult when only a surname is given, or only the initial of a first name with the surname. But the type of information that may be discovered is indicated by the following research suggested by the name of A. Millikin:

We do not find an A. Millikin, and there may have been several, but we do find that this surname appeared variously as Millikin, Milliken, Millingas, Millanges, Mullikin, etc—but always represented the same family and its various branches. As for the Baltimore, Md. branch: "When making an afternoon call, or a day's visit, the Mullikin ladies took their knitting, quilt-piecing, fine sewing; thus uniting sociability and utility." (Ridlon, Gideon Tibbetts, History of the Families Millingas and Millanges, and posterity surnamed Milliken, Millikin, Mullikin, etc-1907).

The quotation from Ridlon corroborates various other writers on Friendship Quilts, also called Album and Autograph quilts:

1) Carrie A. Hull and Rose G. Kretsinger—Patchwork Quilts, Caxton Printers, Caldwell, Ohio, 1935. 299 pp. pp. 22–23- "One custom . . . common in every locality was the making of "Album" quilts. They were highly prized and especially so when made by the women of the congregation as a gift to the minister's wife. Each woman made a block with her name embroidered in the center, then they were set together and a grand quilting bee was given at the home of the minister if he had a local church—but if he was a 'circuit rider' and served many communities the quilting was at the home of one of the members of the congregation . . . much the same as other quiltings . . . except the conversation was apt to take a more religious turn. —Susan B. Anthony . . . delivered her first talk in the cause of "Equal Rights" at a meeting of

this kind. . . . The description of the quilting bee in Harriet Beecher Stowe's book *The Minister's Wooing* is rich in New England lore."

2) Florence Peto, Historic Quilts, N.Y. 1939 210 pp. Chapter 5 - Autograph Quilts or album quilts . . . Theoretically, each block of such bedspreads . . . made by person who signed it using her own preference as to pattern, material and color. Necessarily executed with varying degrees of skill, the result . . . too often a medley of unrelated designs and awkward color contrasts, with little to recommend it except possible sentimental value to the recipient. Many, however, excellent . . . and others because of inscribed names and dates reach beyond the interests of a family and assume importance of historical documents . . . In every dower chest one quilt . . . the bride's . . . on which was expended the utmost skill of the needleworker. Sometimes pieced entirely by the bride-to-be, but quite as often its individual squares were made and signed by her nearest friends, [T]ruly an Album Quilt. In some localities a prospective bride was never permitted to do even an inch of the quilting stitchery on her bride's quilt, because it was very bad luck; she often signed and dated her masterpiece, however, sometimes with initials done in cross-stitch with strands of her own hair! It was equally bad luck for any but a bride to employ the heart-motif; the Dove, symbol of conjugal felicity, appears almost as frequently on bridal quilts as the heart, and on the Baltimore Bride's Quilt, (another Baltimore friendship quilt-n.d. Index Plate TE–177) love birds, in praise and attitudes of mutual adoration, appear fourteen times!

. . . Friendship quilts in the every-one-make-a-block-and-sign-your-name class and, as the name would indicate, made by a group of young women for a mutual friend usually following the announcement of her engagement.

3) Florence Peto, Birds-Quilted Patched and Woven - *Antiques,* Nov '39. The author refers to the "allusion and sentiment" of the "peacock's brilliant plumage . . . the cock's feather considered unlucky . . . In early Christian art (the peacock) was a symbol of Resurrection—depicted with a nimbus—In American . . . taste of epicure and on form the peacock was a 'watch bird' and weather-prophet . . . depicted by Pennsylvania-German in [factors****.]"

And referring again to the Baltimore Bride's Quilt (v.s. p 4), showing an American eagle, peacock and love birds. "From graceful baskets and horns of plenty pour forth full blown flowers and birds in great profusion. The quilt is composed of twenty-five autographed and dated blocks. Love birds appear fourteen times—always in pairs and facing each other in attitudes of mutual adoration. An American eagle assumes protective position in the center of the quilt ... peacock on rosebush ... Needlework ... appliqué technique at peak of elegant finesse ... Small details in opulent flowers, fruits, leaves and birds penned with India ink, not embroidered. Signatures show flourishes and scrolls ... Theoretically, each square in this type of quilt made by a different friend of the bride—i.e. an album piece for remembrance—but it is my feeling that autograph quilts were not always made by those whose name appear on separate blocks. Sewing, like penmanship, reveal[s] personal characteristics. Twenty-five women ... not likely to produce uniformity of style. (But) the possibility of a professional needlewoman in Baltimore specializing in these quilts for bridal trousseau has not been proved."

Figure six in this article illustrates a friendship quilt in which the different blocks were made by different young female acquaintances or relatives of Wm. Henry Vernon of Baltimore, on the occasion of his coming of age in 1840. Such quilts are often known as *freedom quilts*. This quilt assembled in the year of Vernon's marriage included a block commemorating the death of Major Samuel Ringgold at Palo Alto in the Mexican War, in 1846, which was made by Vernon's wife. The other blocks illustrate patriotic and manly virtues in the representation of eagle, flag, ships, guns, horses, dogs and in the symbols of fraternal orders.

• • •

TE-81: Appliqué-quilted coverlet, 1842. Original owner Rev. Joshua K. Ingalls. Made at Southold, L.I., of very delicate appliqué squares. Size 97" x 90".

Florence Peto in *Historic Quilts* describes this quilt:

"The autographed Presentation Quilt ... a popular Token of love and admiration when made by women members of a church congregation and presented to their minister or his wife. Of this type none is earlier than 1840 ... plate 34 ... appliqué quilt for Mr. Joshua K. Ingalls ... made 1842 ... highly esteemed lay preacher, and the quilt made by members of the church where he officiated in Southold, L.I. .... One would venture to say one woman of taste and discrimination directed the work. In this quilt all the wreaths, some square, some round, show delicate foliation interspersed with diminutive birds and flowers; birds lend grace to the central and each of the four corner blocks. Leaves and a cluster of grapes ornament each half-square along the quilt's edge and all the decoration has been raised by judicious padding. Pastel shades further the impression of delicacy; in a majority of the blocks blue has been used for leaves instead of the usual green. Only one block in this assembly seems heavy and out of scale, the *Oak Leaf* . . . but perhaps it complied with the requirement, 'a leaf block', and one can imagine it bore a name not to be omitted from the company of friends. Generally, group quilting shows happier results than group patch making. Half-inch diamond cross-bar quilting backgrounds the wreaths in the Ingalls' spread; a dedicatory verse, penned in ink, is on one of the central blocks, and though there are signatures in ink on every square they have been placed inconspicuously. (In one case, one friendship quilt on the removal of the lining showed each square autographed on the underside)—pp 105, 106.

Charles Burleigh's *The Genealogy and History of the Ingalls Family in America* (Malden, Massachusetts, 1903, 324 pp) gives the following biography of Rev. Ingalls:
"Joshua King Ingalls, son of Elkanah and Polly (Haskell), born Swansea, Mass, July 21, 1816, married Oct. 29, 1837, Amanda, daughter of Elijah and Lydia (Jones) Gray. She was born at Bristol, R.I., Dec. 23, 1819; died at Ellsworth, Kansas, Jan. 1879. At the age of 15 he sought employment in Providence, and soon was apprenticed to learn the trade of sheet metal worker. His evenings . . . devoted to study . . . became an original thinker on religious, social, industrial and economic questions, and a ready debater. . . . Having made the acquaintance of John B. Gough, he (advocated) the temperance cause . . . took up the study of theology and became a preacher in the Unitarian Church, holding pastorates at Southold, N.Y., Southington and Danbury, Conn. His voice failing, he engaged in the manufacturing business in N.Y.C., identifying himself with the land reform movement, was a delegate to the Industrial Congress at Phila., 1848, and soon after became editor and publisher of "The Landmark." Much of his time was given to lecturing thruout N.Y. state. Published many books, "Social Wealth" (1855), "Economic Equities," "Land and Labor," "Work and Wealth," "Reminiscences of an Octogenarian in the Fields of Industrial and Social Reforms." He retired to his country home at Glenora, N.Y., and died Mar. 3, 1899."

There is a portrait of Ingalls in Burleigh's book, app. p. 149: an old, long bearded gentleman, wearing spectacles and skullcap. He has the genial look of the New England poet-preacher and humanitarian.[26]

---

26. Zukofsky's notes reflect a particular interest in Joshua Ingalls as an economic thinker, as Barry Ahearn observes in "Marxism and American Handicraft" (*Upper Limit Music* 83); In-

The following examples from Ingalls' works are typical illustrations of his matter and style:

"Into all production of wealth only two factors enter: (1) the new material—the soil or its spontaneous productions (2) human effort. However complex or extended, in the last analysis only these two elements are found. It is not the carbon and nitrogen, the salts and gases, of which our food and clothing are composed, which we produce as wealth, but that specific form and aptitude for use which our work has wrought or effected" —p. 7, "Work and Wealth," N.Y., 1878.

"Capital—The chief source of Increase . . . divided into *natural* and *artificial*.

Natural capital—The land and the labor. There is in Nature no other source of increase.

Artificial or Institutional Capital—Certain private rights created by custom, statute law, or by the arbitrary will of some conqueror or ruler, which enable one to force an Exchange or command labor without equitable return, through usurped dominion of the land, ownership of the person, or other civil device." —p. 311, "Social Wealth," N.Y. 1885.

• • •

General Material on Patchwork Quilts.
From Agnes M. Miall's Patchwork Old and New, London 1937 120 pp.:
appliqué . . . contains no piecing, but is built up by repeated applications of one material over or next to another, on a thick creamy cotton foundation . . . difficult to distinguish between patchwork and appliqué, for in many cases they merge into each other . . . much modern patchwork is partly appliquéd —p. 15.

American patchwork . . . originally came from England . . . We may separate all patchwork other than crazy into two main classes, pieced and appliqué; and we may say broadly that pieced work, though found both in the Old and New Worlds, originated in England, and that appliqué is peculiar to America —p. 66.

Friendship quilts especially popular in the U.S. (where) all friends in the neighborhood would contribute patches from their piecebag for the bride's memory quilt, or would agree upon a pattern and each make one square or

---

galls is referenced in "*A*"-12 (256–57) as subject of a proposed book entitled *About Some Americans*.

block from their own pieces. A central space was often reserved for the signatures of all the donors, written out in pencil in their own handwriting on white, and worked over in outline stitch to perpetuate it. —p. 25

Quilted patchwork—extra warmth obtained by quilting a padding between the patchwork top and its lining. Quilting not merely an added beauty . . . gives more strength, makes finished item almost uncreasable and holds lining firmly in place. —p. 108–9.

. . . tradition for the quilting to be done by someone who did not piece the patchwork. In old-time America, owing to need for the very large frame, which, when set up, occupied almost an entire room, it was essential for the quilting to be done more quickly than any one worker could. This led to

FIGURE 8. Friendship Quilt

junketings, quilting bees or parties—the padding and lining was bought for the patchwork top and invitations sent out for the quilting bee. No more than eight workers, two to each of the four sides could be accommodated round the frame and one of these would be the hostess or patchworker. The frame consisted of four long strips of wood, clamped together at the corners and arranged at convenient working height by being laid across the backs of four matching chairs . . . As the edges within easy reach were done, the clamps were taken out and the finished parts rolled inwards, so that a new area was brought close to the quilters.

By evening, the work was finished, and the frame taken down. Now arrived husbands, brothers and sweethearts for the chicken or turkey supper which was etiquette at a quilting bee . . . going home afterwards, in pairs . . . and as the old ballad (written by Stephen C. Foster, 1850) suggests:

> In the sky the bright stars glittered
> On the banks the pale moon shone
> And 'twas from Aunt Dinah's quilting party
> I was seeing Nellie home,
> I was seeing Nellie home.

• • •

From Ruth E. Finley—Old Patchwork Quilts, Phila. 1929, 202 pp:
Technically there are two kinds of patchwork. Piecing is sewing of patches of cloth together by means of a seam. Appliquéing is laying a smaller patch of cloth on a larger and then hemming or felling it down. —p. 41
Appliqué technique employed in America from middle of the eighteenth century —p. 118.

Louis Zukofsky
Mar. 14 / 40

11
Research for Broadcast No 11 "The Human Side of Art"
Cotton Historical Prints

I–Index Data Sheet TE–229: Washington Print using Du Simitière's profile portraits
From Edna Donnell, Portraits of Eminent Americans after Drawings by Du Simitière, in *Antiques*, v. 24, July 1933, pp. 17–21, 37–8.

"Chastellux wrote in 1782: 'I was expected in three places by a lover of natural history, by an anatomist, and at the college or rather University of Philadelphia. I began by the Cabinet of natural history. This small and scanty collection is greatly celebrated in America, where it is unrivalled; it was formed by a painter of Geneva called *Comitiere,* a name better suited to a physician than a painter. This worthy man came to Phila. twenty years ago, to take portraits and has continued ever since; he lives there still as a bachelor, and a foreigner, a very uncommon instance in America, where men do not long remain without acquiring the titles of husband and citizen.'"

The drawings for this series were made, for the most part, during the year 1779. In Du Simitière's 'commonplace book' we find this notation

'1779, Feb 1

a drawing in black lead of a likeness in profile of his excellency General Washington, form of a medal, for my collection. N.B. The General at the request of the Hon. Mr. Jay President of Congress, came with him to my house this morning and condescended with great good nature to sit about 3/4 of an hour for the above likeness having little time to spare, being the last day of his stay in town.

Sept. 16, 1799

delivered this day to Monsieur Gerard Minister of France fourteen drawings in black lead, being portraits in profile in the form of a medallion of eminent Persons engaged in the American war and the next day delivered to him a memoir how I should wish the Subscription might be set on foot, as also instructions drawn up in French for the engravers, of both of which I have copies and a list of pictures, delivered. N.B. his own picture to be added to it, and will make fifteen, he had it already before . . .'

—The engravings themselves were executed in Paris by the famous engraver Bénoit Louis Prévost . . . advertised for sale in America in Pa. Journal for Sept. 25, 1782. Pirated by British publishers when in 1783, two different sets, engraved in London, appeared within the space of five days: copies in reverse of French originals. One of these included Benedict Arnold, the other didn't —(in re- Arnold, Simitiére wrote "does not sell in America.") One set published by Richardson, May 10, engraved by Burnet Reading, the other May 15, by Wilkinson, and engraved by 'the most eminent artists' but signed B.B.E (meaning Best British Engravers??). From the latter English industry derived most of the American portraits that it spread so liberally on *printed textiles*, enamels and earthenware—"

—See also Editor's note and Illustration, same no. of Antiques p. 37

Paper Proof from an engraved plate for a printed handkerchief (c. 1783) signed by Talwin and Foster of Bromley Hall, Middlesex. A handkerchief of this pattern was listed in the ms. catalogue of a collection dispersed at the time of the World War. No other example had been published. Owned by John Jay Ide. Border embodies Louis XV rocaille motives, the garlands and ribbons connecting the inner medallions betray a later feeling. The center composition represents "Gen. Washington directing Peace to restore Justice the Sword which had gained Independence to America." The supporting ovals enclose profiles of twelve Americans—all but four of which (i.e. Franklin, Adams, Mifflin, Greene) are apparently copied from the B.B.E. set of *Du Simitiére* portraits.

—For the popularity at that time of the monochrome copperplate textile prints, of which TE-229 is an example, see: *The New York* Gazette and Weekly Mercury." Oct. 29, 1782, no. 1567, p. 3. col. 3.: "There is at William Campbell's Store, the corner of Fly-Market, the Most Compleat Assortment of Superfine Broad Cloth that has been offered for sale in this City since the war; . . . The ladies may likewise be supplied with a very neat assortment of silks, muslins, *chintzes*, lawns, gauzes etc.

• • •

II. Index Data Sheet. TE-204 Printed Cotton with Genre Scenes:

For description, see Esther Lewittes, "A Cotton Travelogue," Dec. 1939, *Antiques* (copy available with Mrs. Skahn, Index Files)

—Editor's Attic, *Antiques*, v. 37, Mar. 1940, p. 117 and Fig. 1, has a further note on this textile plate, entitled *Transportation Textile*. In re-Figure I, the editors says, —"This section of a printed cotton completes the pattern illustrated in Dec. 1939 Antiques." (Figure I is a 1930 reproduction, Coll. of Miss Elizabeth F. Graves, of the original piece which was made about 1830.) "The two scenes in the upper section, not shown here, depict a Conestoga wagon and a canal boat . . . Numerous details of shading and definition in the original . . . omitted from the reproduction . . . Miss Lewittes' surmise that the missing section of the repeat depicted a railroad scene was proved correct. A steam engine pulling a fuel car and two passenger cars puffs past the church and dwellings of a village, attracting the stares of children and their mothers and terrifying a horse hitched to a buggy, this scene may serve to date the original printed slightly later than 1830, but not much. By 1833 railroad cars of the stage coach type were being replaced by cars long enough to seat sixty passengers, and cars approximating the present American were in use as early as 1835.

Carl W. Drappard takes exception to certain of Miss Lewittes' statements as to locale depicted in various parts of the design. Perhaps close identification of these is not permissible. Granting that the artist might have taken liberties with the actualities, the possibility should not be overlooked that he had no specific setting in mind for each of his four scenes, but filled in an appropriate background largely drawn from his imagination . . . Thus, the house in the Conestoga scene need not represent Philadelphia architecture, but merely a house, or a tavern, somewhere in the overland route. The fact that the low-lying landscape along the canal does not, as Mr. Drappard points out, look like the Susquehana Valley need not detract from the validity of the canaling scene. Now that the missing unit of the design has been applied, this cotton travelogue becomes of even greater interest."

— John Santain, (see section III of this report), in "the Reminiscences of a Very Old Man 1808–1897" verifies the *Transportation Textile* as to the kind of conveyances used on his journey from Phila. to N.Y. in 1830 (see p. 138 ff)—mentioning the steamboat, a side-paddle steamboat, four-horse stages, and a projected railroad to N.Y. from Camden, opposite Phila., the South Amboy (N.J., opposite Staten Island) terminal of which is already in existence.

III. Index Data Sheets. TE 222, 203, 191—Printed Cotton with Mexican War Scenes.
1) TE-191-Printed Cotton ca. 1848 engraving by John Sartain after original daguerreotype registered in Pa. 1848. The subject depicted is Zachary Taylor in battle (Battle of Buena Vista ?? N.B. Miss Lewittes doesn't think so.) In re- John Sartain, see above pg. 5, he was a famous engraver, born in England, who became an Academician of the Pa. Academy of the Fine Arts; author of a Brief Sketch of the History and Practice of Engraving, Phila. 1880; sponsor of "Sartain's Union Magazine of Literature and Art Embellished with the finest steel mezzotint and wood engravings, music and col-

ored fashions, edited by Mrs. C. M. Kirkland," N.Y. 1848–1849 (vols. II–IV in N.Y. P.L., Call Mark •DA).

Pg. 21, vol II of "Sartain's Union Magazine" attests to the popularity of Mexican War subjects in engravings of the time—illustrating the "Gallant Exploit of Lieut. Schuyler Hamilton (aide-de-camp of Gen. Scott) near the Dell of Yobla (in 1847) Designed by T. H. Matteson and engraved by T. Doney.

2) TE–222–Printed Cotton (after 1846) showing battle of Resaca de la Palma. Colors: brown with touches of green and yellow. Justin H. Smith, in *The War With Mexico* (vol. 1) (N.Y. 1919) gives the following description of the battle of Resaca de la Palma (May 9, 1846) which may be correlated with a description of the detail in TE–222.

"The chaparral and woods that (Arista's—the Mexican General's—) troops had been seen to enter extended with some interruptions to the Rio Grande, a distance of approximately seven miles, and two hours before noon, after marching about halfway through it, he stopped at the Resaca de Guerrero. The Resaca was an ancient channel of the river, but it now consisted merely of a shallow, muddy ravine, somewhat in the shape of a bow, several hundred feet wide and three or four feet deep at the banks, lying substantially east and west across the route, with its concave side toward Palo Alto. At the bottom of it, both to the right and left of the road, lay narrow ponds, and the space between the water and the banks was rather closely filled with bushes and small trees . . . The woods made in impossible for the Americans to employ (artillery) effectively. The bank of the Resaca formed a natural breastwork, and it seemed likely that the troops, protected in this manner, would be confident and firm. But evidently bold and enterprising enemy could take advantage of the woods to conceal his movements, and evidently, too, Arista's main batteries could fire only in the direction of the road, since there were Mexicans in advance of the Resaca both to the right and left.

. . . Taylor, then, advancing at about two o'clock, after detaching most of the Artillery Battalion and perhaps Kerr's dragoons to guard the train, moved forward to the edge of the woods, and halted at what was called the Resaca de la Palma to await information . . . To right and to left the battle soon raged. All the Americans on the ground, . . . about 1700, were put in. No general guidance could be exercised. Chance was the lord of all save the good right arms of the troops,' wrote an officer. In such woods and thickets lines could not be formed. Even companies found it impossible to remain intact. A field officer was no more than a captain, and a captain no more than a subaltern. All got into the work promptly, and all did their best when there. As fast as they could, singly or in little squads, they pushed on, cheering and shouting. Often it required one's utmost exertions to squeeze through or hack through the dense and thorny chaparral under pelting showers of bullets. Now there was shooting, and now the cold steel struck fire. 'My orders were to make free use of the bayonet,' said the General afterwards, and the orders were borne in mind. Here Lieutenant Meade, the future victor of Gettysburg, had a chance to win his spurs; and he was but one of many heroes, though perhaps the most conspicuous in his quarter . . . . The Mexicans who fought at all this day, fought like tigers . . . A company of Uraga's regiment . . . every man of it either killed or wounded . . . During all this, Taylor, exposing himself as much as anyone, had been fighting at the center. The proper course to adopt there was to charge the Mexican guns on the road with infantry, but for some reason he sent May's dragoons against them. In a way the effort succeeded. Slashing as they galloped, the horsemen quickly ran over the batteries—more than a quarter of a mile beyond them, in fact; and then, coming back in a scattered condition, had a chance to slash again, for the batteries had been reoccupied. But the thickets on both sides were full of Mexican infantry. Against their muskets the dragoons were mere targets—broad ones, too; and before long the squadron, much the worse for its charge, recrossed the Resaca. Taylor was disgusted. Turning to Belknap and the Eighth Infantry he exclaimed, 'Take those guns, and by _____ keep them!' A part of the Fifth joined Belknap; and these men, rushing in furiously all together . . . captured the pieces. But the battle had already been won (i.e. the main body of the Mexican Army under Arista as already retreating across the Rio Grande) . . . An army supposed to out number ours three to one had been scattered, and a prestige of the utmost value at home, in Mexico and in Europe, had been gained." (p. 171–177)

In re-May (above), Smith has this further note, p. 467
"May, very tall and straight, with long black hair and a black beard that reached to his waist, became a newspaper hero, and for reasons that are rather hard to understand, was promoted several times during the war; but he seems clearly to have been essentially a cowardly sham. In this fight he seized a cannon, but only the infantry prevented the enemy from recapturing

it. He claimed the credit of making Gen. Vega his prisoner, but the real cap-
tor was a bugler. By his own account, he could rally only six of his men after
running through the batteries. The horses appeared to have "run away"
with the men. Taylor's report laid stress upon what occurred at the road,
and he does not seem to have known—at that time, to say the least—what
mainly caused the sudden collapse of the enemy, but an abundance of Mexican evidence, partly given under oath, makes the matter clear."

3) TE–203
Chintz with historical scene. ca. 1847, made in U.S.A. according to Elinor
Merrell, owner. Painted in brown with yellow ochre and green in the floral
decoration. The historical scene is of Zachary Taylor at the Battle of Buena
Vista, Feb. 22–23, 1847. Similar piece illustrated and described in *Antiques,*
vol 8, Sept 4, 1925, frontispiece and p. 139: "Size 25" x 18" owned by Mrs.
O. A. Fanning . . . Printed chintz . . . until recently cherished as Revolutionary relic depicting Lafayette. Obviously the Revolutionary association was
incorrect. The costumes would dispose of that. But who was the American
general with a weakness for a stove-pipe hat and for riding side-saddle on a
white horse? According to the American historian Justin H. Smith . . . 'I am
inclined to believe this picture was intended to represent General Taylor.
The horse was meant to be white, I judge, and his favorite charger was *Old
Whitey.* Gen. Taylor liked even in battle, to sit sidewise when mounted':
(battle *probably* Buena Vista). It is not unreasonable to believe that this
chintz was printed in America during 1847 or 1848. Its colors are the somewhat melancholy browns, greens, and ochres characteristic of the period
and doubtless more fully explicable on the ground of some manufacturing
problem than on that of popular esthetic preference."

Miss Lewittes has data supporting the last statement, showing that the
only dyes available to manufacturers at the time this chintz was made were
indigo and the melancholy browns, greens and ochres already mentioned.
(Please ask her for this information). Considering, however, that most of the
Mexican battles shown in our prints had their climaxes at sunset, it would be
interesting to verify, if one could, if the artists of the time had this fact in
mind when they used the indigo, browns, greens and ochres, the only dyes
available to them, i.e. the question is did they consciously use†††† the dyes
to the best advantage of graphic representation and historical accuracy? The
following matter from Justin H. Smith's "The War With Mexico," Vol I,

might be correlated with a direct study of the representational detail of the Mexican War prints: p 143 -(in re- conditions at Corpus Christi, a hamlet on the south side of the Neuces River—the description probably fits other places "on or near" the Rio Grande) " . . . the tents could scarcely keep out a heavy dew; for weeks together every article in many of them was thoroughly soaked; and much of the time water stood three or four feet deep in some. The weather oscillated sharply between sultry heat and piercing northers [*sic*][27] . . . hardly enough wood could be obtained for the cooks, camp-fires usually out of the question; . . . only brackish drinking water could be had."

The landscape of the Mexican frontier:
p. 146 - (Mar. 1846) ". . . the weather was now fine, the road almost free from mud, and the breeze balmy. Frequently the blue lupine, the gay verbena, the saucy marigold and countless other bright flowers carpeted the ground. The cactus and the cochineal excited . . . curiosity. Ducks and geese often flew up from the line of advance. Many rabbits and many deer scampered across the plain; and occasionally wolves, catamounts and panthers were frightened from cover; . . . once a herd of (wild horses), spaced as if to allow room for cannon, were taken for Mexican cavalry. Innumerable centipedes, tarantulas and rattlesnakes . . . the boundless prairie had somewhat the fascination of the sea; and occasionally, when a mirage conjured up a range of blue mountains—clothed with forests and reflected in lakes—that melted presently into the air, one had a sense of moving on enchanted ground."

p. 148. (New Matamoros, Mar. 27/ 1846) "On each side bristled what a soldier described as an irregular, impenetrable mass of 'scraggly, scrubby, crooked, infernally, illegitimate and sin-begotten bristly trees loaded with millions of thompins—that is to say, *chaparral.*' Passing this and a few cabins in the midst of corn, cotton and pomegranates, the troops found themselves at the end of their march. Rio Bravo, the 'Bold river of the North' brown with mud, rolls swift and boiling at their feet, and in plain view about half a mile distant—black with crowded house-tops, gay with flags, and noisy with bugles and barking dogs—lay Matamoros. A rude pole was soon raised; to the music of our national airs the colors went up; and a small masked battery of field guns was planted near them."

27. A sudden, cold gale coming from the west.

p 163 - (near Palo Alto, near Resaca de la Palma, May 1846)

"The shallow, greenish-brown lagoons rimmed with broad, flat oozing banks of mud, the marshes full of tawny grass, and the low ridges mottled with patches of herbage and bald surfaces of gleaming dry dirt seemed interminable, but as hours passed the now sultry air began to be streaked with salt odors, and by noon the panting troops caught the sparkle of blue waves."

In re - General Taylor:

p. 140–141 – "Brevet Brigadier General Zachary Taylor . . . born 1784, had grown up and gained some rudiments of an education amidst the Indian troubles of the Kentucky border. At the age of twenty-three . . . commissioned first lieutenant in the Seventh Infantry, and after showing remarkable coolness and intrepidity in two small affairs during our second war with England and the Black Hawk War, he had won a stubborn flight in 1837 against the Seminoles at the head of some 1100 soldiers. Three years later he was assigned to a supervising command in the southwest, and this included Fort Jessup.

Personally Taylor possessed a strong character . . . neither exhausted by self-indulgence nor weakened by refinement and study . . . The makings of a hero lay in him, and to a large extent the making had been done. He was gifted, too, with solid common sense, not a little shrewdness and ambition, a thorough knowledge of men—the sort of men that he knew at all—a military eye, and a cool resourceful intelligence that was always at work in its own rather ponderous fashion. The sharp gray eyes and the contraction of his brows that made the upper part of his face look severe were tempered by the benignity of the lower part; and the occasional glimmer of a twinkle betokened humor.

On the other hand, everything about him suggested the backwoods man. His thick-set and rather corpulent body, mounted on remarkably short legs, typified barbaric strength. In speech he was rough and ungrammatical, in dress unkempt and even dirty, and in every external of his profession unmilitary. He never had seen a real battle nor even a real army. Ignorance and lack of mental discipline made him proud of his natural powers and self-mastered attainments, and he saw very distinctly the weaknesses of school-taught and book-taught men. West Pointers train[ed] in person and in mind but inferior to him in strength, practical sense and familiarity with men and things, he felt strongly inclined to belittle, and this feeling went so far that he despised, or at any rate frequently seemed to despise, knowledge itself. He could not, however, fail to recognize on occasions the professional superiority of his trained officers, and no doubt found himself unable now and then to defend his opinions. In such cases, being by temperament extremely firm, he naturally took refuge in obstinacy; and sometimes he appears to have been positively mulish, holding to his own view after he must have seen its incorrectness." (ca. 1845)

(Mar. 1846)- ". . . we have a picture of Taylor . . . break fasting at the door of his tent with a mess-chest for table, his rugged countenance flaming with sunburn, his long lips cracked and raw, and his long nose white with peeling skin."
(Battle of Palo Alto, May 1846) "Taylor, sitting unconcerned with one leg over the pommel of his saddle, writing, was notified of this movement (of the Mexican troops) and simply replied, 'Keep a bright lookout for them.'"
p 372-3 - (Jan. 1847, one month before Buena Vista)
"The General's (Taylor's) position in his army was now extraordinary. To the troops, while they gloried in his courage, his achievements had seemed at the time commonplace enough; but sentiment at home as exhibited in the newspapers—reacting from painful anxiety, indulging in the common taste for exaggeration, and instinctively demanding a national figure for this national crisis—had not only done justice to his great qualities, but partly in order to explain victories clearly marked with errors, made him out a genius and a worker of miracles; and all this laudation, read by the army, created an impression which both duty and interest forbade the more discriminating to impair.

The General, moreover, though nursing the mammoth conceit that he was qualified to be President of the U.S., was careful to spare the self-love of all who came in contact with him; and while no one could enter Scott's presence without feeling himself before a superior man aware of his superiority, probably most of Taylor's visitors had an agreeable sense of excelling him in personal appearance, dress, education and talents, and enjoyed also a flattering conviction of their insight, because they recognized that he possessed high merits after all. How the soldiers, oppressed by the lordliness of many generals, adored his plainness we have seen. They felt they could bow down to such a man without losing self-respect, since the obeisance was due to their own choice, not his demand, and when he welcomed one to his un-guarded tent and talked with him about home and friends, or shook a delinquent by the two ears with a kindly warning not to do so again, he established a positive dominance over their minds and hearts... Taylor had thus a double hold on his troops. His black body-servant referred to him as 'De ole hoss,' but would have died for him; and while the army would probably have expressed itself about him as lightly as did the street urchins of Philadelphia:

> 'Old Zack's at Monterey,
> Bring out your Santa Anner;
> For every time we raise a gun,
> Down goes a Mexicanner;'

yet in reality he was now enthroned in the hearts of the soldiers generally as a father, a hero, and almost a fetich."

Buena Vista, Feb. 1847

pg 384 — "... a section of Captain Washington's battery hurried down the slope towards La Angostura ... the mountains on the east flung long shadows across the valley ... this was the twenty-second of February. The bands struck up Hail Columbia. The watch-word "honor of Washington" passed among the men ... (the coincidence of the battle of Buena Vista happening on Washington's birthday, might serve as a connecting link between the material of the Washington prints (section I above) and the Mexican prints, if both are used as the subjects of one broadcast).

p 385– "*the field of battle* ... Running north along the western side of the road ... a creek, which had excavated near La Angostura an amazing network of gullies with almost vertical banks twenty feet or so high, that practically vetoed the passage of troops; and west of this obstruction the ground rose more steeply until it became a line of high hills, parallel to the creek, which resembled a huge wave ready to break. On the other side, between the road and the sierra, there was a space varying from three quarters of a mile to a mile in width, and this was roughly divided by two east-and-west ravines— the more northern of which may be called the long and the more southern the broad ravines—into three parts: the north field, as we may name it, extending to Buena Vista, the middle field or plateau, and the south field extending to La Encantada."

p. 386 "... the engineers reconnoitered actively, and both Taylor and Wool visited and addressed the various American corps."

p. 395 - (The climax of the battle and its significance) ". . . in the narrow valley day was already waning . . ."

"It was an extraordinary battle. On the part of the Americans it began in flight and ended in success. Marred by mistakes and failures, it exhibited even more strikingly both skill and moral grandeur. Taylor seems to have had but little to do with directing it, and that little seems to have been poor work; but he did more than engineer success—he created it. Huddled rather than mounted, a great part of the time, on Old Whitey with arms folded and one leg unconcernedly thrown across the pommel of his saddle, the conspicuous target of the Mexican artillery, yet utterly unmoved even when his clothes were pierced, he was a fountain of courage and energy. In other words, the victory of Buena Vista was due primarily to Taylor's prestige, valor and gift of inspiring confidence."

p. 396 ". . . Our artillery was beyond praise for both daring and skill . . . the batteries served indispensably . . . as rallying points for the infantry. The (Mexican) lancers cantering over the plain and finishing the American wounded, gave great assistance by exasperating and warning our men . . ."

p. 400 (three weeks after Buena Vista) ". . . the tidings of (Santa Anna's) failure exaggerated . . . into news of a brilliant and overwhelming triumph won by a general robbed of his troops, •caused a tremendous rebound. Polk, holding that only Taylor's blundering and violation of orders had created the peril, and that his brave men had rescued him from it, would not permit a general salute in the army; but the nation saluted, and the General's nomination for the Presidency became inevitable."

(•Taylor could not maintain lines of communication; detachments en route were assailed and destroyed by Spanish American robber bands led by Urria.)‡‡‡‡ P.S. Study of Mexican War daguerreotypes and engravings might also serve to establish the historical authenticity in the detail of the scenes rendered in the cotton prints.

See for instance Robert Taft, Photography and the American Scene, N.Y. 1938, p 223: "The earliest photographic records of war now known are some four or five daguerreotypes made during the Mexican War (1846–8) . . . now in possession of Mr. H. Armour Smith of Yonkers Museum of Science and Art . . . probable that they were made by a local daguerrotypist in town of Saltillo, Mexico . . . it may possibly be that one of them is the first photographic record of a battle field, that of Buena Vista." See also note 246c: pp. 484–5 also illust. p. 225; also p. 59: Matthew B. Brady, included a portrait of Zachary Taylor in his Gallery of Illustrious Americans, 1850.

2) John H. Beneval Latrobe, Three Great Battles, Baltimore, 1863—for Portraits of Taylor, Wool, etc. and Engraving of "General Taylor directing Capt. Bragg to use a little more grape."

3) Denison (John Leydard) - Pictorial History of the Wars of the U.S. NY 1859. Chapters 22–24 black and white engraving of "Captain May ordered to charge the Mexican batteries" (in which May is shown with black beard) (see above pg 10, line 1) which TE–222 (see pg 6 ff) does not show; also colored engravings of Battle of Buena Vista, which tho it makes use of bright red, white and pink, besides green and brown is, similar in the detail of foliage and the general feeling of the design to TE–191.

4) Charles J. Peterson—The Military Heroes of The War with Mexico with a Narrative of the War. Phila. 1849: Engraving of Col. May (also with black beard) at Resaca de la Palma - p. 41.

IV. TE–201, 192, 197 - Event handkerchiefs using George Washington portraits. (This material might be related thematically to this material of pp. 1–3 of the report)

Antiques, v. 36, July 1939, Frontispiece: An American Historical Hankerchief [*sic*] c. 1783, copper plate engraving printed in red on white linen, made by *Talwin and Foster, Bromley Hall Mold* (appears above the lower border). This is probably the only cloth print bearing their name. This hankerchief identical in subject and engraving with the *paper proof,* above p. 2. showing profile portraits after drawings by Pierre Eugène Du Simitière, is from the collection of Edwin Lefèvre. An article based on the material gathered by him, in the same issue of Antiques, July 1939, pp. 14–17 contains illustrations of other Washington handkerchiefs, and may be summarized as to general detail as follows:

American *historical kerchiefs* or *events handkerchiefs* include items signalizing [*sic*] persons, battles, or anything else indicative of the social, political, religious and educational trends at various periods of American history. It is more accurate to speak of historical kerchiefs, rather than handkerchiefs, for many of the most striking examples are too large to be of pocket size. (Some were worn around the neck) The date of the earliest American kerchief is unfixed—none could be accurately ascribed to the Colonial period. The earliest are all of foreign make, and American only as to subject—e.g. those celebrating or commemorating Geo. Washington.

Louis Zukofsky

Apr. 4 / 40

Editorial Notes

* Significant variations in the format of the scripts have been preserved. Abbreviations for speakers have been standardized.

† slowly] slowing

‡ This address overscored in the manuscript: ~~1088 E. 180 St., N.Y., N.Y.~~

§ Typescript is undated; autograph version in the Harry Ransom Humanities Research Center, University of Texas, archive has: "Louis Zukofsky / Nov. 22/39."

** This and subsequent scripts have been transcribed from autograph manuscript. Earlier pieces were presumably hand-drafted, sent to a typist, and then copyedited by Zukofsky. Of a later date than other Index materials, the scripts bear signs of varying degrees of revision but little editing; all lack the usual signature indicating Zukofsky had proofread them after composition.

†† clothing] cloathing

‡‡ Manuscript has this line with deletion marks preceding it: "So he was a mechanical toy, our binnacle figure? And with mercuric (sic) eyes? Or . . ."

§§ The passage above (from "It may seem . . .") was inserted from reverse, as per Zukofsky's edits. It is impossible to tell whether the next sentence should begin a new paragraph.

*** Manuscript illegible.

††† Manuscript illegible.

‡‡‡ New England was not to begin with the center of stoneware manufacture that it was later with] New England was not the center of stoneware manufacture to begin with that it was later . . .

§§§ parallel] parallels

**** Manuscript is uncertain; "Factors" is supposition.

†††† use] used

‡‡‡‡ This note is presented in exactly the form it takes in Zukofsky's notes.

AFTERWORD

John Taggart

Moving on to the Beginning

To begin moving on to the beginning, to one of the beginnings of Louis Zukofsky's life and time as a poet which, the poetry, is itself the beginning (as motivation) of this volume and of all the other volumes in The Wesleyan Centennial Edition of Zukofsky's critical writings, consider "The Seer."

> Throughout the winding, torpid day I heard
> The onward-sipping undertones of voices
> Fall about me, and laughter that rejoices
> In the transient glory of a transient word.
> Now I have heard the seer—the mystery
> Of rarer, starlit regions in his face—
> Lay bare in music, in a fitting space
> Of time, words reaching to infinity....
>
> I am fulfilled of music, perfect chords
> That linger. And I think of studded hordes
> Of moonbeams, trickling on dark shrouded trees,
> Like threaded tears; and of a dark stream, twining
> Over jet ledges, when the moonbeams freeze
> It silver, and it flows on purling, shining....
> *Columbia Verse* (1924)

One of the beginnings is a sonnet. In its discombobulated and decorative imagery, in its slight and polite manipulation of the conventions of the most traditional of all traditional verse forms, it reveals itself as what it is: student work. It thus comes trailing clouds of English romantic poetry, clouds dwindling at the close of each stanza to a not so much romantic as Victorian rhetorical "dying fall" of ellipsis. After all, if you've heard the seer and if you're fulfilled of the music laid bare by the seer's words, what more is there to say?

The sonnet reveals that its writer has not yet caught up with modern poetry as practiced by the two poets who were to become his actual seers, Ezra Pound and William Carlos Williams. It also reveals that Zukofsky was not a genius. Gertrude Stein had defined a genius as someone who doesn't need to know the two hundred years of history that everyone else needs to know. This is especially so if, before any consideration of history, you're beginning as a modern American poet with Yiddish as your first language. Basil Bunting: "Zukofsky is the only considerable English poet . . . who did not have English as his mother tongue" (*Basil Bunting on Poetry* 151). Zukofsky learned his English and history first at Columbia and then at the one-man university that was Ezra Pound. It was "at" Pound that he learned a history much more encompassing than any two favored centuries and that he learned English beyond the academically distilled conventions of such centuries. It was from Pound that he learned his craft as a poet, a modern as contemporary craft at once based on a rejection of the romantic/Victorian past and on a careful testing of the poetry of many centuries (and in languages other than English).

If Zukofsky learned, was stimulated to begin the gradual making of himself into a modern poet by Pound, there was one thing or aspect about the modern that he more particularly learned from Williams. This thing or aspect is America. For, contra Bunting, Williams saw not speaking English as an advantage. ". . . I did not speak English . . . that should be the basis for a beginning, that I spoke a language that was my own and that I would govern it according to my necessities and not according to unrelated traditions" (*Selected Essays* 177). But, as Williams has one of his characters say in *A Voyage To Pagany*, "America . . . casts a veil, a pallor rather, on everything." And one of the agents of this veiling is none other than American higher education:

> Their dreadful, dreadful colleges with no inkling of where knowledge begins nor where it ends, actually teaching, thinking they can teach the young—the hopeless young, deceived as to history, their own history, misled as to their governors—never an inkling of actuality, but to gather up a hod of small facts of "general information"—looking for day with a candle. (161)

If American colleges cannot properly teach the American young as to the actuality of their own history, Williams, in the case of Zukofsky, could. Or not so much teach, as Pound was always "teaching" in his own antic/manic version of the old professor, but rather design, design as verb, i.e., point a finger. And Williams's finger pointed not to yet another revised curriculum—the academic resquaring of the circle of the English/European past—but to the actuality and actualities of American history.

If a finger points, it's useful for there to be another pair of eyes to take note of its pointing and of what it points toward. Zukofsky had quick eyes. As he writes in a 1928 review of *A Voyage To Pagany*, "What is intended to be a novel becomes in structure an animated itinerary. There is practically no design, since the aim impelling the book is—to move on to the Beginning" (*Prepositions* 53). There is practically no design in Williams's novel and in the entirety of his work if design is taken as a noun in itself, a "proper" name for proper as traditional English/European history (and language and writing). Design in Williams is a verb, a pointing toward and encouragement to begin to move on an animated itinerary to "the Beginning": the beginning of beginning to be aware of American historical actuality, the beginning of beginning to be a modern American poet.

A Voyage To Pagany was published in 1928. "The American Background" (a section from the essay "America and Alfred Stieglitz") was published in 1934. By this latter date Zukofsky was working for the New York City WPA Art Project, working on what would become *A Useful Art,* collected and published here for the first time in the Wesleyan Centennial Edition. The later essay, essentially a reflection and refinement upon the novel and upon Williams's personal "revisionist" study of American history, *In The American Grain* (1925), is ambitious. It attempts nothing less than an understanding of the laws and conditions involved in the historic evolution of American culture as well as a critique of American culture. It is neither simply nationalistic nor backward yearning. "Nothing is good because it is American, as nothing survives merely because it is authentic." Nonetheless, one of its key claims champions the desirability of the small American community of early settlers as opposed to the city developed in the interests of wealth. Such a community represents "the culture of immediacy, the active strain, which has left every relic of value which survives today" (*Selected Essays* 148). The culprit is wealth, what wealth achieved in its accumulation (purchase of a nonnative, past art and culture) and what it took away or displaced (the native, the local). "The insecurity all men felt in the predominance of this purchased culture, unrelated to the new conditions, made them rush for security in money all the more" (150). Williams does not simply castigate wealth, does not simply write as proto-"reflectionist" Marxist (or displaced Southern Agrarian). He concedes that more was involved, i.e., that the development of cities was also fueled by a growing "spiritual impoverishment of the outlying districts." The one brought about the other, and the other contributed to the one. This negative symbiosis brought about another form of worship: "the actual, the necessity for dealing with a condition as it existed, seemed to become unnecessary because of mystical powers represented by money" (151).

In hindsight and in relation to Williams's unflagging exasperation with Eliot's "The Waste Land," there's considerable irony in his version of American culture. For both poets read "the situation" similarly. There are, however, differences. Eliot's culture is the great tradition of England and Europe, and his reading results in a hoarding of fragments from that culture. The end of "The Waste Land" is recusant, a holing up in a private museum of private sensibility; it is a dead end from which nothing new can begin. Significantly, there are no American fragments in his museum (or mausoleum).

In contrast, I would cite a very different set of "fragments" mentioned in passing by Williams in his American background essay.

Against this heavy tide, the real cultural forms might take on an unconscious beauty of refinement in the lines of fast ships and, in more conscious form, the carved and painted figureheads of the ships themselves. It might produce glassware, such collectors' items as the wooden marriage chests of Pennsylvania workmanship, an architecture old and new, and many other things as well exemplified as anywhere by the furniture in white pine and other native woods built by the Shakers in their colonies along the New York–Connecticut border. Beautiful examples are these of what could be done by working in a related manner with the materials at hand; they are plastically the most truthful monuments to the sincerity of the motives that produced them that could be imagined. (*Selected Essays* 150)

Williams's real cultural forms connect directly and specifically with much of what we find in Zukofsky's *A Useful Art*. Directly and specifically: the carved and painted figureheads of the ships themselves, the Henry Clay figurehead discussed in the first of the radio scripts. Direct, specific connection *and* difference.

Williams's relics and real cultural forms are mentioned in passing as examples of what could be produced despite the enervating and inevitable "heavy tide" of capitalism. Zukofsky's radio script focuses in detail on ship figureheads, the history of their development beginning with the Egyptians and their post-1900 demise, and in particular on the political history of Clay and of his figurehead's involvement in the 1852 wreck of a steamboat named after him. Like his *Test Of Poetry* in relation to the tests and exhibits of Pound's *ABC of Reading*, Zukofsky's *A Useful Art* "goes one better" than his other seer's passing reference. While Zukofsky's prose projects might not have happened without these earlier pointings, as his poetry—the later, non-student poetry that is distinctively his own—might not have happened, the point is that he did heed their pointings and that he did act upon the actualities pointed toward. His action, as indicated by the distinctive quality of his poetry, transcends the gravitational effects of influence. It is formerly inventive (Pound), it is American (Williams), and it is finally its own.

The Centennial Edition has come into existence because of the existence of Louis Zukofsky's distinctive poetry. An interest in the poetry has provoked an interest in the prose. If only because the two are inextricably intertwined, the prose—and *A Useful Art* in particular—is of value. (The reader will find detailed linkages established between the poetry and *A Useful Art* in Kenneth Sherwood's helpful editorial introduction to this volume.) As Zukofsky observes in his radio script, ". . . a ships' figurehead becomes a guide not only to all ship's figureheads that preceded it, but a reason for creating sculpture in our time." A past work of American "unconscious" art becomes a guide to a past beyond its own historic moment and a rationale for the creation of "conscious" art in the present. It is thus doubly useful. Further, the figurehead ceases to be a museum piece or collector's item when its image is circulated among people who will "demand an effort from contemporary art that will yield a comparable pleasure to the living." It can only be hoped that the publication of *A Useful Art* will lead to a greater sense of the "use value" of early American culture and to a greater sense of the pleasure to be gained, based as it may be on that culture, from contemporary American art. A like hope exists for the distinctive "sculptural" poetry of Louis Zukofsky. The implicit imperative for both past and contemporary culture is attention. In the old advisement to schoolchildren at street crossings: stop, look, and listen!

In Zukofsky's radio script, a ship's figurehead can become a guide. The word "guide" takes us back to Pound, to his *Guide To Kulchur,* and to his sense of the word's meaning as helping others to get "there." Dedicated in part to Zukofsky as a struggler in the desert, Pound's *Guide* nonetheless implies that he, writing from Rapallo, has already arrived and that culture resides in Europe or anywhere else other than America, America as cultural *deserta. A Useful Art* challenges such implication as it challenges the implication of Gertrude Stein's famous "no there there." It is perhaps easier to be American as an American in Paris, even as Wallace Stevens was imaginationally such an American. It is perhaps more difficult to achieve an awareness of "there" in the midst of one's own here and now. Guided as he was by Pound and Williams, Zukofsky got there by staying here, a here that allowed him to move back, beyond America, in history, and forward into his own poetry.

While Pound writes from Rapallo (and Venice and London and Paris), he does not ground his sense of arrival "there" with geographic location but with performance. "The violinist, agonizing over the tone, has not arrived. The violinist lost in the melodic line or rather concentrated effortlessly on reproduction of it has arrived" (209). Only Pound's performer—as Zukofsky's son Paul, a widely recognized violin virtuoso, could have informed him—is concentrated on a *reproduction.* Culture is defined by Pound as being able to do "the thing without strain." If what's so done is one's own line of melody, a line perhaps guided by past lines of American design, then there is such a thing as American culture, a culture that in turn can be a resource of guidance for performers in the present intent upon their own performance. Zukofsky's poetry offers such guidance, and *A Useful Art* itself is a guide as to where guidance can continue to be found. Both his poetry and "the useful arts" (the phrase occurs in a 1937 letter referring to the Index of American Design project from Zukofsky to Pound) are guides for those who would make their own gradual beginnings toward that which is, now, more than merely and subserviently "postmodern."

· · ·

It's spring as I write. It's a rampantly green world outside my study windows. Thinking and writing about Zukofsky's *A Useful Art,* I often pause to look out: across the road and a stretch of lawn the top of a foundation can be glimpsed. Limestone, three-sided, it's all that remains of a once flourishing grain and lumber mill. Ceasing operation in the late 1940s, the top three wooden stories eventually torn down, its salvageable parts and more curious bric-a-brac given away (or stolen), the mill became a midden with nearly full-grown maples sprouting up here and there. So my wife and I found it on moving here ten years ago. Several of those years were spent cleaning it up. Cutting down the trees, breaking up hulking and no longer operable cast-iron grinding machines, hauling out endless wheelbarrow loads of broken machine belts, wooden beam sections, piles of worn-out hand files, bits of crockery, square-headed nails, the odd shoe sole and shampoo bottle, hundreds of pieces of shattered glass. *Then* digging out and sifting mounds of dirt that had accumulated in the foundation corners. Watching me work one day, a passerby asked if I'd discovered any buried treasure. I hadn't. Not a single old coin. In fact, what I'd "discovered" were many of the same things mentioned in *A Useful Art.*

But the walls stood, revealed for the first time since their construction. Hardly Machu Picchu, not much more than seven feet tall, having to be re-built and patched up in places, they nevertheless stood. And stand. The cleaning up has taken several years. Struck by their own revealed and immediate actuality, we've been slow to plant anything that would obscure their chunks and blocks of limestone, grey-yellow seams of mortar running between them.

Likewise, I've been slow to write about or "from" them as I've been slow to realize that this—where I live, what's actually and immediately outside my windows—is my culture. It's a local, found and foundational culture. And a culture, as a foundation, is to be built upon. Of course, a culture can be not only cleaned up and restored but also re-enacted (as Civil War battles are re-enacted at nearby Gettysburg). Yet to be alive in the present, not dead, not merely historically and authentically American, something new has to be built. If you're a poet, it can be a poem, a poem that in its newness will be more than a reproduction/restoration/re-enactment of past local color.

It's taken several years to clean up the foundation. It's taken even longer for me to begin to realize what is my own culture as both noun and verb. *Noun:* as this collect of things (collected by a gradual accumulation of consciousness itself), the chunks and blocks of stone and all that surrounds them, all of what makes up the there of my here: the mill-race, twenty-five feet across and six feet deep, stretching back into the woods where birds dart among leaves and shadows to the Condoguinet Creek, swollen brown rush and sometimes bright glitter of the Creek in early spring, hayfield on the other side of the race with its one lone walnut tree, the silver maple woods on the far side of the field that was once pasture land and before that woods again among which Indians once camped but didn't stay long into the summer (too humid and too many mosquitoes), far edge of the woods coming right up to the Creek from whose mucky banks I pulled mountain stones during last summer's drought for a set of steps. *Verb:* as the thing done on that foundation, which could be the story of one's stories, stories told by neighbors and passers-by, the story of a heavy spring run of carp in the Creek getting into the race and clogging the mill's machinery and having to be pulled out with pitchforks, story of young students from the Shadyside School (just down the road, a one room brick schoolhouse, deserted now) coming to our house each morning to fill their single bucket of drinking water, story of Chloe Failor—daughter of John Failor, operator of the mill from 1913 until its closing—who could carry a sack full of grain under each arm, story of someone trying to burn down the covered bridge (detected and put out just in time by a neighbor). Near the northwest corner of our property, the bridge is named after Jacob Ramp, who built the house in which we live. It was Ramp's great-grandson, now an older man himself, who came from Oregon to see the place for the first time and, standing with us and his own children and grandchildren at the edge of the mill foundation, openly wept. Stories, stepping stone stories. Or, if you're a poet intent upon steps as rhythm, lines perhaps of melody perhaps without strain.

Following and furthering the finger pointing guidance of Pound and Williams, Zukofsky came comparatively much more quickly to such realization. Or his gradual making of his beginning was much less gradual. In this regard and on reflection, he surely deserves genius status. Not Gertrude Stein's genius, but rather a genius of beginning (to be American, to be modern as contemporary, to be a poet whose work—whatever its own foundation in history—lives on in its own continuous present). More than an uncanny anticipation of current academic interest in "material culture," *A Useful Art* is of value as a design, a pointing toward where and how some of his beginning began and of where and how others may begin to move on to their own beginnings to the fulfillment of their own music.

Works Cited

Bunting, Basil. 1999. *Basil Bunting on Poetry*. Ed. Peter Makin. Baltimore: Johns Hopkins University Press.

Pound, Ezra. [1938] 1970. *Guide To Kulchur*. New York: New Directions.

Williams, William Carlos. 1928. *A Voyage to Pagany*. New York: The Macaulay Company.

———. [1954] 1969. *Selected Essays*. New York: New Directions.

Zukofsky, Louis. 2000. *Prepositions +*. Hanover, N.H.: Wesleyan University Press.

About the Authors

Louis Zukofsky (1904–1978) is widely considered a significant American modernist and one of the primary forerunners of contemporary avant-garde writing. His many books include *"A," Complete Short Poetry, Prepositions +,* and *A Test of Poetry.*

Kenneth Sherwood is Assistant Professor of English at the University of Texas of the Permian Basin.

John Taggart is Professor Emeritus of Literature and Creative Writing at Shippensberg State University, and the author of *When the Saints* (2000).

DATE DUE

JUL 1 8 2008		
OCT 1 0 2008		
GAYLORD		PRINTED IN U.S.A.